This is the Day the Lord Has Made
by Sue Reidell
Copyright © 2015 Sue Reidell

All rights reserved. This book is protected under the copyright laws of the United States of America. This book may not be copied or reprinted for commercial gain or profit.

The Holy Bible: New International Version ©1978 by the New York International Bible Society, used by permission of Zondervan Bible Publishers. All rights reserved.

The Holy Bible: New Living Translation ©1996, 2004, 2007, 2013 by Tyndale House Foundation. Used by permission of Tyndale House Publishers Inc., Carol Stream, Illinois 60188. All rights reserved.

The Holy Bible: New American Standard Bible® ©1960, 1962, 1963, 1968, 1971, 1972, 1973, 1975, 1977, 1995 by The Lockman Foundation. Used by permission. All rights reserved.

The Holy Bible: New King James Version® ©1982 by Thomas Nelson. Used by permission. All rights reserved.

ISBN 978-1-63360-022-5
For Worldwide Distribution
Printed in the U.S.A.

FOREWORD

There are many trials and tribulations we have to go through in our walk with the LORD. But each day can be considered a blessing, no matter what occurs, as long as we seek the presence of the LORD before we begin our day.

This is the Day the Lord Has Made was written because I had a desire to help others understand that as human beings, we are called to complete the mission work the LORD has sent us, as His faithful servants, to glorify the Kingdom of Heaven. We can take the Word of God to others who are still trapped in the darkness, and so desperately need to be guided to the light of Jesus.

But we tend to get lost in our own self-importance before we even begin our journey for the LORD! Simply put, our pride and arrogance, make us think we know better than the LORD does about how to run our own lives. So we venture off the path the LORD has set for us and do our own thing worshipping the idols of this world. Then one day, we come to our senses, realizing we made a HUGE MESS OF OUR LIVES! When we are "sick and tired of being sick and tired," do we humbly hit our knees and make atonement to the LORD asking for forgiveness from Him for violating His covenant.

I am talking from experience when I say that I know what it means to think I have control over my life! I would be the first one to admit that since I came to my senses twenty-eight years ago, and realized that I allowed the evil idolatry of this world to hold me captive in the bondage of sin that had captured my soul. When I surrendered my life over to the LORD, He cut the chains of bondage with His unfailing, love, mercy, and grace, and set this prisoner free! Sometimes I still go off the path where the Lord is, but I quickly seek His presence for comfort and peace. Each day now is filled with joy and serenity, regardless of what happens in my day.

    May these precious words of scripture, which are dear to my heart, uplift you with peace that defies all understanding: *"And we know that all things work together for good to those who love God and have been called according to His purpose."* Romans 8: 28 (NKJV)

    God bless you,
    Sue Reidell

January 1

THIS IS THE DAY THE LORD HAS MADE

This is the day the Lord has made; let us rejoice and be glad in it. Psalms 118:24 (NASB)

Every day should be a day of rejoicing. Just the fact that the Lord, your God, woke you up this morning is a blessing that you can rejoice and praise God for. You have a marvelous God who enjoys giving you treasures from heaven. He delights in making you happy and fulfilled. His greatest miracles are the ones that you don't see. They come every day to you, wrapped in invisible paper that you need to search out and find.

Some gifts you receive and don't always recognize are: the birds waking you up with a pleasing melody of singing; the sun shining in your window to awaken your body to its glorious warmth of healing for your heart and soul; the fluffy marsh-mellow clouds in the sky which wrap around your body to comfort you like your favorite security blanket. *This is the day the Lord has made; let us rejoice and be glad in it.* Praise the Lord in thanks for this day!

I want to thank you Lord for every day you give me. Each day is a marvelous blessing Lord God. I praise and worship you, Father God, with my hands lifted up to the heavens and with singing and dancing erupting from my heart and soul. This is the day You have made Lord, let me rejoice and be glad in it. Amen.

January 2

BE STRONG IN THE LORD AND HIS MIGHTY POWER

Be strong in the Lord and his mighty power. Put on all of God's armor so you will be able to stand firm against all strategies of the devil. Ephesians 6:10-11 (NLT)

When you are under attack by the Devil, you can *be strong in the Lord and his mighty power.* If you call on the name of the Lord, He will come and fight the evil one. When you have the Lord in battle with you, nothing the Destroyer can do will seriously harm you. He is your strong and mighty fortress that surrounds you from all sides and is keeping you safe and secure.

You know when the devil feels it is necessary to attack you, you are doing the will of God. The father of lies is trying to use any strategies he can think of to throw you off your mission for the Lord. Think about it! If you were doing what the god of this world wanted, he wouldn't need to attack you! He would not divide his own house. So feel privileged when the Devil is frustrated with you. He knows if you succeed in what God has set before you that you are going to damage to his kingdom. Eventually it will fall under the strong hand of the Lord. Be proud to do the will of God!

O Loving Father of my heart, I am delighted to be your faithful servant. Continue to ask me to do anything for You and I will happily do your will. Thank You, Devoted Friend, for trusting me with th important task of working for Your kingdom on Earth. I will be strong in Your mighty power God, and not allow the devil and his minions to defeat me. I know that I call on Your Precious Name Father, You will save me. Amen.

January 3

THE SURE THING

The thief comes only to steal and kill and destroy; I came that they may have life, and have it abundantly. John 10:10 (NASB)

Jesus is the sure thing! The One and Only Savior for all mankind. Jesus' unfailing love redeemed you from eternal Hell, where you would have been cut off from the sunlight of His Spirit forever. Jesus paid the penalty for your transgressions against God by sacrificing His life on the cross so that you could live a life of freedom from sin. Jesus is the only way you can be born again, and live forever in heaven.

If you live in Jesus, and surrender your life over to Him, you *may have life and have it abundantly*. As you spend time in His glorious presence you discover peace like you have never known before!

Dear Heavenly Lord Jesus, I know You are the sure thing! Ever since I invited You into my life Jesus, life has taken on a new meaning for me. Never have I felt such contentment and peace Jesus! Thank You for saving me from my sins, Lord. Amen.

January 4

ENJOY YOURSELF

So I concluded there is nothing better than for people to be happy and enjoy themselves as long as they can.
Ecclesiastes 3:22 (NLT)

God has shown us mercy and grace every day of our lives. So why not enjoy yourself to the fullest, and appreciate the blessings you have been given by God?

Why do we always have to look back on our past and regret what we have done? If we could only take a good look at our life and see that God has already taken care of our past by forgiving us of our sins, we could forgive ourselves and enjoy what blessings we have today. Another thing we have a habit of doing is concentrating on the future and worrying ourselves into distress and panic. By trying to figure out what's going to happen tomorrow, instead of being grateful for everything we have today you should *be happy and enjoy yourself* today. Life is too short to worry and fret about things you have no control over. God wants you to delight in the blessings He gives you. Be thankful to God for everything He has so graciously bestowed upon you. God wants to see your heart erupting in joy today for all the blessings you have.

I don't know why Lord I worry about what is going to happen tomorrow and regret what happened yesterday. Help me to stay centered in You God. If I place You, Father God, in the center of my life, I will enjoy what has been given joyously to me. If I don't appreciate what I have, it can be taken from me by You Precious One. So let me be grateful, O Lord, and thank You all the time. Amen.

January 5

YOU CAN TRUST JESUS TO HAVE YOUR BACK

Jesus Christ is the same yesterday, today, and forever.
Hebrews 13:8 (NKJV)

You can trust Jesus to have your back whenever trouble invades your home like an intruder in the night. But you have to invite Jesus into your life. Then He will stand guard over your heart and soul so the enemy can't disrupt your inner sanctuary.

All you need to do is call on the Precious Name of Jesus, and He will be there to save you. As you make it a habit to seek the presence of the Lord, you will be blessed with the assurance and confidence of having a Devoted Friend who delights in giving you comfort. You just need to remember that *Jesus Christ is the same yesterday, today, and forever.* That is a promise you can place in your heart and soul knowing you have a Savior who doesn't change. You can be reassured that Jesus will never leave you nor forsake you. He has been with you since the beginning of time, and He will be with you always.

Jesus, our Precious Redeemer, I trust You to have my back always. I never have to fight battles alone. When the enemy invades my life, I can call on Your Sacred Name, Jesus, and You will be there to defeat the enemy and save me. I am so blessed to have a Devoted Friend who will never abandon me in my time of need. Amen.

January 6

DRAW NEAR TO GOD

But it is good for me to draw near to God; I have put my trust in the Lord GOD that I may declare all you works. Psalms 73:28 (NKJV)

Only God can satisfy all your needs. He waits patiently for you to come to Him. You can draw near to God anytime. You don't have to wait until problems happen to seek God. You can come to God in the morning and throughout your day to find comfort in His presence and lay in His gentle arms, delighting in just being near Him.

When you *put* your *trust in the Lord GOD* you have a dependable friend you can count on to be there for you no matter what happens in your life. When you have a good day, God rejoices with you. When you have a day that is hard and draining, God will come to you with a relaxing massage that rejuvenates your mind, body and soul with warm, soothing, healing ointment.

I praise You, Lord, for always being a dependable friend to me. Where would I go, or what would I do without You O God? This world I live in is so scary and dark Lord! I can't walk my days on this earth without You as my Precious Comforter beside me. When I draw near to You God, nothing can seriously upset me. Thank You for Your unfailing love Lord, that is everlasting to everlasting! Amen.

January 7

I WILL PRAISE THE LORD

The Lord is my strength and song, and he has become my salvation; this is my God and I will praise him.
Exodus 15:2 (AMP)

The Lord is my strength and song, so I will praise the Lord! He is my strong fortress, where I can find shelter from my enemies. My Lord protects me by placing me underneath His everlasting wings of salvation. I feel safe in the mighty presence of My Lord knowing He will not let any harm befall me. I will tell of His marvelous deeds to everyone I meet!

I will worship and praise My Lord, shouting hallelujah, hallelujah, glory to the One and Only Name above all names! He is the Keeper of my life! My Lord is the only God that brings joy and happiness into my heart and soul. How thankful I am that He is My Lord!

I delight in praising You Lord, and shouting from the rooftops, what a glorious God I have in my life. You are a God who saves me! You protect and shelter me from all of my enemies Lord. Thank You for always being there for me when I seek Your presence O Lord. Amen.

January 8

SEEK THE PRESENCE OF THE LORD

You will go out in joy and be led forth in peace; the mountains and hills will burst into song before you, and all the trees of the field will clap their hands.
Isaiah 55:12 (NIV)

It can be difficult for you when things happen beyond your control. You know you can't change or fix anything. The only solution you have is to seek the presence of the Lord in prayer. He will walk with you through the pain, and even carry you when it is too difficult for you to walk because the pain leaves you unable to move. Visualize at this moment the Lord carrying you to a grassy knoll where He places you on a soft blanket, where *the mountains and hills will burst into song before you,* to comfort you with sweet melodies of peace.

Lord, it is very hard when the pain comes. It hurts so badly Lord! Please comfort me as I seek Your Glorious Presence, Lord. Only You, Lord, can take my pain away as You hold me snuggly in Your gentle arms. Amen.

January 9
A CHILD OF GOD

Yet to all who did receive him, to those who believed in his name, he gave the right to be children of God— children born not of natural descent, nor of human decision or a husband's will, but born of God.
John 1:12-13 (NIV)

The sins that caused suffering bound you up in chains of guilt, remorse, and shame. Jesus released you from them upon His death on the cross. Your chains were broken and you were set free to live an inheritance as a child of God for eternity in the kingdom of heaven.

To those who believed in his name, he gave the right to be children of God. As such, you are entitled to all the privileges of royal descent. You will receive the crown of faithfulness upon your head, wear a robe of righteousness on your glorified body, and sandals of peace upon your feet. The rivers of living water will flow forever through the city of gold!

Precious Heavenly Father I am very thankful to be Your child! What a glorious life I will have with You in your royal kingdom. I am looking forward to enjoying never-ending peace forever in Your Sacred Presence, Lord. Amen.

January 10

GOD SEES YOU

Hagar referred to the Lord, who spoken to her as, "the God who sees me," for she said, "I have seen the One who sees me!" Genesis 16:13 (NLT)

Hagar is frightened and scared after her mistress, Sarai mistreated her. So she runs away into the wilderness and encounters God when she stopped at the springs of water. He tells Hagar she will have a son, and his name will be Ishmael. That is when Hagar said, *"I have seen the one who sees me."* Can you relate to Hagar? She was in distress, and felt she didn't have any other options but to run away from Sarai. She knew slaves didn't have any rights to speak up for themselves.

Have you felt like running away from a problem? Isn't this when God always finds you and comforts you? God sees you. He makes it a point to know everything about you. The truth is, God knew what was going to happen in your life when He formed you into His most precious creation. So you can say with confidence, "My God *sees me,*" and takes care of all I need because He loves me unconditionally.

I am so grateful to know I have an intimate relationship with You, O God. You see me Lord! Your unfailing love for me Father God, meets all my needs. Thank You God for taking such good care of me. Amen.

January 11

WHEN YOU ARE TEMPTED BY THE DEVIL

The temptations in your life are no different from what others experience. God is faithful. He will not allow the temptation to be more than you can stand. When you are tempted, he will show you a way out so you can endure. 1 Corinthians 10:13 (NLT)

When you are tempted by the devil, God *will show you a way out so you can endure.* God will never leave you stranded in the darkness to find your way out alone. He will be your experienced guide, leading you to safety. After you are secure, God will fight the enemy and restore your peace and serenity. Then you can enjoy the comfortable presence of God surrounding you with a soft cocoon of warmth.

Praise and honor and glory, are Your special names, O God! You came to my rescue and saved me from the temptations of the devil. I was lost in the darkness Lord, until You came and led me out of the darkness and into Your healing light. I will praise You Devoted Friend, always! Amen.

January 12

GRACE MERCY AND PEACE

Grace, mercy, and peace, which come from God the Father and from Jesus Christ-the Son of the Father- will continue to be with us who live in truth and love.
2 John 1:3 (NLT)

When you *live in truth and love*, God is able to work through you to help others in need. You are a witness to the marvelous blessings God has given you. When people see how you trust God with your life, even when problems arise, they will be willing to surrender their lives over to the care of God. By grace, mercy, and peace, they will be forgiven of all their sins by God the Father of Jesus Christ.

How can people have a relationship with Jesus Christ if they were never told about Him? You are called by God to talk to others about Jesus Christ and lead them out of the darkness and into the healing light of truth and redemption for their souls. What a glorious gift that is; when you see others embrace the Lord Jesus with their hearts and souls. You see the remarkable change in their lives. They go from a person who is empty inside, to a person who is fulfilled with the unfailing love of Jesus Christ.

Gracious Lord, thank You for sending Your Son Jesus Christ from heaven to earth to save me from my sins. I am forever grateful to You, Father, for that precious gift of peace. Your mercy, grace, and peace granted a sinner like me the opportunity to be set free, so I can go out and be a witness to others, and guide them out of the darkness and into the healing light of Jesus Christ. Amen.

January 13

THE HOLY WORD OF GOD

All Scripture is inspired by God and is useful to teach us what is true and make us realize what is wrong in our lives. It corrects us when we are wrong and teaches us to do what is right. 2 Timothy 3:16 (NLT)

When you are discouraged about your life and don't know what to do, the Holy Word of God will help you discover what you need in your life to make you feel more fulfilled and content. For the Holy Word of God says: *"All Scripture is inspired by God and is useful to teach us what is true and to make us realize what is wrong in our lives."* God will direct you to what He wants you to read and incorporate into your life from His Holy Word. Your life can become filled with His presence so that God's will can be done in your life.

When you try to control your life it becomes a total mess, which you are unable to clean up by yourself. You need God to help you sweep up the broken pieces of your life, and repair the damaged pieces to make your life whole again. This is why the Holy Word of God is so vital to your life. It helps to correct what is wrong in your life, and shows you how to live your life for God. Then and only then, will you find peace and serenity.

Holy Father God, life can become difficult at times. I become lost in the transactions of day to day life. I know what to do at O God. But when I read Your Holy Word Lord, I find a solution for the problems that trouble me and I am able to feel peace again. Thank You Wonderful Counselor, for always guiding me to Your Holy Word so I can correct what is wrong in my life and make it better again. Amen.

January 14

THE MIGHTY POWER OF GOD

So humble yourselves under the mighty power of God, and in his good time he will honor you. Give all your worries and cares to God, for he cares about what happens to you. 1 Peter 5:6-7 (NLT)

You have an awesome God who deeply cares about you! His unfailing love for you is always available to comfort you when your worries and fears become overwhelming. Submit yourself to God as you understand God, and watch the mighty power of God take control over all of your needs. *And in his good time he will honor you,* and praise you for trusting Him with your life. God will give precious blessings to you, for being faithful to Him.

You are an Awesome God, who is always good to me! When I have concerns and fears, O Wonderful Provider, You come and rescue me. Your mighty power, God, protects me and makes me feel safe and secure. Thank You, Lord, for always being there for me. Amen.

January 15

TRUST IN THE LORD WITH ALL YOUR HEART

Trust in the Lord with all your heart, and lean not on your own understanding; in all your ways acknowledge Him, and He shall direct your paths.
Proverbs 3:5-6 (NKJV)

When the Lord directs you to do something do you dismiss what He is telling you to do? Do you sit still and listen to what the Lord is saying for you to do? It takes a lot of faith to trust the Lord. But if you are willing to commit yourself to God, *He shall direct your paths*. When you trust in the Lord with all your heart, your paths are smooth and your steps are secure. Nothing can make you stumble and fall when you are holding on to the righteous right hand of the Lord. Whether you are having financial problems, or are unemployed, or seeking new employment, the Lord will walk with you, and help you solve your problems. The Lord doesn't close a door without opening up a better one. Have confidence that the Lord will walk through the door with you. He will never leave your side.

O Heavenly Father, thank You for always guiding my path. I know I can depend on You, Lord, to never leave me nor forsake me. I trust in You with all my heart Lord. I don't want to lean on my own understanding, because I will fail miserably Lord. I need You so much Lord to be a part of my life. I can't do anything without You beside me Lord. Amen.

January 16

HOLD FAST TO THE LORD

But you are to hold fast to the Lord your God, as you have done until now. Joshua 23:8 (NIV)

No matter what happens in your life, *you are to hold fast to the Lord,* and allow Him to take control over the circumstances you are dealing with. Often when life is going good God can be placed on the shelf until a problem comes into your life that you can't handle by yourself. Then you take God off the shelf, dust Him off, and ask Him for His help. If you would only stay in close proximity to God and develop a relationship with Him, you would have a Devoted Friend by your side always.

Lord God, You are my Constant Companion! A Devoted Friend I can depend upon, in good and bad times. I want to remain in Your Glorious Presence forever. God, You satisfy all my needs! Amen.

January 17

GOD WILL ALWAYS WELCOME YOU BACK HOME

So he returned home to his father. And while he was still a long way off, his father saw him coming. Filled with love and compassion, he ran to his son, embraced him, and kissed him. Luke 15:20 (NLT)

Our heavenly Father uses this scripture about the Prodigal Son returning to his father after squandering his money to illustrate how his father welcomed him home with arms opened wide with love for his son. This also describes how your Father in heaven will always welcome you back home, even when you have committed all types of sins against Him.

So when he was still a long way off, his father saw him coming. Filled with love and compassion, he ran to his son, embraced him, and kissed him. Isn't this how God loves you? When He sees you coming, He runs to you, shows you deep compassion, and takes you in His arms, holding you in His embrace. God is a forgiving God! He is filled with tenderness and love when you come back to Him and repent of your sins. He treats you like nothing has happened. Your sins are erased from His memory. God's mercy and grace sets you free.

Gracious and Merciful God, thank You for always loving me unconditionally. I praise and honor Your Sacred Name, God, forever. You always welcome me back home when I repent of my sins against You, O Lord God. Nothing on this earth can keep You from me, Father God. I am your prized possession. You cherish me God, above all the creatures You have made. I am so blessed to be Your child, Father! Amen.

January 18

MY SOUL THRISTS FOR GOD

As the deer pants for the water brooks, so my soul pants for You, O God. My soul thirsts for God, for the living God. When shall I come and appear before God? Psalms 42:1-2 (NKJV)

My soul thirsts for God, for the living God. I have so much to do today that I know I won't be able to accomplish anything without the presence of God beside me. I have learned that if I want my day to be filled with happiness and joy instead of stress and anxiety, it is easier to have God helping me complete each task I need to get done. God is such a blessing in my life! Every hour of each day I need God. He is my Life Mate, and Soul Companion!

God, My God. The living God. Oh how I need You! Your presence gives me such joy and happiness, O God. You are beautiful and precious to me My God! My soul thirsts for You to hold and love me. I find such peace and serenity in Your arms, Father God. You are the only way to eternal life. For each day I am alive on this earth, I need You, My Strong Tower of Refuge and Strength, to be with me always! I adore You! Amen.

January 19
STAND TALL

Even when I walk through the darkest valley, I will not be afraid, for you are close beside me. Your rod and your staff protect and comfort me. Psalm 23:4 (NLT)

Isn't it amazing that when painful situations occur, you start blaming God and screaming, "Why did you let this happen Lord?" Instead of thanking God for being there for you *through the darkest valley.* You need to realize God is always close beside you and He will never leave you.

You can stand tall through the pain and suffering you are going through, and be reassured that God is feeling all the pain you are experiencing. He is a God of compassion and sensitive to all your needs! He will protect and comfort you through the darkest valley until you reach the top of the mountain and find peace.

Precious Heavenly Father, thank You for being my comfort and peace through my darkest valley of pain. I can stand tall knowing You will never leave me. I am blessed to have a God who is sensitive to all my needs, and just wants me to find joy. Amen.

January 20

JOY IN YOUR LIFE

Always be full of joy in the Lord. I say it again—rejoice! Let everyone see that you are considerate in all you do. Remember the Lord is coming soon.
Philippians 4:4-5 (NLT)

Life is what you make it! You can choose to *be full of joy in the Lord*, and let others see how much God brings delight and joy into your life. Or you can walk through life with a chip on your shoulder, feeling you haven't received what you deserve, and be miserable. The choice is yours. Choose wisely! Life speeds way too fast. You don't want to have regrets at the end of your life. Seek God and find peace for your heart and soul.

I am so relieved to be able to call You my friend, O Lord. I just hope and pray, I will continue to seek You, Lord, and have joy in my life. I don't want to be miserable my entire life, Lord God. I want others to see a light in my eyes when I talk about You my Precious Comforter. Amen.

January 21

THE LORD IS YOUR HOPE AND SALVATION

But if from there you will seek (inquire for and require necessity) the Lord your God, you will find Him if you [truly] seek Him with all your heart [mind] and soul and life. Deuteronomy 4:29 (AMP)

Don't get distracted and allow your focus to be taken away from the Lord, your hope and salvation, when life becomes out of control. When you do this, your mind becomes cluttered with worries and fears. When this happens, you are unable to function properly, because your mind is on overload. *But if from there you seek (inquire for and require necessity) the Lord your God, you will find [truly seek Him with all your heart [mind] and soul and life.* The Lord will revitalize you, and surround you with His powerful energy. Then you will be able to refocus your thoughts on Him. Nothing can overwhelm you and cause you to fear when you place yourself in the care of the Lord. He will take your burdens upon Himself, and give you peace that defies all understanding.

O My God, how I need You! You are the only dependable God in my life! When I seek You, Lord, I find hope and salvation. When I let life control me, when I need to lose myself in You, I become overwhelmed and lose myself in things, to share Wonderful Comforter. I love You, so much Lord! I am so grateful to You, Father God, for always surrounding me, and protecting me when life gets too much for me to handle alone. You are My Precious One! Amen.

January 22

GLORIFY GOD

So then, whether you eat or drink, or whatever you may do, do all for the honor and glory of God.
1 Corinthians 10:31 (AMP)

You have an awesome God, who gave up His Only Son Jesus, to die for you, and set you free from the bondage of your sins. Jesus suffered a horrible death on the cross. You were given a new Life in His Father. What are you going to do today to glorify God? This is a question only you can answer. What does it mean to be set free and to live a blessed life because God showed you mercy and grace? If you don't know God these can be tough questions to answer. They can be easy questions to answer because you give your life up daily to God.

How you live your life can be a sacred testimony that you give to God. Or you can choose to worship idols of this world instead of worshipping God. The truth is, you should do everything *for the honor and glory of God.* He gave up way too much for you to live your life any way you feel like it. Repent and come clean to God and He will be with you, and walk beside you always.

O Father God let my life be lived as a living testimony to glorify You. You give up Your Only Son Jesus, so my sins could be wiped clean forever, God. When I sin against You Lord, I pray that I will repent of my sins and surrender myself totally to You. You are the Joy and Laughter in my life Lord. Nothing else this world has to offer me will satisfy me. I love You. Amen.

January 23

THE LORD LOVES YOU

May the LORD bless you and protect you. May the LORD smile on you and be gracious to you. May the LORD show you his favor and give you peace.
Numbers 6:24-26 (NLT)

The Lord loves you so much! He only wants the best for you. What an amazing Lord you have on your side! He stands by you no matter what you go through. Be thankful you have a Father who adores you. *May the Lord show you favor and give you peace.* All the rest of the days of your life you will never have to walk alone. What a marvelous blessing has been bestowed upon you by the Lord, your Father. Enjoy your life abundantly!

What a glorious and blessed day this is Father! To know that You love me Lord, makes my heart sing with joy and gladness. I have a Father who thinks of me always with compassion and unfailing love in His heart. What an Awesome Comforter I have in my life! Amen.

January 24
GREATER IS THE ONE INSIDE OF YOU

The Word was with God, and the Word was God. He existed in the beginning with God. God created everything through him, and nothing was created except through him. The Word gave life to everything that was created, and his life brought light to everyone. The light shines in the darkness, and the darkness can never extinguish the light.
John 1:1-5 (NLT)

The Word of God is Jesus Christ. He brings peace and healing to those who believe in Him. His *light shines in the darkness and the darkness can never extinguish the light.* What hope that gives you! When the prince of darkness surrounds you, trying to destroy the light within you by telling you lies, don't believe him. He is the deceiver of the truth. His main goal is to convince you to lose your faith. Trust in Jesus Christ so you can come over to his side and worship him. But greater is the One inside of you, than the one who is in the world! If you stay strong in Jesus Christ to the end of the ages, He will destroy the evil one, and you will live forever with Him in Heaven.

Oh what a friend I have in You, Jesus! You are the light that shines in the darkness, and the darkness can never extinguish the light of your Holy Spirit living inside of me. I know that when the devil comes calling with all his lies. I just have to call on Your Name, Jesus, and the enemy has to flee. I am looking forward to spending eternity in Heaven with You Jesus. Amen.

January 25

GOD TURNS BAD THINGS INTO GOOD

It will lead to an opportunity for your testimony.
Luke 21:13 (NASB)

In life, there will we bad things you will have to go through. Don't lose hope. God will use those bad experiences for a good purpose in your life. When something traumatic and painful happens to you, you will be able to comfort another person who is going through a similar thing you went through. In this way, you let the other person know they are not alone.

This also can *lead to an opportunity for your testimony* describing how God was there with you the entire time, shielding you with His blood of protection, when you were going through the traumatic and painful situation. In this way, you can lead the other person to God and healing

Thank You, for being there with me, Father God, when I was going through the traumatic and painful situation in my life. At the time, all I could feel was anger and despair, Lord. Now I realize You protected me with your shield of blood. You turned my bad experience into a good one Lord, because I can help others going through the same thing, and lead them to You, and healing. Amen.

January 26

NEVER STOP PRAYING

Rejoice always, pray without ceasing, in everything give thanks; for this is the will of God in Christ Jesus for you. 1 Thessalonians 5:16-18 (NKJV)

Never stop praying. You must continue to seek God often if you want joy and peace in your life. So seek the Lord God, as you would seek a friend, and discuss your hopes and dreams with Him. He is not just there to run to when you have problems. God wants a relationship with you.

Rejoice always, pray without ceasing, in everything give thanks; for this is the will of God in Christ Jesus. Without the constant refreshment of prayer to God your life would become very dull and unbearable to live. Prayer to God adds enjoyment to your life. God is fun to be around! He adds laughter to your day, which you can never find in the world. He delights in you! What a perfect gift God is! When you unwrap God, your eyes will light up with pleasure. Seek God often.

Holy Father God I delight in Your presence! I will never stop praying to You, O God. My life is filled with joy and peace because I seek You often Lord. Thank You for being My God and never being too busy to listen to me. Amen.

January 27

HAVING CONFIDENCE AND TRUST IN THE LORD

But blessed is the one who trusts in the Lord, whose confidence is in him. He will be like a tree planted by the water that sends out its roots by the stream. It does not fear when heat comes; its leaves are always green. Jeremiah 17:7-8 (NIV)

Having confidence and trust in the Lord, doesn't mean that you will not get upset when trouble comes you way. It means you will seek the Lord immediately to walk with you, and comfort you through the rough patches of life. You are not meant to handle problems on your own. That isn't how God made you. He wants you to depend on Him, and have faith He will be with you always, never to leave you to walk alone. If you trust the Lord you *will be like a tree planted by the water that sends out its roots by the stream. It does not fear when heat comes; its leaves are always green.* Just like the example of the tree that doesn't fear the heat, when faced with difficulties that come into your life, you won't fear, because you know the Lord has everything under His control.

All I can say Lord, is thank You, thank You, for being My Shelter. When the storms of life sweep in and try to drown me in the waters of despair and worry, I no longer have to fear, because I have confidence and trust in You Lord, to take care of me. You are the Master of my life! It is Yours to do what you want with it. Amen.

January 28

GOD WILL NEVER LEAVE YOU

I will be your God throughout your lifetime—until your hair is white with age. I made you, and I will carry you, and I will care for you. I will carry you along and save you. Isaiah 46:4 (NLT)

God's unfailing love is eternal. This means that God with never leave you nor forsake you. No matter where you go, or what you do, God will always be beside you. *I will be your God throughout your lifetime—until your hair is white with age.* What a comforting truth this is! God made you and therefore, He will never abandon His masterpiece. He will polish it until it shines. He will display His precious craftsmanship to the world so they can marvel at such fine art work.

Think about how valuable you are to God! You are His child, and as such, He will do what any father would do. He will provide for all your needs, and make sure no one harms you. When you come to Him with your tears, because someone hurt you, God will wipe your tears away, and hold you in His arms to comfort you. He will be there, watching over you, until you return to heaven to be with Him for eternity.

God, You are so precious to me. When you call me Your child, I am so honored to be a child of the King of Kings, and Lord of Lords! YOU ARE THE GREAT I AM! Sometimes it is hard to grasp how valuable, a redeemed sinner, I am to You Lord. But I know my body was washed cleaned by Your blood. So I am forever righteous in Your sight, O Lord. And as Your child, You will never leave me, and always watch over me. Amen.

January 29

GOD IS ALWAYS FAITHFUL

And we know that in all things God works for the good of those who love him, who have been called according to his purpose. Romans 8:28 (NIV)

God is always faithful to those *who have been called according to his purpose.* If you believe in God and His Son, Jesus Christ, God will see to your every need. If you reject God, and His Son, Jesus, God will reject you. God wants you to come to Him on your own. God will not force Himself on you. He gave you free will to choose Him or the things of this world. What are you going to do today? Will you give yourself totally over to God, and find everlasting peace? Or will you continue to worship the things of this world, and find dissatisfaction in your life? God loves you, unconditionally, and wants you for His own. Choose God and find happiness and joy. All you have to do is seek God, and surrender your life over into His care. It is that simple! Then you will have God beside you and in you always!

Dear Heavenly Father, I want a relationship with You. But, I don't know how to approach You, O God. Please help me to surrender all of my life over into Your hands, Lord. I know You will be faithful to me, if I believe in You, and Your Son, Jesus Christ, Father. I know this world is evil, and can't satisfy my needs, Lord. Only You can satisfy all my needs. Amen.

January 30
THE FRUIT OF THE HOLY SPIRIT

But the Holy Spirit produces this kind of fruit in our lives: love, joy, peace, patience, kindness, goodness, faithfulness, gentleness, and self -control. There is no law against these things! Galatians 5:22-23 (NLT)

When Jesus Christ redeemed you of your sins by sacrificing His body as a blood offering, He made you one with God. Because you and God make up a whole body together, your life is no longer yours, it belongs to God. God demands that you listen and follow the guidance of His Holy Spirit inside of you. He calls you to be His servant for the people of this world, who are lost and never heard the name of Jesus. That means you must live the fruits of the Holy Spirit: *Love, joy, peace, patience, kindness, goodness, faithfulness, gentleness, and self-control.* God knows you are not perfect. But He does require that you demonstrate Jesus, by how you conduct your affairs. People will not follow you if they see you acting like the father of this world. They need proof that Jesus is alive in you. You are the only proof that they will ever see.

Thank You, God, for Your Holy Spirit inside of me. As I listen and follow the guidance of the fruits of the Holy Spirit, I will be able to bring people to You, by practicing what You have taught me to do, God, as I mediate on Your Holy Word. I want to be a devoted servant to Your people Lord. Please continue to help me be the best example of Jesus, to a lost and destitute people. Amen.

January 31

GREAT IS THE FAITHFULNESS OF THE LORD

The unfailing love of the Lord never ends! By his mercies we have been kept from complete destruction. Great is his faithfulness; his mercies begin afresh each day. I say to myself, "The Lord is my inheritance; therefore, I will hope in him!"
Lamentations 3:22-23 (NLT)

Great is the faithfulness of the Lord! *We have been kept from complete destruction...his mercies begin afresh each day.* You are exceedingly blessed, over and over again! God's unfailing love for you will never end. God gets complete and utter joy in giving you happiness and peace in your life.

When you seek the Lord, because you love him, He delights in you. God loves holding you in His arms and showering you with hugs and kisses. He is your devoted soul mate anticipating seeing you again so He can worship every part of your body. Never will God stop showing you how much He loves you. Seek God with your whole heart and soul often. You never will be disappointed!

I delight in Your presence, O God. You are my sunshine when skies are gray! I love You so much Lord! Never do I want to be apart from You, Father God. I find such joy and happiness in Your presence, Wonderful Comforter! Great is Your faithfulness Lord! Each hour of every day, Lover of My Soul, You give me countless mercies and blessings! Amen.

February 1

FACE THE TRUTH

The Lord detests lying lips, but he delights in those who tell the truth. Proverbs 12:22 (NLT)

Quit lying. Start being honest with yourself and others. *The Lord detests lying lips,* so be truthful always. If you want to be a follower of God, then you need to clean up your act. If you don't change how you are living your life, you will be stuck in believing your own lies. That is like trying to steer a boat without the wheel.

Face the truth. When you lie, you are doing what the god of this world wants you to do. Be honest with all the affairs of your life, and the Devil will not have a hold over you any longer. Seek the presence of the Lord, and admit your sins to Him. He will forgive you, and redeem you. Your heart and soul will feel such relief! Peace and serenity will once again walk with you. When you have God with you, He settles all the discontent inside of you with His healing waters of salvation.

I am so blessed to have a Devoted Friend like You Lord! I can seek Your presence at any time and surrender all of my transgressions to You, Precious Father. When I face the truth in my life and quit lying to myself and others, the devil will not have a hold over me any longer, O God. I am so grateful to You Lord, for welcoming me back into Your presence. Amen.

February 2

OVERWHELMING

Now to Him who is able to keep you from stumbling, and make you stand in the presence of His glory blameless with joy, to the only God our Savior, through Jesus Christ our Lord, be glory, majesty, dominion and authority, before all time and now and forever. Amen. Jude 1:24-25 (NASB)

It is overwhelming to comprehend that God, through His unfailing love for you, would take everything you have done against Him, and wipe the slate clean, remembering your sins no more. That means that all the shame, remorse, and guilt that you have felt, despite the things you have done, you can now stand before God, *blameless with joy, to the only God,* who has given you mercy and grace. Now you can forgive yourself. Just to know that you are set free from all your sins is a tremendous burden that is lifted from your heart and soul. All the filth and dirt in your soul was wiped clean from its walls by the atoning blood of Jesus Christ.

It is overwhelming to realize, Beautiful One, You would accept me back into your presence after all the sins I have committed against You! I will praise Your Name to everyone about how Your mercy and grace has saved me, a filthy sinner. You are good all the time Lord, You are good! Amen.

February 3

THE LORD IS ALWAYS COMPASSIONATE AND KIND TO YOU

May the Lord bless you and protect you. May the Lord smile on you and be gracious to you. May the Lord show you his favor and give you peace.
Numbers 6:24-26 (NLT)

The Lord is always compassionate and kind to you. He looks out for your wellbeing always. There is nothing for you to fear, because you have the Lord with you wherever you go. Life can be rough at times, but *the Lord will smile on you and be gracious to you.* God is your Constant Companion! Whether you walk through the valleys or go up to the mountains, the Lord walks before you and behind you, shielding you from all harm. Just keep seeking the presence of the Lord and He will be the Shining Sun to warm your steps and fill them with peace and serenity!

Gracious and Merciful God, You are always compassionate and kind to me. Going through this evil world in which I live Lord, I don't have to fear and be afraid, because You will shelter me. This life is filled with rough spots and stumbling blocks, but when I have You with me, O God, You make my steps smooth and even, so I don't fall. You are my Strong Fortress, when life intrudes on my peace and contentment. I worship and praise You always, Lord! Amen.

February 4

BE GRATEFUL

Naked I came from my mother's womb, and naked shall I return there. The Lord gave, and the Lord has taken away; blessed be the name of the LORD.
Job 1:21 (NKJV)

When things don't go as expected, do you find yourself getting rebellious at the Lord? Do you try to control things? Remember, the Lord is the only Perfect One! So He knows what you need. When you find situations that are not as you want them to be, be grateful to God. You have just avoided a catastrophe! Praise the Lord for taking charge over your life. Say with unrelenting Joy, "The Lord gave, and the Lord has taken away; blessed be the name of the LORD." Shout to the Lord, thanking Him for making your life so good.

Lord, You are so glorious to me! You take charge of my life, and give me many blessings. I am so grateful I have a God who watches over me, and sees what I need. I could never repay You, O Lord, for all the blessings You have graciously given me. I can never out give You, God. So I will worship and praise You, Father God, for the rest of my life. Your kindness is deeply appreciated, My Lord! Amen.

February 5

IN THE PRESENCE OF THE LORD IS JOY

Those who look to him for help will be radiant with joy; no shame will darken their faces.
Psalm 34:5 (NLT)

In the presence of the Lord is joy. Some days are easier to find joy than others. When circumstances crowd your soul, get rid of them. Replace them with the divine furniture of the Lord's presence and be *radiant with joy,* as you sit on the love seat of comfort.

How delightful and joyous is a day spent in the loving presence of your Best Friend! He knows all the secret places of your heart and soul. There is no room for pretense, when you are in His presence. No one understands you better than your Creator. God has been there for you before you were born. God continues to be there through all your ups and downs in life, until you come home and enjoy everlasting peace with Him.

Every day in Your presence, Lord, is wonderful and freeing for my soul! The joy I find in Your presence, Lord, rejuvenates every cell in my body with living waters of peace. Never do I want to leave Your comforting presence Lord, because I could never find contentment anywhere else. I love You Lord! Amen.

February 6

TRUST IN GOD

Trust in me in your times of trouble, and I will rescue you, and you will give me glory. Psalm 50:15 (NLT)

You need to pray to God when conflict and strife comes your way. In *times of trouble,* God will never leave you nor abandon you to fend for yourself. The Lord is always faithful, even when you are not faithful to him. Many times you think you can handle life's problems on your own. But you instantly realize in doing this, you bring more problems upon yourself You find you are trapped as the problems all fall at your feet. Then you have no choice but to call on the precious name of the Lord to help you.

You make life so complicated at times, when life can be so simplified! You just need to get your priorities straight and seek the presence of the Lord to walk beside you, guiding you along pathways to peace and serenity. For instance, instead of trying to accomplish every problem on your own, you can have God as your refuge and strength, in times of trouble. What an amazing blessing that would be for you! Now you just need to make God a part of your daily life.

Precious Heavenly Father, show me the way to Your presence every day. Help me to seek You, Lord in times of trouble. Life can be difficult at times, but if I call on Your Precious Name, O God, You will gladly help me. Your unfailing love for me, Father God, is always there for me to draw upon at all times. Thank You, Constant Companion, for always walking with me. Amen.

February 7

LET ANGER FEND FOR ITESELF

And we know that in all things God works for the good of those who love him, who have been called according to his purpose. Romans 8:28 (NIV)

You can get so caught up in who is right and wrong, and how entitled you are to your feelings. Expressing yourself, especially when you feel you were disrespected, allows anger to control your life. You should let anger fend for itself! What do I mean by this? Anger is the dominating factor in so many broken relationships today. Anger destroys maliciously! It doesn't leave survivors unless you engage anger in battle by calling on the Precious Name of God to help you defeat it. The reality is, the devil loves to put anger between you and those you love. It is his main strategy that he uses all the time. But the truth is, the enemy is not mightier than God.

God is an Awesome Provider! He takes care *of those who love him, who have been called according to his purpose.* Amen.! God will never let you down. He knows everything about you, and will give you what you need to handle all life throws at you. So why let anger get the upper hand on you? You can seek God's Mighty Presence to help you defeat anger. You just need to retreat, rethink and react differently, knowing God is right beside you cheering you on to victory!

Lord God, thank You for helping me defeat anger. I can now let anger fend for itself. I don't have to let anger into my life to control me. When I have You, Holy Father, by my side fighting for me the devil will not gain a foothold as I seek Your presence, Lord. Amen.

February 8
MIND BLOWOUT

Do you not know? Have you not heard? The Everlasting God, the Lord, the Creator of the ends of the earth does not become weary or tired. His understanding is inscrutable. He gives strength to the weary, and to him who lacks might He increases power. Isaiah 40:28-29 (NASB)

Instead of letting your mind blowout from over thinking about the future, you can surrender all your weary thoughts to God. All you can control is your reactions to today. Let Him take care of the future and handle everything else. Of course, you need to do the footwork if you need something. God will only help you obtain what you need. Prayer without action will not work! God *gives strength to the weary, and to him who lacks might He increases power.* For instance, if a light bulb blows out, you replace it. That is what God does for a weary mind. He revitalizes it with healing light of salvation, restoring peace and contentment once again.

God clearly states you should only concentrate on the problems of today. When you think about this, you can see how hard it is to get through the difficulty of life just for today. So why do you borrow trouble for yourself? Let God take care of what is His responsibility, and you can take care of yours! With the assistance of God beside you, it can be done.

Holy Father God, help me concentrate on today's problems. I always need to seek Your presence before I do anything. Then I won't have a mind blowout, which makes me so weary and unable to function properly. I am glad You are my Constant Companion! Amen.

February 9

WHEN YOU SEEK THE LORD, HE IS YOUR COMFORT AND STRENGTH

Search for the Lord and for His strength; continually seek Him. 1 Chronicles 16:11 (NLT)

When others make you feel insignificant, and unworthy of love, seek the Lord. He is your comfort and strength. The Lord calls you His precious child entitled to the royal inheritance of the throne of God. God loves you so much He made you in His image! He sees deep into your heart and soul, so therefore, He knows you. Others see your outward appearance and are sometimes quick to judge you. But you don't have to despair, for Your Lord God is always there for you.

You can pray with a sincere heart for those who wrong you. God will give you many blessings. The key to discard the bitterness you feel, is to continue to pray with a thankful heart, asking God *for His strength* to endure. Bitterness only causes decay to rot your heart and soul. So those who made you feel insignificant and unworthy of love, take them to God in prayer, asking for forgiveness for them. Then you will feel peace and serenity fall down to your heart and soul, healing them. This is the glorious fulfillment that cleanses your body with unfailing love from Your Magnificent Creator.

Oh how I love thee Lord! You are My Holy Father, who made me in Your precious image. I praise Your Glorious Name, O Lord God, for Your mercy and grace that saved me, so I can worship at Your royal throne forever. I praise Your Sacred Name, that I am your beloved child! When I seek You, You are my comfort and strength in times of hurt and sorrow. I can find comfort in Your gentle embrace, Devoted Father. Amen.

February 10
I AM GOING TO PRAISE YOU LORD

Praise be to God and Father of our Lord Jesus Christ! In his great mercy he has given us new birth into a living hope through the resurrection of Jesus Christ from the dead, and into an inheritance that can never perish, spoil or fade—kept in heaven for you, who through faith are shielded by God's power until the coming of the salvation that is ready to be revealed in the last time. 1 Peter 1:3-5 (NIV)

I am going to praise you, Lord. I am going to praise your Holy Name, above all names! I am going to lift up my hands high and thank you, Lord God, for the wonderful blessings I enjoy every day. You, O Lord, have blessed me beyond what I deserve.

You have given me *a living hope through the resurrection of Jesus Christ from the dead.* In this hope, I have been born again into a life of freedom from my sins. I can say with confidence, that one day I will live forever with you, O God, in heaven. That is why I will continue to praise you Lord, while I am on earth, to everyone I meet. All I can say is, hallelujah, hallelujah! My Lord is worthy to be praised!

I want to praise and glorify Your Precious Name, Holy Father. Please accept my praises as a gift offering of our appreciation for all You do for me Lord. I could never walk alone through this scary, evil world without Your presence beside me O Lord, guiding me. The blessings I receive daily are not in material possessions, but that I have Your unfailing love to always know My Life Mate will never leave me or forsake me. What joy I have in You, Our Redeemer! Amen.

February 11

YOU CAN'T HAVE PEACE UNLESS YOU KNOW JESUS

The thief comes only to steal and kill and destroy; I have come that they may have life, and have it to the full. John 10:10 (NIV)

You can't have peace unless you know Jesus. The ruler of the world offers you death and destruction. The evil one *comes only to steal and kill and destroy* you. Your Lord Jesus Christ comes to give you eternal peace and joy in your life. If you follow Jesus, He will be with you to the end of all the ages of time. What a glorious miracle that is! To have Jesus with you always.

Unless I know You Jesus and follow You, I can't have peace in my life. I have to surrender my life over totally into Your keeping Jesus, to have peace and serenity. Otherwise, I will continue to have darkness in my life, as I follow the evil one. Thank You Jesus, for Your unfailing love that saved me from my sins. Amen.

February 12

HAVING FAITH WITHOUT WORKS IS DEAD

What does it profit, my brethren, if someone says he has faith but does not have works? Can faith save him? If a brother or sister is naked and destitute of daily food, and one of you says to them, 'Depart in peace, be warmed and filled,' but you do not give them the things which are needed for the body, what does it profit? James 2:14-16 (NKJV)

The above scripture is a reminder of the importance of demonstrating your faith by just not talking about it, but actually showing those in need that you will be glad to help them. It is easy to talk to others about the faith you have in Jesus Christ, but look the other way when you see someone hurting and in need. You can tell yourself, someone else can take care of that person. You are too busy to stop and help them. Having faith without works is dead. *"What does it profit, my brethren, if someone says he has faith but does not have works?* When you ask yourself this question, hopefully you can say that you are being faithful to Jesus by being a good disciple; going out and helping His children, no matter what it cost you in time or money. You need to give it away, in order to keep being filled up with blessings by the Lord!

Holy Father God, help me to show compassion and kindness to Your children, because faith without works is dead! I don't want to talk faith to others, and not show them faith in my walk, Lord. Amen.

February 13
WHEN YOU TURN YOUR RECEPTORS OFF

Pay close attention to what you hear, The closer you listen, the more understanding you will be given—and you will receive even more. Mark 4:24 (NLT)

Jesus used parables to help us understand the word of God He was preaching to the people in different towns He visited. But a lot of people heard the word but didn't apply it to their lives. Some allowed Satan to take away the teachings of Jesus. Others started to incorporate the Word of God in their lives but got distracted with worldly possessions. They stopped doing what the Word of God told them to, so their lives could be peaceful and joyous. Basically, they did their own will, instead of obeying God's will for their lives.

Is this how you live your life sometimes? You allow outside influences to come between you and your relationship with God. You turn your receptors off and can't hear the voice of the Holy Spirit speaking to you. *"The closer you listen, the more understanding you will be given—and you will receive more."* When you take the time to closely study the Word of God, you are able to hear the voice of the Holy Spirit guide you through life and you will feel more peace and serenity.

O God, You are my hope and salvation when I get lost in worldly possessions! Please help me hear Your voice instead of tuning into what the world has to offer. When I do this, Lord God, all I receive is empty promises that can't satisfy my needs. Only You can satisfy me, Father! If I spend more time studying Your Word I will be able to hear the voice of the Holy Spirit guide me through life to find peace and serenity. Amen.

February 14

GOD IS WITH YOU WHEREVER YOU GO

Be strong and courageous. Do not be terrified; do not be discouraged, for the LORD your God will be with you wherever you go. Joshua 1:9 (NIV)

You do not have to fear when problems attack you, because God is with you wherever you go. So you can *be strong and courageous*, knowing God will save you from the mighty winds and onslaughts of torrential rains as the storm tries to sweep you away. God is an awesome warrior who you can depend on to be your shelter in the storm. He will pull you up into the boat, and take you safely to shore, where you can bask in the sunlight of His spirit.

I praise You and worship you, O Lord, My Strong Warrior who protects me always! I know You, O God, will go with me wherever I go. Problems may come to invade my peace and serenity, and try to take away my joy, but if I call on You, Lord, You will come instantly to help me through the storms of life. I am safe and secure in Your comforting embrace, Father God. Thank You for always being there for me. Amen.

February 15

DO YOU KNOW WHERE YOU ARE GOING WHEN YOU DIE?

Therefore my heart rejoiced and my tongue exulted exceedingly; moreover, my flesh also will dwell in hope [will encamp, pitch its tent, and dwell in hope for in anticipation of the resurrection].
Acts 2:26 (AMP)

Do you know where you are going when you die? If you have not surrendered your entire life to God and asked for atonement for your sins, you should do it now. You don't have time to waste! The Lord Jesus could be returning today. You need to get ready for His return. Think about it. To be raptured and reuinited with Jesus Christ would be an awesome experience you don't want to miss! There is no reason to be afraid or scared. Approach the Lord, and tell Him you are sorry for sinning against Him and want forgiveness. Be willing to give your life to Him and you will be guaranteed an inheritance into the kingdom of God forever.

Like king David elegantly said, *"Therefore my heart rejoice and my tongue exulted exceedingly; moreover, my flesh dwell in hope."* King David knew that after He died, his soul would be in heaven with the Lord. Only his body would remain in the ground. As you savor this Holy Word of God, know you are a precious child of God, and He prepared a room for you in heaven.

I want to live in heaven for eternity, Lord. Please help me to trust in You and put my faith in You. You are the only way to find salvation for my soul, Jesus. No other way will guide me to heaven! I want to know where I am going when I die. I don't want to burn in Hell forever after I die. Amen.

February 16
THE LORD IS WORTHY TO BE PRAISED

The Lord is my strength and defense; he has become my salvation. He is my God, and I will praise him, my father's God, and I will exalt him. The Lord is a warrior; and the Lord is his name. Exodus 15:2-3 (NIV)

The Lord is worthy to be praised! He never leaves you, or abandons you. The Lord cherishes you above all the creations He has made! It is very obvious when you look at everything the Lord has so graciously given you. He didn't need to give you anything, considering all the times you have gone against God's will for you, and worshipped worldly things, instead of worshipping God the Father. You are very blessed to have a Lord that loves you so much! You can say with absolute assurance, *"He is my God and I will praise him."* How can you not be shouting for joy to the Lord all day long, thanking Him for how good your life is?

I want to praise You and exalt your Holy Name, Lord! My Lord of lords, and King above all kings! Never have I had such a delightful relationship before You came into my life, Lord, and swept me off my feet! I love You so very, very, much Lord! Amen.

February 17
MY SALVATION COMES FROM THE LORD

But I will offer sacrifices to you with songs of praise, and I will fulfill my vows. For my salvation comes from the Lord alone. Jonah 2:9 (NLT)

Happiness and contentment comes from the merciful heart of the Lord! His unfailing love for you will never end. So when you wake up in the morning, remember to thank the Lord for the day ahead of you. Because you know the Lord will walk with you all through the day. Nothing that happens in your day can distress you if you can say, *"My salvation comes from the Lord alone."* I will enjoy my day with my Constant Companion by my side. Before you go to sleep, thank the Lord for the wonderful day He gave you.

Lord, I know that my salvation comes from You. I will not have a heart of fear, O Lord. Nothing can seriously upset me if You are by my side! I enjoy our time together! You are a delightful friend, Lord! I never want to walk alone again, because I get so much more joy with you being my Life Mate. I praise and honor You, for all the blessings I receive in Your presence. Amen.

February 18
GOD OF HOPE

May the God of hope fill you with all joy and peace as you trust in him, so that you may overflow with hope by the power of the Holy Spirit. Romans 15:13 (NIV)

God gives you infinite masterpieces that He created, so that you will be filled *with all joy and peace as you trust in him.* Some examples are: A fresh batch of snow; making snow men out of the snow with your children; the trees turning green after a long winter; the flowers blooming in your back yard; a butterfly dancing around you with its multitude of colors; sitting on your porch on a warm summer night, enjoying the breeze that hits your face; the leaves turning brilliant colors of reds and oranges as the fall season comes in; making a scarecrow with your children. You have a God of hope, who gives you these beautiful creations, so in the middle of the storms of life, you will remember all the blessings He has given you. Your heart will leap for joy once again!

Gracious Heavenly Father, I could never, ever, see everything You have created for me to enjoy to my heart's content! I am grateful You are a God of hope, because then I can find joy in the midst of suffering and pain. You knew as you created me, O Lord, what was going to happen in my life. That is why You created such breath-taking artwork for me to gaze upon and enjoy. I can't stop praising Your glorious name, Father! Amen.

February 19
WILLING TO FORGIVE

Make allowances for each other's faults, and forgive anyone who offends you. Remember, the Lord forgave you, so you must forgive others. Colossians 3:13 (NLT)

When someone offends you, it can be hard sometimes to forgive them. Especially when they don't have a heart of repentance. But God says, *"Make allowances for each other's faults, and forgive anyone who offends you."* When you are able to pray for the person who offended you, ask God to bless them abundantly for two weeks. After the two weeks are up, you will find you are willing to forgive that person. Then God will reward you with blessings of peace and contentment in your heart and soul.

I need Your help, Holy Father. It isn't easy to become willing to forgive someone whose heart isn't filled with repentance for offending me. But, as Your Holy Word says. "Remember, the Lord forgave You, so You must forgive others." Please help me to forgive them Lord. I want to be a faithful follower of Your Holy Word. Amen.

February 20
BROUGHT NEAR TO GOD

But now you belong to Christ Jesus, though you were once far away from God, now you have been brought near to him because of the blood of Christ.
Ephesians 2:13 (NLT)

    You were once lost in the folds of the world's idols, which had you trapped inside their inner layers of broken promises telling you that you would receive happiness if you worshipped them. Some examples are: Drinking alcohol to excess to have a good time, looking at pornography as a source of comfort, and having sex with others to find intimacy and love. These things only leave you empty and unfulfilled. But now you belong to Christ Jesus, who surrendered His body over to death on a cross, so your sins were forgiven by His Father. Through Jesus' sacrifice, you have been brought near to God, and a blessed life in His comforting presence.

    O Precious Comforter, I am happy and excited to be back in Your presence again! Being near You, O God, has been the greatest treasure in my life! My life is now complete because You are part of it again. I love You! Amen.

February 21

STRONG IN YOUR FAITH

I can do all things through Christ who strengthens me.
Philippians 4:13 (NKJV)

You know you are strong in your faith, when you trust the Lord will all facets of your life. As you continue to seek the Lord, you are able to walk with confidence and assurance, knowing that the Lord Is your invisible shield that nothing can penetrate. When trials and tribulations occur this enables you to feel peace that surpasses all understanding. The world will never comprehend that *you can do all things through Christ who strengthens* (you). Keep on believing in your faith that transcends all knowledge, and you will have a gold mine you can never spend in this lifetime, because God is a priceless nugget that keeps on giving!

O Lord over my life, I thank You for being my faithful friend! I know that my faith wouldn't be this strong, if I didn't believe totally in You, Lord Jesus. I never want to lose Your unfailing love for me, Father God. It is in Your unfailing love that I have found wholeness for my soul. I can never repay You, Lord, for all You have given me. That is the point, I'm not expected to repay You for all the blessings You gave me, O God. All you want is my loyalty and love. Amen.

February 22
FRIENDSHIP

The wise are known for their understanding, and pleasant words are persuasive. Proverbs 16:21 (NLT)

If you have a close friendship with another person, it is more precious than rare pearls! It is unmeasurable and more valuable than gold or silver! When you have a true friend you can trust, you have a relationship with someone you can weather the storms of life with. This is God's most treasured blessing for you.

The wise are known for their understanding, and pleasant words are persuasive. That is what a true friendship is, knowing you can count on someone having your back, no matter what happens in your life. Thank God for your friendship with that remarkable and special person who is in your life.

Dear Heavenly Father, thank You for the special friendship I have. I have someone that is always there for me. I praise You, O Lord, for giving me someone to share my life with! Amen.

February 23

CHANGE

God is our refuge and strength, always ready to help in times of trouble. Psalm 46:1 (NLT)

Change is inevitable! That is what life is all about. When you have to make a decision to change any part of your life, ask God to help you. He will be your *refuge and strength*, all through the process of making the choice to change what is wrong in your life, so your life will become better. You will eventually see that in the long run, your life has never been as good as it is now.

I have struggled, Lord, with change. I hate change! But, I can now see that change was exactly what I needed, O God! I have never been so happy since I made better choices in my life. Thank You for walking with me through it all, God. Amen.

February 24
THE LIVING ONE

Do not be afraid; I am the first and the last, and the living One; and I was dead, and behold I am alive forevermore, and I have the keys of death and Hades.
Revelations 1:17-18 (NASB)

It is so exciting to imagine a life in heaven with the Living One forever. No more pain and suffering. Just endless peace, joy, happiness, love, and gentleness; exciting times to savor all that is offered by God, to your heart's content! But that is something not everyone is entitled to. You have to work for it. It can be hard work sometimes, but the pay-off is a life forever in the presence of the Father, the Son, and the Holy Spirit. Just surrender all that you are to God God is *the first and the last, and the living One,* the GREAT I AM! Can you contain the thrilling expectations that are leaping for joy in your heart right now? You will always be this excited! To see the GREAT ALMIGHTY GOD every day forever. Wow!

O My King, how I love You! I can't wait to be with You, Lord forever and forever more. You are the Living One, the First and the Last, the Alpha and the Omega, the King of Kings and Lord of Lords! You have the key to my heart, God. I want to be Yours, and no and not belong to anyone else. Amen.

February 25

ACCEPTANCE

Your word is a lamp unto my feet and a light for my path, Psalm 119:105 (NIV)

Acceptance isn't an easy thing, but it is the best solution for you. When you can accept life as it is, and not as you want it to be, you have learned a valuable lesson! You have learned that it is better to have peace and serenity in your life, instead of distress and anguish. Life will throw you enough curve balls that you can't hit. So why bring more stress and despair over a problem that is not yours to solve? Trust in God and He will be a *lamp unto your feet, and a light for* the path you will travel in this life.

Lord, I am so thankful You are always available for me, when I call on You in prayer. You are the reason I can, most of the time, accept things in my life, Lord. I know I can't control what is going to happen in this life. But I do know You will be there for me, lighting my way, when I seek You, Father. Amen.

February 26
THE GREATEST SHOW ON EARTH

Who is a God like You, Who forgives iniquity and passes over the transgression of the remnant of His heritage? He retains not His anger forever, because He delights in mercy and loving-kindness.
Micah 7:18 (AMP)

God is the greatest show on earth! You can never say your life is dull after accepting God into your life! God takes a lowly sinner and makes you a part of His inheritance forever. Who does this? No one in this world. That is for certain! But here comes God into your life, with a full pardon. He forgives your *iquity.... He delights in mercy and grace and loving-kindness,* because of His unfailing love for you. He wipes the slate clean, and rewards you with blessings every day. You could never find anything to top this!

O Merciful God, I glorify Your Blessed Name, above all names! I will praise and worship You all the days of my life. I will tell every one of your marvelous deeds, Father. You are the greatest show on earth, Lord! Amen.

February 27

A NEW HEART

I will give you a new heart, and I will put a new spirit in you. I will take out your stony, stubborn heart, and give you a tender, responsive heart.
Ezekiel 36:26 (NLT)

God is so compassionate and kind to you that He would *take out your stony, stubborn heart, and give you a tender, responsive heart.* What an amazing God you have in your life! He gives you a new heart, free of charge. He is the Great Physician, who wants to make sure your heart is functioning properly, so you can love others, and lead them to a blessed life with Jesus Christ. As you continue to do this, your life will be more fulfilling and rich in the knowledge that you have saved countless souls to live with God forevermore.

Father God, I didn't think I needed a new heart, until I realized my life was empty and unfulfilled. Thank You, Lord, for waking me up, and showing me a more promising way of life. I now feel so blessed to be able to help others find fulfillment in You, My Friend! I love You! Amen.

February 28
WHAT IS GOD CALLING YOU TO DO?

Remember, it is sin to know what you ought to do, then not do it. James 4:17 (NLT)

What is God calling you to do? Only you can answer this question. God won't force you to obey His will. He gave you free will. *Remember, it is sin to know what you ought to do, then not do it.* It is easy to submit to the world's expectations of how you should live your life. But when you do this, your life will be filled with all kinds of problems. Only God can offer true peace and serenity! Come back to God, and He will show you the right path to follow, so you can get your life back on the right track again.

I need You God! I am so lost! I need You to rescue me Lord, from the world, and its expectations of how I should live my life. I want to come back into Your loving presence Lord, and do your will. I am ready to do what You are calling me to do, Father. Amen.

February 29

SEEK JESUS WHO UNDERSTANDS YOUR NEEDS

For we do not have a high priest who is unable to emphasize with our weaknesses, but we have one who has been tempted in every way, just as we are—yet did not sin. Hebrews 4:15 (NIV)

In this life you will have many challenges to overcome. But you don't have to try to accomplish them alone. Seek Jesus, who understands your needs. Some challenges may be hard, but don't allow the evil one to convince you to give up. He loves to whisper in your ear, and try to get you to quit striving for your goal, even before you start on your way. Don't believe him! ACall on the name of Jesus, *who has been tempted like you in every way,* to help you go all the way to the finish line and become victorious.

You are an amazing God, who I can always depend on when I am struggling through something! The challenges I face in this life are hard sometimes, Jesus, but I know You understand my needs. That is why I have confidence You will help me, Jesus, through it, and guide me to the finish line to success. Thank You, Jesus, for never being unavailable when I need You to rescue me. Amen.

March 1

PRAYING THIS WAY

Pray, then, in this way: 'Our Father who is in heaven, Hallowed be Your name. 'Your kingdom come. Your will be done, on earth as it is in heaven. 'Give us this day our daily bread. 'And forgive us our debts, as we also have forgiven our debtors. 'And do not lead us into temptation, but deliver us from evil. [For Yours is the kingdom and the power and the glory forever. Amen.'] Matthew 6:9-13 (NASB)

The above prayer is so vital to say when you are struggling with taking matters into your own hands. This prayer will guide you along the right path to sanity. Because it is insane behavior to even attempt to do anything on your own. It only leads to futility! But don't despair when you find yourself going out alone. The blessing is, you can come to God at any time and surrender it all into His capable hands, and feel relief surround you. Remember to say this: "Your will be done, on earth as it is in heaven." By praying this way you are set free from your own destructive thinking.

My Father in heaven, thank You for this wonderful prayer of salvation. When I pray this way, I feel all my problems just resolve themselves in Your capable hands, Lord. I love You, so much, Father! Amen.

March 2
A WRECKING BALL

And I am convinced that nothing can separate us from God's love. Neither death nor life, neither angels nor demons, neither our fears for today nor our worries about tomorrow-not even the powers of hell can separate us from God's love. Romans 8:38 (NLT)

What is so hard to see sometimes, when you are so caught up in trying to solve the problems of your life, is that you fail to notice that God is there waiting for you to seek His presence. He can take the control you are clinging tightly to, and resume charge over your life. It is like you are taking a wrecking ball through your life and destroying everything useful in sight. You do this when you separate yourself from the loving and caring presence of God. Then you find yourself lost and alone in this dangerous, scary world.

Neither our fears for today nor our worries about tomorrow-not even the powers of hell can separate us from the love of God. This is such a powerful statement from God to you! This Holy Word of God, lets you know you are never alone. God is always waiting and willing for a chance to be of service to you. The truth is, God delights in taking care of all of your needs. Just let go of everything you are holding tightly to and give it all freely to God.

O Precious Redeemer, I need You so much right now! My life is a mess, Father God! It is like I have taken a wrecking ball through it. I need You now, Lord, to help straighten out my life. I can't handle anymore, O God. Please help me! I surrender control to You. Take my life and do what You want with it, My Friend. Amen.

March 3

YOUR DAYS ARE FILLED WITH PEACE AND REST

Your castles and strongholds shall have bars of iron and bronze, and as your day, shall your strength, your rest and security, be. Deuteronomy 33:25 (AMP)

When you walk with God, instead of walking alone through your life, your days are filled with peace and rest. When problems arise, and you start to feel anxious and distressed, you have the luxury of the Lord to comfort you, guiding you through anything that is bothering you. The Lord God is your trusted friend, who wants you to come to Him with all your worries and fears. He wants you to be dependent on Him, so you will need to come to Him frequently to get a refill of strength and energy. *Your castles and strongholds shall have bars of iron and bronze, and as your day, shall your strength, your rest and security,* will be found in the loving arms of the Lord your God.

O My God, My Friend, and Constant Companion, what would I do without You? You are My Wonderful Comforter, who fills my days with peace and rest, as I walk with You. I need you always, My Lord, to be a part of my life! Amen.

March 4

THANK THE LORD BY PRAISING HIM

I will thank the Lord because he is just; I will sing praises to the Most High. Psalm 7:17 (NLT)

Thank the Lord by praising Him *because he is just.* He makes your days fun and delightful! Even when you find strife in your day, laughter and fun will soon arrive with the Lord. You will find warmth and joy in the sunlight of His spirit.

Praise the Lord with all your heart and soul! He deserves to be worshipped with singing and dancing. Shout to the heavens showing God how much you appreciate all He has done for you. Thank God for every blessing He graciously gives you daily.

You deserve to be praised and worshipped, Lord! Thank You so much, Father, for taking delight in making all my days filled with joy and happiness. I want to shout from the rooftops for everyone to praise the Lord Most High! Amen.

March 5

THE PERFECT ANTIBIOTIC

If a man has a hundred sheep and one of them wanders away, what will he do? Won't he leave the ninety-nine others on the hills and go out to search for the one that is lost? Matthew 18:12 (NLT)

This illustration that Jesus is using describes how God loves you. God sent Jesus to you and saved your life, when you were lost in the corruption of this world. If God wouldn't have loved you unconditionally no matter what you did, He could have let you be tormented in Hell forever by the devil and his minions. Instead, God sentenced His Only Son, Jesus, to die in your place on the cross. Jesus was the perfect antibiotic that healed your soul sickness! As Jesus says, *"If a man has a hundred sheep and one of them wanders away.... won't he leave the ninety-nine others on the hills and go out to search for the one that is lost?"* You are the one sheep that is lost. God felt you were important enough to rescue you and bring you back to His other sheep in His kingdom.

Father, God, thank You for sending Your Only Son, Jesus, to be the perfect antibiotic that cured the soul sickness inside of me. I love You, Lord, so much! You are the Lover of My Soul! That is why every morning I praise You and thank You, O Lord, for all you have done for me. I find enjoyment in praising Your Sacred Name, Father! Amen.

March 6
DRAW CLOSE AS YOU WANT TO GOD

Draw near to God and He will draw near to you. Cleanse your hands, you sinners; and purify your hearts, you double-minded. James 4:8 (NKJV)

You can draw as close as you want to God. He is patient and will be waiting for you. When you decide to leave the distractions of the world behind, *draw near to God and He will draw near to you.* The enemy of the world loves to manipulate your thoughts, by having you focused on worldly things, instead of focusing on God. But don't despair. God will not abandon you. Ask God and receive His presence over you.

Please My Devoted Friend, help me to come back to You, so I can draw close to You again. I need to be close to You God. There is no other alternative for me Lord! I just need to seek your presence, Lord, and concentrate more on Your beautiful face, rather than the things of this world which draw me away from You. Amen.

March 7
ATTITUDE FILLED WITH THANKFULNESS

So, then, just as you received Christ Jesus as Lord, continue to live in him, rooted and built up in him, strengthened in the faith as you were taught, and overflowing with thankfulness. Colossians 2:6-7 (NIV)

When your attitude is filled with thankfulness for the Lord, you *continue to live in him, rooted and built up in him, strengthened in the faith as you were taught.* When your faith is strong in the Lord, nothing you encounter can cause you to stumble and fall, because the Lord has a strong hold on your hand guiding you through the rocky crevices that hinder your passage through life. What a marvelous guarantee that is!

What a glorious relationship I have in You, My Lord! You are the strength I feel when I put my faith in You, O Lord. When I have an attitude filled with thankfulness for You, Father God, I discover that my day goes smoothly and is filled with absolute peace, no matter what happens that day. Amen.

March 8
PLEASING GOD

And the one who sent me is with me-he has not deserted me. For I always do those things that are pleasing to him. John 8:29 (NLT)

When you go through your day, and you find things that need your attention, ask yourself, are you pleasing God by doing these things? God desires for you to seek Him first. If you are struggling to figure out whether the thing you want to do is from God, or from the ruler of this world, ask Him. You can say to yourself, God *has not deserted me*, so I will turn my attention to Him and seek approval before I do anything today.

Precious Heavenly Father, I need Your help today. I am struggling with some things that I am not sure are from You, or the evil one of this world. Please show me whether they are from you, Lord, or the devil. I want to do things that are pleasing to You, O Lord God. Amen.

March 9
GLORY TO GLORY

But we all, with unveiled face, beholding as in a mirror of the glory of the Lord, are being transformed into the same image from glory to glory, just by the Spirit of the Lord. 2 Corinthians 3:18 (NKJV)

What an amazing thing to anticipate, being transformed into the same image from glory to glory, just as by the Spirit of the Lord. When you think about being born again by the power of Jesus' blood, can you remember being overwhelmed to realize your life would never be the same again? To live your life for the Lord is wonderfully unique! Being a servant of the Lord, is an honor and a privilege not very many people choose to enjoy.

You no longer live your life as a prisoner to the king of this world. Bowing down and worshipping him, only kept you in chains of shame, remorse, and guilt. Now your life is blessed in the unfailing love and mercy of your Creator.

Holy Father God, I am honored to be a servant of the greatest Master who ever lived! Glory to glory, I delight in the presence of Your Holy Spirit. My life is wonderfully filled with abundant peace and serenity, O Lord, because You are always with me! Amen.

March 10

ALL THINGS ARE POSSIBLE

Looking at them Jesus said. "With people it is impossible, but not with God; for all things are possible with God." Mark 10:27 (NASB)

This life is not for the faint-of-heart! It is a rough life filled with trials and tribulations. But there is hope in the Lord to get you through every one of them. When you trust in the Lord with all your heart, mind, body, and soul, *all things are possible* to handle. Because the Lord wraps you in His light of strength and upholds you through the most difficult times in your life. But you must seek Him on the narrow road you will travel through your life.

Nothing is impossible to handle in my life when I have You with me Lord. I delight in Your loving presence, O God! You are the love of my life, My Devoted Life Mate! Amen.

March 11

THE HOLY WORD OF GOD

For if you listen to the word and don't obey, it is like glancing at your face in a mirror. You see yourself, walk away, and forget what you look like.
James 1:23-24 (NLT)

  The Holy Word of God is very important for you to not just read it, but incorporate what it says to do into your life. Do you find yourself reading the Holy Word of God like a ritual you must do every day? Or do you actually enjoy meditating on God's Holy Word? There is a big difference! God wants you to *listen to the word* and use it faithfully in your life, and follow all of His commandments. If you do this, your life will be so blessed and filled with all the righteousness that God intended for you to have.

  O Gracious and Merciful God, I am so very sorry I made Your Holy Word not important in my life. I have made it a farce! I ritually find myself reading your Holy Word, Lord, just to get it over with, like a daily chore. Please help me to be faithful to You, O God, by reading Your Word, and also incorporating it in my life. Thank You, Lord. Amen.

March 12

LAUGHTER: THE MASTER KEY

To shine on those living in the darkness and in the shadow of death, and to guide our feet into the path of peace. Luke 1:79 (NIV)

Life is what you make of it! You can choose how you will go about you day. Either you will begin each day with prayer and meditation with the Lord. Or you will get out of bed and start going about you day without consulting the Lord first. One way brings peace and serenity. The other way brings chaos and mayhem. Which pathway will you walk today?

When you surrender the day to God, your find laughter is the master key to your heart! When things do require your immediate attention in your day, and you walk with God to deal with these problems, He will guide your *feet into the path of peace.* Then you will find your heart and soul rejoicing with happiness and contentment, because nothing you had to deal with was a struggle for you, with the Lord by your side. When you go alone trying to handle anything, you find that everything you touch falls apart, leaving you screaming in frustration.

Lord, I have made a complete mess of my day! I tried to accomplish everything I had to do without You by my side, Lord. Now I admit defeat. I am crying out to You, Lord God, to help me. I promise if You help me, Lord, I will begin each day with You by my side. I want laughter to be the master key to my heart, God. Laughter and joy will only be possible if I surrender my life to You, O Lord. Amen.

March 13
COMFORT AND STRENGTH

Be strong and of good courage, do not fear nor be afraid of them; for the Lord your God, He is the One who goes with you, He will not leave you nor forsake you. Deuteronomy 31:6 (NKJV)

God is your everlasting comfort and strength, throughout your entire life. He is a strong tower of refuge when you face threatening opposition. Never fear or be afraid because the strong arm of God will shelter you and protect you against the mightiest giants that come to fight you. *He is the One who goes with you and will never leave your nor forsake you.* God is a powerful warrior who will defeat all your enemies.

Lord God, I want to thank You for always fighting my enemies. You are always faithful. Lord You never abandon me when I am in trouble. I can always depend on You to fight my battles, Lord. You, O God, are my comfort and strength against the mightiest giants who come to do me harm. I love You, Lord! Amen.

March 14
DAILY SIN

For all have sinned; all fall short of God's glorious standards. Romans 3:23 (NLT)

Each day you sin. Whether it is being prideful, or having angry outbursts, or being envious of someone, or being lustful, or wanting more than you deserve. If it wasn't for God's merciful grace, you would be left surrounded by your sins for eternity. The fact is, you *fall short of God's glorious standards.* Thank God that there is hope for you! You would be lost in the darkness. Now God's spirit will light your passage into heaven to be with Him forever.

Thank You so much, God, for your merciful grace which has saved this lowly sinner. I know I sin daily, Lord, but when I repent of my transgressions against You. Your unfailing love for me grants me forgiveness. I am so blessed that Your heart Lord, is very tender where I am concerned! Amen.

March 15
GOD VS THE SMART PHONE

Great is the Lord and highly to be praised, and His greatness is unsearchable. Psalm 145:3 (NASB)

God doesn't need to be charged again every time you use Him, like your smart phone does.

You don't have to seek your Devoted Friend through your contacts on your phone, like you do with an earthly friend.

When you lose God, you don't have to search for Him with a built-in GPS system, like you do when you lose a smart phone. Just seek the Lord and He will be immediately there for you.

God is not an app you have to download, like on the smart phone to give you pleasure. God delights in giving you special blessings without you even asking Him.

You don't have to pick God up and turn Him on, like you do on the smart phone, because God is already turned on inside of you, willing to guide your every move.

Great is the Lord and highly to be praised, and His greatness is unsearchable. So depend on God more than you depend on your smart phone and God will make all of your days prosperous.

God, You are more available to me than my smart phone. I just need to use you more in my life, Lord, than I use my smart phone. I am sorry I neglected You, Father. Please forgive me. Amen.

March 16
GOD'S LOVE

But if one loves God truly [with affectionate reverence, prompt obedience, and grateful recognition of His blessings], he is known by God [recognized as worthy of His intimacy and love, and he is owned by Him]. I Corinthians 8:3 (AMP)

God is the magnificent Creator, who loves you with an unfailing love that can never be taken away from you. All God demands from you is your devoted love and obedience to Him only. God is a jealous God, who gets angry when you worship other gods. His anger is quickly taken away when you come back to Him asking for total forgiveness and repentance.

If you love God *truly [with affectionate reverence, prompt obedience, and grateful recognition of His blessings],* God's love will shine down upon you forever and ever, with total devotion and reverence for you His precious child.

I love You so very, very much, My Lord God! I can't imagine my life without You in it, O God. Your love, God, sweeps over me with gentle warmth and comfort when my body gets weary. I depend on You, Lord, always being there when I need you. Please remain with me always, My Devoted Companion. Amen.

March 17

THE BREATH OF LIFE

Then the Lord God formed the man from the dust of the ground. He breathed the breath of life into the man's nostrils, and the man became a living person.
Genesis 2:7 (NLT)

God *breathed the breath of life into* you, His marvelous masterpiece. He wanted you to be His most precious of all His possessions on the earth. God took His time forming you so you would be fearfully and wonderfully made in His own image. God loved you above and beyond all of His creations. God finds you enjoyable to look upon. He watches over every step of your life, ensuring you are safe and secure always. Never does God leave you. He loves walking beside you, guiding your steps to joy and happiness. Praise God for making you so special and unique!

O Holy Father, I am overwhelmed by Your beauty and majesty! I can't comprehend why God, You considered me to be the most precious of all Your creations. I am deeply humbled in Your presence, Lord! Thank You for breathing the breath of life into my body. Every day I wake up, Lover of My Soul, is a blessed gift I receive from You. I deeply love You, Lord! Amen.

March 18

WISDOM, KNOWLEDGE AND UNDERSTANDING

For the Lord gives wisdom; from His mouth comes knowledge and understanding; He stores up sound wisdom for the upright; He is a shield to those who walk uprightly; He guards the path of justice, and preserves the way of the saints. Proverbs 2:6-8 (NKJV)

Wisdom, knowledge, and understanding are the important key words of the Lord. His ways are not your ways, but they are always the best ways possible for a contented life. When you trudge up the steep and perilous mountain cliffs of life, you will find comfort in the understanding of the presence of the Lord. He will give you *sound wisdom* and knowledge so you will have a resolution that can solve the problems that are making you weary and stressed.

Lord Your understanding, wisdom, and knowledge have been so beneficial to me. I need these important concepts from You, Lord, to solve the problems that are making me stressed and very tired. Thank You for coming always to my rescue, Father God. Amen.

March 19

UNLIMITED TREASURES

I will give you the treasures of darkness, riches stored in secret places, so that you may know that I am the Lord, the God of Israel, who summons you by name.
Isaiah 45:3 (NIV)

When you surrendered yourself to the Lord, your God, He gave you unlimited treasures *stored in secret places* of your heart and soul. Theses glorious riches are seen when you touch other's hearts by the unconditional love you give away to them. It is a love that gets transferred from one person to another, causing a ripple affect which spreads all over the world. The effect of you touching one heart is the unlimited supply of God's blessings, which heals their inner being, like He healed yours.

Dear Lord, I am so grateful and thankful I surrendered myself to You! It has been the best thing I have ever done in my life! Now I can bless others with unlimited treasures Lord, by passing on to them what You have so freely given me. Amen.

March 20

FULLY UNDERSTANDS YOU

*If we are living by the Holy Spirit, let us follow
the Holy Spirit's leading in every part of our lives.
Galatians 5:25 (NLT)*

God is the only one that fully understands you. All the walls you have built to protect yourself from being hurt, can slowly be taken down and replaced with allowing the Holy Spirit inside of you, to surround you with His gentle arms of compassion.

When you can finally feel safe underneath the ever loving arms of God, you will find an eternal peace which you have never experienced before in your life. You will know without a shadow of a doubt that you *are living now by the Holy Spirit's* guidance. That gives you an unfailing love in your heart and soul which just feels so good and right!

I have never felt so loved and accepted before You became a vital part of my life, O God! You are the only one who fully understands me. I will always need You, Lord! And someday I will enjoy life for eternity with You, My Life Mate. I love You so much! Amen.

March 21
THE GOD OF HEALING

Indeed, the darkness shall not hide from You, but the night shines as day; the darkness and the light are alike to You. Psalm 139:12 (NKJV)

When your past haunts you, and causes you to be overwhelmed because someone harmed you, don't lose hope. The God of healing will cover your heart with cleansing waters of comfort. You may feel like the darkness is closing in on you, but the *darkness and light are alike to* God. He will sweep the darkness out of your mind, and ease your troubled heart with His gentle kiss of love. Then His light of deliverance will surround you with His peace.

God of Wonders and Miracles, I thank You for Your unconditional love that covered my troubled heart with Your healing light. I am feeling much better now God. You came quickly to comfort me, Lord. I praise You, O Lord God, because at all times You are good! Amen.

March 22
DESPERATE FOR GOD'S PRESENCE

Yet I still belong to you; you are holding my right hand. You will keep on guiding me with your counsel, leading me to a glorious destiny. Psalm 73:23-24 (NLT}

There are some things in life you must do. For instance, when you are given a job by your supervisor at work, the whole time you are doing the job assigned to you, you may be grumbling angry words of frustration under your breath. You find yourself desperate for God's presence. If you look, you will see God right beside you, *holding your right hand.* Imagine God taking you to a grassy knoll where He spreads a blanket and tells you to rest your head in His lap where God gently rubs all your frustrations and anger away until only peace remains.

My dear, dear, Devoted Friend, You are always there when I desperately need you! As I bask in Your endearing presence, Lord, I feel all the tension and frustration just melt away. Calmness and peace are seeping into my innermost being from Your miraculous touch, Glorious Father God. Amen.

March 23

GOD WILL EXULT OVER YOU

For the Lord your God has arrived to live among you. He is a mighty savior. He will rejoice over you with gladness. With his love, he will calm all your fears. He will exult over you by singing a happy song.
Zephaniah 3:17 (NLT)

Every day can be very challenging, especially when you have so many things to do. When you choose to accomplish all these things, without taking the time to rest in the presence of the Lord, is when you find yourself on an unfamiliar road totally lost. Take a deep breath and seek the Lord, and *He will exult over you by singing a happy song.* Immerse yourself in the delightful arms of the Lord, and He will rejoice at having you with Him.

Precious Lord God, thank You for sweeping me up in Your gentle arms of comfort. I am so happy to be in Your delightful presence again. I am so blessed to have You, God exult over me with a delightful smile. You are my Greatest Blessing! Amen.

March 24

A RED LIGHT

"For I know the plans I have for you," says the Lord. "They are plans for good and not for disaster, to give you a future and a hope." Jeremiah 29:11 (NLT)

Sometimes when you are running around in circles of deep anxiousness, because you are taking too much responsibility upon your shoulders, the Lord will give you a red light. This is a signal that the Lord wants you to slow down and relax. He never expected you to solve all the problems of the world. That is His job. The Lord says, *"For I know the plans I have for you…they are plans for good and not for disaster, to give you a future and hope."* You can't control anything. You can do nothing without the constant help of the Lord.

I am so grateful You slowed my wayward thoughts down Lord! I really needed the red light You placed in my path. Sometimes I can go way overboard in trying to control things that are none of my business in the first place, My God. Amen.

March 25
YOU ARE VERY IMPORTANT TO GOD

The Lord is near. Be anxious for nothing, but in everything by prayer and supplication with thanksgiving let your requests be made known to God. And the peace of God which surpasses all comprehension, will guard your hearts and minds in Christ Jesus. Philippians 4:5-7 (NASB)

When no one understands the hurt and pain you are feeling, you can go to God; know He will always listen to you and comfort you with His unfailing love. You are very important to God. He doesn't find you insignificant or unworthy of His devotion. He cries for you when you don't feel you can find anyone who will be emphatic to your needs. God wants you to seek His presence to unload all your feelings, so He can give you *peace....which surpasses all comprehension,* as God tenderly holds you in His arms and comforts your aching heart.

My Trusted Friend, I am so eternally thankful for being able to talk to You. You are never too busy to listen to me Lord. I am so grateful I am so very important to You God. I feel that I can't talk to anyone. They don't understand or empathize with all the pain I am feeling Lord. I am glad I have You, Father, to come to when I am hurting emotionally. Amen.

March 26

LIVE IN THE MOMENT

The thief's purpose is to steal, and kill, and destroy. My purpose is to give them a rich and satisfying life.
John 10:10 (NLT)

Life is too precious to waste on not living in the moment. God wants you to enjoy *a rich and satisfying life.* That doesn't mean your life will be absent from problems. Of course not! It means, whether you have a good day or bad day, you can still appreciate life to the fullest, enjoying each moment you are alive. Laugh outrageously. Happiness is obtained in all the richness of blessings God has given you.

Holy Father God, I need to live in the moment more. Life is too short to waste on being complacent with sadness all the time. I need to enjoy all the marvelous blessings You have given me Lord, to the fullest. You want me to laugh more and be happy. Thank You, Lord, for all You have so graciously given me. Amen.

March 27

GOD, WHO IS YOUR SAFE HAVEN

"The Lord is my rock, my fortress and my deliverer; my God is my rock, in whom I take refuge, my shield and the horn of my salvation." 2 Samuel 22:3 (NIV)

Trust God completely when conflicts between another person and you makes you feel anger and despair. Lift up your hands and surrender the whole affair to God, who is your safe haven of comfort and peace. He will reach down, take a hold of your outstretched hands, and place you securely in His intimate embrace. As your body relaxes against God, you feel safe, because God is your *fortress and* (your) *deliverer.* God will never leave you nor forsake you.

God, You are my safe haven when other people get me down in my spirit. I know You will always welcome me into your intimate arms of peace, Lord. I never need to feel alone, when I have You to lean upon, My God! Amen.

March 28
EASY DOES IT

And let the peace that comes from Christ rule in your hearts. For as members of one body you are called to live in peace. And always be thankful.
Colossians 3:15 (NLT)

The first thing that you should do, is pray to God for those in need, then for yourself. *And always be thankful* for all He has given you. This simple formula will make it easier for you to come to God in prayer.

Easy does it, should be your motto each time you pray. You can think of God as a trusted friend, who is always happy to hear from you. So when you seek God in prayer, when He hears your voice you can imagine God's face lighting up with a big smile of pleasure.

Lord God Almighty, Creator of heaven and earth! It has been hard for me, with all the titles from Your Holy Word, to see You as a friend. But now through getting to know You Lord, I have found it very easy to communicate with You in prayer. Easy does it, is the key to an uncomplicated prayer time with You, O God. Amen.

March 29

GRACE, MERCY, PEACE

Grace, mercy, and peace will be with you from God the Father and the Lord Jesus Christ, the Son of the Father, in truth and love. 2 John 1:3 (NKJV)

You have the richness of the Holy Spirit of God living inside of you. This is the perfect treasure given especially to you by God, because of His unlimited supply of *grace, mercy, and peace.* God not only saves your life from eternal damnation, but He also puts His Holy Spirit inside of you, upon the death of His beloved Son, Jesus Christ. What compassion and unfailing love God has for you! He gives you the precious gift of His Holy Spirit to watch over you and guide you to do His will. Praise God's Glorious Name!

You are the most wonderful and generous friend to me, God! I am honored and humbled by Your grace, mercy, and peace Lord, which from Your unfailing love, You granted me the privilege to have. I am so blessed by Your marvelous presence, Father God! Amen.

March 30
NOTHING CAN SEPARATE YOU FROM GOD

Who shall separate us from the love of Christ? Shall tribulations, or distress, or persecution, or famine, or nakedness, or sword? As it is written: "For Your sake we are killed all day long; we are accounted as sheep for slaughter." Romans 8:35-36 (NKJV)

It is a fact that absolutely nothing can separate you from God. No matter if you are going through *tribulations, or distress, or persecution, or famine, nakedness, or sword.* God is in the middle of it all, fighting your battles with you. Lean not on your own understanding, but let the perfect understanding of God evaporate inside of you, to guide you forever in the right direction throughout all of your life.

I am so grateful nothing will be able to separate me from Your loving presence, Lord. Your unfailing love with remain with me forever! I love You so much, O God! Amen.

March 31

SAVED THROUGH FAITH

For by grace you have been saved through faith, and that not of yourselves; it is a gift of God, lest anyone should boast. Ephesians 2:8-9 (NKJV)

Many things in your life have gone wrong because you made a choice to live your life in the world instead of following in the footsteps of God your Savior. The result was tremendous suffering and heartache you felt every time you did something that you knew wasn't sanctioned by God. Then, one day God grabbed hold of your soul and healed it by the sacred blood of His Son, Jesus Christ. You were *saved by faith,* believing God could renew the inner parts of your body making them more shiny and polished than they were before.

My soul was so blackened and charred by sin, Lord, before I surrendered all of my life over into your keeping. It was my faith in You, O God, which saved me and healed my broken and damaged soul. Today I feel peace and joy in the wonderful relationship I have with You, My Awesome Counselor. Amen.

April 1

DON'T IGNORE THE TRUTH

"Do you thus repay the Lord, O foolish and unwise people? Is not He your Father who has bought you? He has made you and established you.
Deuteronomy 32:6 (NASB)

Does the above Holy Scripture of God bring into your heart and soul an awakening of how foolish you have lived your life? Do you see areas you need to change? Are there areas which will make you and your life more complete and whole? If you answered yes to these questions, don't ignore the truth any longer. Cry out to the Lord, and ask Him to help you to change all that is disrupting your life. All of this makes you lack serenity or peace inside of your heart and soul. *Is not He your Father that has bought you?* He bought you with the shedding of His Son Jesus' blood on the cross. Seek His Holy Presence to find contentment and healing.

O Precious Lord, I am crying out to You! I have lived my life so foolishly without any thought of You, My Redeemer. I don't want to ignore the truth of how selfish I have been! I am asking You, Father God, to please help me change my life and make it more complete and whole. I need You so much, Healer of My Heart and Soul, to patch up all the broken pieces of my inner being. I want to enjoy peace and serenity in my life, O God. Amen.

April 2
A KISS

Love is patient and kind. Love is not jealous or boastful or proud or rude. It does not demand its own way. It is not irritable, and keeps no record of being wronged. It does not rejoice about injustice but rejoices whenever the truth wins out. Love never gives up, never loses its faith, is always hopeful and endures through every circumstance.
I Corinthians 13:4-7 (NLT)

God gently breathes a kiss of love into your innermost being all day long. *Love never gives up, never loses its faith, is always hopeful and endures through every circumstance.* This is a perfect example of how God loves you. God considers you very precious to Him! You are God's most valued creation, His perfect masterpiece! He loves to show the world how very special you are to Him. Even when you abandon God, He never abandons you. God was waiting for you to come back to Him. That is why He considered you so important to Him that He gave His Only Son, Jesus, to suffer a horrible death. This was so you could be set free from your sins.

I don't understand why I am so precious to You O God. But I am certainly glad I am loved unconditionally by You, Lord. Thank you, Glorious Father, for breathing a kiss of love into my innermost being all day long. I am so filled with gratitude to You, O Lord, for creating me, to be valued more precious than all your other creations. I love You God, so much! Amen.

April 3

FILLED WITH THANKFULNESS

*That my heart may sing your praises and not be silent.
O LORD my God, I will praise you forever.
Psalm 30:12 (NIV)*

There is so much you can be joyous for every day. When you look around at all the Lord has given you, how can you not be filled with thankfulness? For one thing, everything you have belongs to the Lord. But He graciously permits you to use all He has given you so you can have a blessed life. God also expects you to share what He has given you with others. Doesn't that make you want to shout praises and *sing….and not be silent,* and let others know what an awesome God you have?

Glory hallelujah, praise and honor are Yours, My Wonderful Savior! I am so filled with thankfulness to You, O God, everything You so graciously have given me. It is a great pleasure to share with others the abundant blessings You, Lord, gave me! Amen.

April 4

NOTHING HAPPENS IN GOD'S WORLD BY MISTAKE

Nothing in all creation is hidden from God. Everything is naked and exposed before his eyes, and he is the one to whom we are accountable to.
Hebrews 4:13 (NLT)

Nothing happens in God's world by mistake. He knows everything that you are going to do before you do it. When God formed you in the secret place, He formulated a full-proof plan to help and guide you, no matter what you will experience. *Nothing in all creation is hidden from God.* He will be there to hold you right hand and support you through the best and worst of times in your life.

What a precious gift I received O God, when You became a vital part of my life! Nothing that happens in Your world God is a mistake. You see everything that I experience throughout my life Father God. I am so blessed and thankful Lord that You watch over me! Amen.

April 5

THE LORD IS YOUR COMFORT

May God our Father and the Lord Jesus Christ give you grace and peace. God offers comfort to all.
2 Corinthians 1:2 (NLT)

Consider it pure joy when you go through trials and tribulations for the Lord. Because this will give you strength and endurance. Don't allow the enemy of God to convince you that God doesn't care what happens to you. Instead, when the voice of the devil invades your mind with his darkness, don't lose faith. Remember the Lord is your comfort of *grace and peace* always.

Holy Father God, I consider it pure joy when trials and tribulations come. I know I am doing Your will during these times, because the devil is causing these problems to happen to me. I know You are with me Lord, so I can endure anything. I know You, Lord, delight in giving me comfort, when I am weary and tired. I love being in Your gentle and compassionate embrace God! Amen.

April 6
LIVING FOR GOD

God has called us to live holy lives, not impure lives.
1 Thessalonians 4:7 (NLT)

God has called us to live holy lives, not impure lives. Living for God is a privilege, not a dreaded chore you hate doing. God has been a Devoted Friend, who loves you with an unfailing love that is from everlasting to everlasting! He is the One who sees into your heart and soul. He knows the real you. You are a unique and special person in God's sight! Your life should represent God in everything you do. God's excellent teachings in His Holy Word will guide you along the right path through life.

How could I not live my life as a praise offering to You, O Devoted Friend? You have been my saving grace Lord. Aside from You, Father God, I can do nothing. Every good thing I have is because of Your unfailing love for me my Precious and Beautiful Redeemer! I love You Lord! Amen.

April 7

NEVER GIVE UP

Therefore since we are surrounded by such a huge crowd of witnesses to the life of faith, let us strip off every weight that slows us down, especially sin that so easily trips us up. And let us run with endurance the race God set before us. Hebrews 12:1 (NLT)

When God directs you to do something, even though you are scared, keep your eyes on God and never give up. Because you know that God will never give you something to accomplish without Him remaining by your side, helping you to achieve miraculous works. So *strip off every weight that slows you down, especially sin that so easily trips* (you) *up*, and keep striving to finish the job God set before you to do.

Holy Father God, thank You so much for guiding me to keep faithfully holding on to You when I was afraid. It has been a thrilling journey Lord, with You leading the way! I am glad I never gave up trusting You, My Life Mate, to take me to exciting places. My life, O Lord, is so very blessed because of You! Amen.

April 8

THE GREAT I AM

And God said to MOSES, I AM WHO I AM and WHAT I AM, and I WILL BE WHAT I WILL BE; and He said, You shall say this to the Israelites: I AM has sent me to you. Exodus 3:14 (AMP)

God is THE GREAT *I AM*! As such, you should lift your hands up in praise and worship to God all the time. God is the Glorious One who is worthy to be praised! God doesn't skimp on the blessings He so delights in giving to you. So you shouldn't skimp on the praises and worship you give to God. If you truly love God with your whole heart and soul, you will find that you can't stand to be away from God's divine presence for even a second. Be desperate to seek Him, fall into His arms, and kiss His beautiful face in hallelujahs and Amen.s.

Praise and honor and glory I want to give You always, My Blessed Savior! I love You so very much, O Lord! You are THE GREAT I AM and the ALMIGHTY GOD of all creation! I will bow down before You and praise your Glorious Name forever. I can't be away from Your loving presence God. I need You more than I need air and water, Father God. You are the Beautiful One! Amen.

April 9

THE SHEPHERD KING

He will feed his flock like a shepherd. He will carry the lambs in his arms, holding them close to his heart. He will gently lead the mother sheep with their young.
Isaiah 40:11 (NLT)

You were not made by God to control events in your life. God made you weak so you would need Him to care for all your needs. You were never meant to do things on your own. When you attempt to manipulate any situation, you only cause yourself undue complications, which leads only to chaos and mayhem.

When you are frustrated to the point of exhaustion, call on the Shepherd King, and He will come and save you. You are one of His lost sheep. He carries you *close to his heart* because He is overjoyed that He found you.

Precious Heavenly Father, my pride and ego causes me so many problems. I convince myself, O Lord, that I have control over the situations in my life. Then I find myself surrounded by obstacles that hinder my progress. This leads me to become lost in my own self-importance God. This is when I need to seek You, my Shepherd King, to come and find me, and bring me back safely to the flock. That is where You will care for all of my needs. I love you, Lord! Amen.

April 10
GOD DESIRES A RELATIONSHIP WITH YOU

Come, let us go up to the mountain of the LORD, to the temple of the God of Jacob. He will teach us his ways, so we may walk in his paths. Micah 4:2 (NIV)

You can come to God when you are angry, happy, sad, desperate, filled with fear just to name a few emotions you may be feeling at any given time in your life. The point is this, God desires a relationship with you. He knows you intimately. So come to God as you are. God's presence is your refuge and strength when the problems of life become too much to handle. God is also there when life is going really fantastic for you. *Go up to the mountain of the LORD* and let Him surround you with His glorious light of warmth for your heart and soul. Realize you need the glorious presence of God in all circumstances of your life.

What a friend I have in You God! The amazing part of our relationship is I can come just as I am. What a blessing that is Lord! You accept me just as I am. I am so glad You desire a relationship with me God, always. I can't live without You being a part of my life O Lord! I can't do this scary life alone. When I walk beside You, Father God, I feel peace and contentment surround me, no matter what is happening in my life. I truly am in love with You, Precious Father! Amen.

April 11

TAKING THE EASY ROAD

You can enter God's Kingdom only through the narrow gate. The highway to hell is broad, and its gate is wide for the many who choose that way. But the gateway to life is very narrow and the road is difficult, and only a few ever find it. Matthew 7:13-14 (NLT)

God's way to travel is taking the 'easy road' through life! When you allow yourself to be totally out of control, and depend only on God, your life becomes joyous and peaceful. That doesn't mean there won't be hardships in your life, but you will be able to surrender them immediately to God, because you have complete faith in God to be your shelter through the storms that come.

The highway to hell is broad, and its gate is wide for the many who choose that way. It is paved with good intentions that go seriously wrong! Don't allow yourself to be led by the devil to travel that way. He is the great deceiver and father of lies. He wants to get you off your divine walk with God to everlasting peace. Don't allow the evil one to win. Keep on walking the narrow road through life, and at the end of your life, you will be rewarded with a crown of glory for a job well done.

God, at various times in my life, I didn't find your way to be taking the easy road! I was so confused and I allowed the evil one to side track me, and that lead me away from Your loving arms, O Lord. Now I am convinced Your way, Holy Father, is the easy way to travel. I can't imagine traveling any other way except with You, My Constant Companion! Amen.

April 12
A FANTASTIC DISPLAY

Let the heavens rejoice, let the earth be glad; let the sea resound, and all that is in it. Let the fields be jubilant, and everything in them; let the trees of the forest sing for joy. Let all creation rejoice before the LORD, for he comes, he comes to judge the earth. He will judge the world in righteousness and the peoples in his faithfulness. Psalm 96:11-13 (NIV)

What a fantastic display will appear all over the world when the Lord returns to take you home with Him! There will be angels singing praises to the Great Creator, blowing the one and most important trumpet call of your life. So you can gather in the clouds beside Jesus. *Let all creation rejoice before the LORD, for he comes, he comes to judge the earth.*

Make sure your house is in order, because the Master of your house will be returning. You don't know at what time He will be arriving home. If you have been a lazy servant, He will throw you out of His house, where you will be doomed to live forever away from the sunlight of His Spirit.

Gracious Heavenly Father, I want to be a witness to a fantastic display of Your Glorious Appearance to take me home with You. I just hope I continue to follow Your will for my life, Father God. I don't want to be left here on earth to be forever cut away from your Magnificent and Beautiful Presence, Lord! I love You so very, very much, Father God! Amen.

April 13

FORGIVING THE UNFORGIVEABLE

Even if that person wrongs you seven times a day and each time turns again and asks forgiveness, you must forgive them. Luke 17:4 (NLT)

Forgiving the unforgiveable is not an easy thing to do! Especially when someone has done horrible things to you. The reason you are supposed to forgive others is for your own benefit. If you don't forgive, you are the one that is held prisoner in the blackness that corrodes your innermost parts until they rust. Forgiveness is what sets the prisoner free! Forgiveness doesn't mean you forget what has been done to you. It means that you are willing to forgive someone, the way God forgave you of all of your sins. Like it directs in the Holy Word above, *'Even if that person wrongs you seven times a day and each time turns again and asks forgiveness, you must forgive them.'* Forgiveness takes away all the resentments you are feeling, replacing them with peace and contentment.

Holy Father God, I am struggling with forgiveness. I was severely hurt by another person's actions, Lord. I don't feel they are showing repentance for what they did to me. But, Heavenly Father, You call me to forgive the unforgiveable. So I will forgive them, O God. I need You with me Lord, when I make my forgiveness. I can't do it alone! Amen.

April 14

FOLLOW GOD'S EXAMPLE

And on the seventh day, God ended His work which He had done, and He rested on the seventh day from the work which He had done. Then God blessed the seventh day and sanctified it. Because in it He rested from all the work God had created and made.
Genesis 2:2-3 (NKJV)

In this fast paced world you feel a need to keep busy, finding more and more things to do, until your body becomes exhausted. You feel so stressed, peace becomes nonexistent. Even God took time after He created the world: *"And on the seventh day, God ended the work which He had done, and He rested on the seventh day from the work which He had done."* If the GREAT I AM knew He needed to revitalize His weary body by resting, then you must follow God's excellent example. Value your body by giving it quality attention and comfort by taking the time to relax. When you make it a priority to do this, peace will surround you, making stress nonexistent.

Teach me to rest, God. I am always finding more and more things to do. I am so stressed out God, I can't find peace anywhere! I need to follow Your example God, and rest more often when I am tired. In this way, I will find peace down deep into my soul, and heal my tired body from stress. Amen.

April 15

A NEW THING

See, I am doing a new thing! Now it springs up; do you not perceive it? Isaiah 43:19 (NIV)

Each day you receive many blessings from God. These blessings are God's way of doing *a new thing* in you. For example, through God's mercy and grace, you have an opportunity to live a special life through God's unfailing love. You can pass it on to others by showing them love and acceptance. In this way, the Kingdom of God will continue to grow. Each kind act you give away has a domino effect. Eventually everyone will show love and kindness to each other. By believing in God, you have made the world a better place to live.

Dearly Heavenly Father God, I rejoice in You and praise You for all the blessings that You have graciously given me! From my heart I sincerely thank You, O God, for doing a new thing in me. I have never felt such joy in my heart, Lord, as when I am giving of myself to others in love. To know you God, is to know peace that defies all understanding! Amen.

April 16
CALL OUT TO GOD

For you are my hiding place; you protect me from trouble. You surround me with songs of victory.
Psalm 32:7 (NLT)

Sometimes your best intentions can turn into your worst nightmare! But you have an incredible God, whom you can seek when you feel like just disappearing to a place where no one can find you. Call out to God with all your anguish and heartache, and let Him *surround* (you) *with songs of victory*, which will seep peace and serenity into your innermost being.

Holy Father God, I am downcast in my heart and soul! I tried to do the right thing Lord, but it ended up turning bad. So I am calling out to You, God, to save me from the snare the devil set for me. Please, O Lord, hold me tenderly in Your arms and comfort me and take this pain I am feeling away. Amen.

April 17

SPIRITUAL NOURISHMENT

You will show me the way of life, granting me the joy of your presence and the pleasures of living with you forever. Psalm 16:11 (NLT)

As you walk through this difficult journey of life, trust in the Lord to be your spiritual nourishment. God will satisfy all your cravings and restore your peace and serenity. You will never receive spiritual nourishment from the ruler of this world. He will lead you astray with empty promises of fulfillment if you worship him and the many idols he is offering you. Before you realize it, the enemy has lead you to a dark and dismal existence. But don't despair, because if you seek God will all your heart and soul and repent of your sins, He will *show* (you) *the way of life granting* (you) *the joy* of His everlasting presence forever.

I have never felt such joy and peace, O Lord, since I atoned for my sins against You. The spiritual nourishment You give me satisfies my craving heart and soul. Every time I read Your Holy Word, Father God, and apply it to my life, never-ending harmony and serenity surround me. I am so grateful for the privilege of Your Glorious and beautiful presence in my life, God! Amen.

April 18

WHY HAVE YOU ABANDONED ME LORD?

O Lord, how long shall I cry, and You will not hear?
Habakkuk 1:2 (NKJV)

Why have you abandoned me Lord? Have you ever said this to the Lord? Think back to a time when you were going through a tremendous burden, and you kept praying to the Lord for help, and He didn't seem to hear you. Maybe you said, *"O Lord, how long shall I cry, and You will not hear?"* But, do you think you were trying to take control over the situation you were dealing with? Maybe the Lord was right beside you. But, because you were so focused on your problems you didn't see the Lord was already there holding your hand. The Lord promised in His Holy Word that He would never abandon you nor forsake you.

O Wonderful Comforter, when I am so caught up in trying to control situations, I don't see you standing beside me. I get frustrated and cry out, "Why have you abandoned me Lord?" I fail to remember You have never forsaken me or ever abandoned me Lord. Never have I walked through this life alone without You. You are My Constant Companion by my side. I am sorry I got impatient and wasn't still enough to listen for Your sweet voice of comfort O Father God. Amen.

April 19

DO NOT LEAN ON YOUR OWN UNDERSTANDING

Trust in the Lord with all your heart and do not lean on your own understanding. In all your ways acknowledge Him, and He will make your paths straight. Proverbs 3:5-6 (NASB)

Place all your fears into the Lord's hands, and *trust in the Lord will all your heart and do not lean on your own understanding.* All your fears do is cause you extreme anxiety! Everything that happens to you is seen by the Lord. He knows how scared you are right now. You can only see what is in front of you. The Lord can see everything. He knows what the results will be with the situation you are facing right now. So surrender everything to the Lord, and you will feel the Lord surround you with a cocoon of warmth and unfailing love.

O My Lord and Savior, I am so afraid! This situation I am facing scars me to death! I need You so very much, Lord, to comfort me. The tears keep falling from my eyes. Please take every tear and hold each one in Your loving hands, My Precious Comforter, and give me peace in Your tender care. I promise to trust You, Father, and not to lean on my own understanding. When I am so filled with fear Thank You, Loving Friend, for always being my comfort. I love You, Lord! Amen.

April 20

BLESSED BE YOUR GLORIOUS NAME

Blessed be your glorious name, and may it be exalted above all blessing and praise. You alone are the LORD. You made the heavens, even the highest heavens, and all their starry host, the earth and all that is on it, the seas and all that is in them. You gave life to everything, and the multitudes of heaven worship you. Nehemiah 9:5 (NIV)

My Lord God Almighty, I honor you above all gods. You are worthy to be praised! Precious is one day in your house than a thousand elsewhere. *Blessed be your glorious name O Lord,* the GREAT I AM! You are My Prince of Peace and My Everlasting God.

I can depend on you, My Sacred Father God, for all of my days to be blessed on this earth. Everything I have that is good in my life comes from you My Wonderful Savior! This is why these praises of glory are sent to you, My Constant Companion and Faithful Friend, because I can't make one day alone without you by my side, My Life Mate. I find such abundant blessings in your beautiful presence, Lord.

I dedicate praise and honor and glory to You, My Compassionate and Loving friend. You are the Lover of my heart and soul! You take all the damaged places inside of me and repair them with your unfailing love, My Savior God. Blessed be Your Glorious Name, above all names, O Lord! I love You so very much, My Life Mate! Amen.

April 21

THE GREAT POWER OF GOD

God's voice is glorious in the thunder. We can't even imagine the greatness of his power. Job 37:5 (NLT)

God is very aware of everything that occurs in your life. You have a compassionate and loving Father who watches over you. God protects you from all that disturbs your life. The great power of God is always vigilant to stop the evil one from harming you.

Your enemies don't want to be in a furious battle with God. When they hear *God's voice...glorious in the thunder,* your foes surrender you to God, and run for their lives. They know that one word uttered out of God's mouth, and they will be vanquished to the nether regions forever.

Great and powerful God, I am thankful that You are on my side! You always protect me from the evil one's harm. I am filled with gratitude, God, for Your unfailing love. I am safe in Your precious care, O Lord. Amen.

April 22

REVERENTLY SERVE THE LORD

Anyone who wants to serve me must follow me, because my servants must be where I am. And the Father will honor anyone who serves me.
John 12:26 (NLT)

In everything you do, reverently serve the Lord. Don't do your own will, because whatever isn't from the Lord, isn't worthy of your time. It only causes strife and despair to be your constant tormentors. Every day you should seek to do the will of the Lord so God *the Father will honor* you with countless blessings for following in the footsteps of His Son. Then you will find that peace and serenity will replace strife and heartache to be your new best friends.

You are the love of my life, O Lord! I reverently will serve You, Lord, in everything I do. I delight in pleasing You Lord and Heavenly Father. I find that when I am doing Your will, I have peace and serenity in my life, God. When I do my own will, Father, I find despair and strife to be my constant tormentors. Please guide me to do Your will in my life, Lord, each day. Amen.

April 23

YOU CAN'T SEE GOD

Now faith is the assurance (the confirmation, the title deed) of the things [we] hope for, being the proof of things [we] do not see and the conviction of their reality [faith perceiving as real fact what is not revealed to the senses]. Hebrews 11:1 (AMP)

You can't see God, but you know He is with you because you have confidence in your faith that God is real and active in your life. When you have been in a jam, God came and rescued you. When you experienced good times in your life, God was right there cheering you on. So in both circumstances, your *faith is the assurance…of the things (*you) *do not see and the conviction of the reality,* that God, as your Constant Companion, walks behind you and before you, surrounding you from all that happens in your life.

I can't see You, God, but I have faith that You are always there with me. My faith is very strong in the assurance that I never walk alone, because You, My Life Mate, are vigilant in Your protection of me. You see me, Lord, no matter where I go! I know without a shadow of a doubt, that I have an Awesome God that loves me unconditionally and You would never leave me. Amen.

April 24

REMAIN FREE IN JESUS CHRIST

Stand fast therefore in the liberty by which Christ has made us free, and do not be entangled with a yoke of bondage. Galatians 5:1 (NKJV)

Remain free in Jesus Christ, *and do not get entangled with a yoke of bondage.* Anything that you worship other than Jesus Christ, will enslave you. There are no exceptions to this fact! Think about what you have brought into your life for comfort purposes. In time, didn't you find you were addicted to it? Some examples of known addictions are: work, food, shopping, gambling, sex, alcohol, drugs, cigarettes, and caffeine to name a few. Other less noticeable addictions are control, fear, and anger. You can't serve Christ and your idols also.

Holy Father God, I am so very sorry that as I worshipped idols I forgot about You . I am asking for Your forgiveness Jesus. I want to come back to You, Jesus, so I can be set free from the yoke of slavery that has me in bondage. It started out as an innocent thing, but Lord, it turned into an addiction. I need Your help getting free. Please help me to be free again in You, Jesus. Amen.

April 25
INNER STRENGTH OF THE SPIRIT OF GOD

I pray that from his glorious, unlimited resources he will empower you with inner strength through his Spirit. Then Christ will make his home in your hearts as you trust in him. Your roots will grow down into God's love and keep you strong.
Ephesians 3:16-17 (NLT)

Life is riddled with trials and tribulations. They are like an infectious disease that keeps spreading through your life. The only cure is the inner strength of the Spirit of God living inside of you. When you trust the Holy Spirit, *your roots will grow down into God's love and keep you strong.* But you need to depend on the Holy Spirit's guidance and direction to make your pathways smooth, keeping your steps upright, so you don't stumble and fall when obstacles block your passage through life.

God, You are My Precious Helper through all life's trials and tribulations. I can't make it without Your guidance and strength, My Wonderful Counselor. Your inner Holy Spirt of strength, God, is the only solution to a peaceful and joyous life! I need to be silent so I can hear your Spirit speaking to me, and helping me to be strong in the midst of difficult situations. The unfailing love of Your Spirit, My God, is my comfort that surrounds me, and provides a shelter of protection when the storms of life sweep over me. I love You, Lord! Amen.

April 26

PROTECTED FOREVERMORE

He who dwells in the secret place of the Most High shall abide under the shadow of the Almighty. I will say of the LORD, "He is my refuge and my fortress; my God, in Him I trust." Psalm 91:1-2 (NKJV)

You never have to fear when the evil one comes calling with accusations against you. When he tries to convince you that you don't measure up to the high standards God expects from you, don't fall for his manipulations. The devil has nothing new under heaven to work with! The enemy is just trying to stop you from completing the mission God sent you on.

Have total confidence that you are protected forevermore by the Lord. *You can say of the LORD, "He is my refuge and my fortress; my God, in Him I trust."* Don't permit the devil to gain a foothold over your life. Seek the protective presence of the Lord, and the enemy will have to flee. Then continue on your pathway of service to God. Finish the race set before you!

Gracious Heavenly Father, I know I am protected forevermore by Your unfailing love. Nothing the devil does can deter me from completing the assignment You gave me to do for You. I will continue on the journey set before me, My Precious Savior, and finish the mission You called me to do. I would do anything You ask me to do Lord, because I love You very much! Amen.

April 27

THE DEVOTED SERVANT

Look at my servant, whom I have chosen. He is my Beloved, and I am very pleased with him. I will put my Spirit upon him, and he will proclaim justice to the nations. He will not fight or shout; he will not raise his voice in public. He will not crush those who are weak, or quench the smallest hope, until he brings full justice with his final victory. And his name will be the hope of all the world. Matthew 12:18-21 (NLT)

Jesus Christ is the redeeming *hope of all the world.* Without Him, no one would have a reason to be joyous at the end of their lives without the faith for everlasting life in Him. He is the devoted Servant of His Father, but also your devoted Servant! He enjoys blessing and fulfilling your life. He rewards you daily for being His faithful follower.

Jesus is always available for counsel when you need someone to talk to. The marvelous revelation in talking to Him is He will never judge or condemn you. He listens, like a compassionate father with his children. You never need be afraid when you seek His presence. And Jesus has enough unfailing love to surround your hurting soul with healing light of salvation and grace.

I am so blessed, Jesus, to have You be a part of my daily life. I want to praise and worship you, Lord, for dying on the cross, so my sins could be forgiven. I am glad you willingly accepted Your Father's plan as His devoted Servant to save all of humanity. I am one very grateful and devoted follower of Yours, Jesus. I gladly will do anything for You, Lord! Thank You for giving up Your life, Jesus, so mine could be saved. Amen.

April 28

LOVE OTHERS LIKE GOD LOVED YOU

No one has seen God at any time; if we love one another, God abides in us, and his love is perfected in us. By this we know we abide in Him and He in us, because He has given us of His Spirit. We have seen and testify that the Father has sent the Son to be the Savior of the world. 1 John 4:12-14 (NASB)

You don't have to go to another country to be a missionary. You can be a missionary where you live. There are plenty of people in your community that have never heard about Jesus Christ. They are living in the darkness without a light to guide them out. You can be their saving light. You are called to love others like God loved you. You *have seen and testify that the Father has sent the Son to be the Savior of the world.* So take your miraculous testimony, and tell others the wonderful news of the Savior that redeemed your life, and set your free from the bondage of your sins. By doing this, you will lead others to a joyous life of freedom with Jesus Christ as their Savior.

Jesus, You have blessed my life the day I accepted You as my Savior. Now I want to love others like God loved me, by telling them how your Father sent You to earth to be their Glorious Redeemer. I want to see them free from the darkness of their sins that holds them in chains of bondage, Jesus. Please guide me to those who need a Savior. I will praise and honor Your Glorious Name, Jesus, by letting them know what a wonderful Savior they have, who loves them with an unfailing love. Amen.

April 29

DO NOT FEAR

So do not fear, for I am with you; do not be dismayed, for I am your God. I will strengthen you and help you; I will uphold you with my righteous right hand.
Isaiah 41:10 (NIV)

So many times when you are faced with a dilemma in your life, you get very anxious and scared. When this happens, seek the Lord. You were created by God to be dependent on Him for all your needs. When you are totally out of control, and God takes over, that is when peace and serenity will be the new furniture in your inner being. Throw out the old love seat of stress and the old recliner of fear. The Lord says, *"So do not fear, for I am with you; do not be dismayed, for I am your God."*

Gracious Heavenly Father, I am so thankful that You are in my life! I willingly surrender everything over into Your hands, Father God. I no longer need to control my life. When I try to control things, O Lord, my life becomes a mess. When I seek Your awesome presence, My God, I do not fear any problem that comes my way. I love You so much, God! Amen.

April 30

THE INFINITE VALUE OF KNOWING CHRIST JESUS

Yes, everything else is worthless when compared with the infinite value of knowing Christ Jesus my Lord. For his sake I have discarded everything else, counting it all as garbage, so that I could gain Christ.
Philippians 3:8 (NLT)

Think about all the material possessions you have. Would you give them all up if Jesus Christ asked you to? That should be an easy question, if you consider Jesus Christ to be more important than anything you have in your life. But, if you have reservations about whether Jesus Christ is your Savior, it can be a hard question to answer .

Search yourself, and see if you would say, *"Yes, everything else is worthless when compared with the infinite value of knowing Christ Jesus."* Do you know with complete confidence that Jesus Christ died for your sins? Have you surrendered your life over to Him? Only you can answers these questions. But know that Jesus Christ desires a relationship with you. Just come as you are. Jesus Christ wants the real you! He sees you, and knows everything about you. He loves you very much!

Dear Jesus, I want to get to know You better. Please help me to have an intimate relationship with You, Jesus. The infinite value of knowing You, Jesus, will be great! I want You to be more important in my life than all the possessions I have, Lord. Thank You, Jesus, for taking the time to listen to me. Amen.

May 1

PERFECT PEACE

You will keep in perfect peace all who trust in you, all whose thoughts are fixed on you. Trust in the LORD always, for the LORD GOD is the eternal Rock.
Isaiah 26:3-4 (NLT)

As you awake today, seek the Lord with joyous praise for the gracious blessings He has given you. For instance, when you look out your window on this glorious morning, thank the Lord reverently for the magnificent sun shining in the beautiful sky above. The Lord created this for you, so you could experience the *perfect peace* of His precious masterpiece seep down deep into your heart and soul, refreshing you with His holy springs of living water.

What magnificent blessings I enjoy every day, Lord, from You. I want to sing and shout praises to Your Glorious Name, My Divine Creator. You are always thinking of me with unfailing loveand delighting me with the perfect peace of Your glorious masterpieces. I thank you, Father, for being precious in Your eyes. Amen.

May 2

LISTEN FOR GOD'S VOICE

They said, "Look, the LORD our God has shown us his glory and greatness, and we have heard his voice from the heart of the fire. Today we have seen God can speak to us humans, and yet we live!"
Deuteronomy 5:24 (NLT)

Just like the Israelites, if you listen for God's voice, He will speak to you, and advise you, as you walk through your day. Never think that God isn't concerned about you. He wants to be in the middle of all your plans, even the small ones. Nothing you do is insignificant to God.

God has shown (you) *his glory and greatness*, every time you have huge problems that you can't solve on your own. When you seek God and ask Him for His help, God takes the monstrous problems that have invaded your peaceful sanctuary and battles them for you, until they vanish right before your eyes. Trust in God, and He will make all your days joyous!

O Faithful Friend, I am so very grateful for all that You do for me. You are my Constant Companion! Never do I have to fear when problems invade my life, O Lord. When I listen for your voice, God, I am strengthened in Your steady hand that holds me upright through the most difficult of circumstances. Thank You, my Life Mate, for always being in the middle of my life. Amen.

May 3

CASTING ALL YOUR CARES UPON GOD

Therefore humble yourselves under the mighty hand of God, that He may exult you in due time, casting all your care upon Him, for He cares for you.
1 Peter 5:6-7 (NKJV)

The reality is, there will always be suffering in this world. But, it is how you handle it that matters to God. God knows you are going to be upset when suffering comes. *Therefore humble yourselves under the mighty hand of God, that He may exult you in due time, casting all you care upon Him, for He cares for you.* Then God can be your strong tower of refuge and strength which you can lean upon to find comfort and peace for your weary soul.

Holy Father, I am so grateful that Your unfailing love covers me, especially when suffering becomes a part of my life. I just don't know what to do sometimes, O Lord, when I am hurting in my heart and soul. I want to come to You, My God, and place all my burdens upon You, but I find myself holding on to them. I need Your help, to cast all my cares upon You God, immediately. If I seek Your presence, Mighty God, and give my suffering to You, I will have more peace and serenity in my life. Amen.

May 4
NO PRETENSES

Though he was God, he did not think of equality with God as something to cling to. Instead, he gave up his divine privileges; he took the humble position of a slave and was born as a human being. When he appeared in human form, he humbled himself in obedience to God and died a criminal's death on a cross. Philippians 2: 6-8 (NLT)

How would you feel if you were taken away from your family and placed with strangers? Even though Jesus Christ was doing the will of His Father, don't you think He missed His home in heaven? Especially when the world rejected Him as the Son of God. Yes, you might say, "Jesus was prepared to die for you, so your sins could be forgiven." Still, the Word of God tells you, Jesus wanted the cup to be taken away. (Matthew 26)

When he appeared in human form, he humbled himself in obedience to God and died a criminal's death on a cross. What a humbling and unselfish act Jesus Christ did for you. This was the pain and the suffering He endured so you could be set free from the bondage of your sins. Jesus died with all your sins upon His body. There was no pretenses about Jesus. He lived and died a sinless life, as His Father's Beloved Son!

O What a gift I have been given in You, Jesus. Your unfailing love for me took away all my sins. But, the very sad fact is, Jesus, You died a prisoner's death, so I could have eternal life with You forever. There were never any pretenses about You, God! You were human and God at the same time. Never did You sin. You were innocent of all crimes against You, Jesus. Thank you, Jesus, for giving up your life to save mine! Amen.

May 5

EVERYDAY HAPPINESS

Take delight in the LORD, and he will give you the desires of your heart. Psalm 37:4 (NIV)

When you seek the Lord first in the morning, you can have everyday happiness. The Lord is always there for you. He waits patiently for you to seek His presence. So before you begin your day with countless chores that you feel need to be done, *take delight in the LORD, and He will give you the desires of your heart.* The Lord has a compassionate heart that waits in anticipation for you to communicate what you need to Him. And everything that the Lord knows is prosperous for growth in your life, He has available in His warehouse of blessings. Ask the Lord to your heart's desire, and you will discover that the Lord has an unlimited supply of blessings for you to receive out of His unfailing love, mercy, and grace.

Everyday happiness, My Lord, comes to me wrapped up in unfailing love, compassionate, and humble devotion for me, from Your sacred heart to mine. All I need to do is communicate my needs to You, Holy Father, and You take your unlimited supply of mercy and grace, and give to me my heart's desire. You will give me much more than I ever expected to receive, O God. Thank You, My Devoted Friend, for all the blessings You graciously grant me daily. Amen.

May 6

THE LORD SHOULD BE WORSHIPPED AND PRAISED

After all these things I heard a loud voice of a great multitude in heaven, saying, "Alleluia! Salvation and glory and honor and power belong to the Lord our God!" Revelations 19:1 (NKJV)

The Lord should be worshipped and praised above all gods. *"Alleluia! Salvation and glory and honor and power belong to the Lord* (your) *God!"* He is a Divine Healer of your soul. He is the Redeeming Breath that awakens your heart to His unfailing love. The Lord is the Sunlight of His Spirit that shines brightly within you. The Lord is the One and Only Great Artisan that can take your worn out body and replace it with a glorified body, adorned with a pure, ivory robe, interwoven with the rarest pearls; and upon your feet will be slippers made with the finest diamonds; and upon your head will be placed the crown of righteous by the Lord, for your excellent servitude.

You are worthy to be praised, Lord! You are the LORD GOD ALMIGHTY and the GREAT ARTISAN of every living thing on the earth! Because of You, O Lord, sacrificing Yourself on the cross for me, I now am entitled to a royal inheritance in the kingdom of heaven. I wait in anticipation until the glorious day I can see You face to face in heaven. I will fall to my knees in reverent honor and praise, O Lord, My Perfect Creator. I love You God! Amen.

May 7

WISDOM FROM ABOVE

But the wisdom from above is first of all pure. It is also peace loving, gentle at all times, and willing to yield to others. It is full of mercy and the fruit of good deeds. It shows no favoritism and is always sincere.
James 3:17 (NLT)

God loves all his people. He shines the sunlight upon those who do evil, as well as, those who do good. He *shows no favoritism and is always sincere.* God hates the deeds of those who don't do His will and cause harm to others, but He loves them with an unfailing love and devotion. All are His creation and therefore His children. That is why wisdom from above is perfect and impartial. God punishes those who need to be punished, like a human father would punish his children for doing wrong. And when his children do good, they get rewarded and praised. That is exactly how God loves you; with an unfailing love of unimaginable prisms of exploding magnitudes of compassion, kindness, and gentleness upon you, as you seek His glorious presence!

Gracious Heavenly Father God, I am so overwhelmed with Your unfailing love for me. I can't imagine the depths of Your everlasting love for me. I have sinned against You, God, daily, and You still love me. What an amazing gift, O Lord, You give me daily. Your wisdom from above sees down deep into my soul, Father, and knows me intimately. So, I shout praises to the Father who sees all of me! Amen.

May 8
GIVING UP CONTROL

For everything that was written in the past was written to teach us, so that through endurance taught in the Scriptures and the encouragement they provide we might have hope. Romans 15:4 (NIV)

Giving up control of everything to the Lord God Almighty, is the only way to enjoy total peace and serenity in your life. By reading the Holy Word of God, you will find examples of people like Abram, who was led to Egypt by the Lord. But Abram's fear that he would be killed if he presented Sarai as his wife to Pharaoh and his officials caused Abram to use poor judgment and he led them to believe Sarai was his sister which aroused God's anger, sending plagues down upon the Egyptians.

If you can learn from the examples of men and women in the Holy Bible, who have gone through similar circumstances as yours; *through endurance and encouragement of the Scriptures,* you will discover that when they trusted God, and surrendered their lives to Him, life became easier and more joyful. They still struggled with problems, but they could endure with the presence of God by their side.

It can be so hard at times to give up control to You, O Lord. But once that I surrender everything to You, I feel peace and joy take the place of stress and annoyance, Father God. I am asking You, my Constant Companion, to please help me to get better in this area of my life. Amen.

May 9

UNION WITH THE LORD

I am the vine; you are the branches. Whoever lives in Me and I in him bears much (abundant) fruit. However, apart from Me [cut off from vital union with Me] you can do nothing. John 15:5 (AMP)

When you find yourself spinning out-of-control like a broken top, reach your hand out and grab onto the righteous right hand of God, and He will help balance you, until you are steady again. Then you will be able to continue on the pathway through life, assured that everything will be OK, because you aren't walking alone, but have a Life Mate walking the trail of life with you.

Jesus says, *"I am the vine; you are the branches… apart from Me [cut off from vital union with Me] you can do nothing."* Union with the Lord, is the only way you can make it through this world in which you live. This world is getting worse every day! You can see for yourself, as God is taken out of more and more people's hearts, how tragic this world has become. God has been replaced with the evil one of the world.

Lord, I can't make it through this dark, scary world without You beside me. Union with You, O Lord, is the only way I can live in this world where the evil one rules. All of my days on earth, I need to be surrounded by your unfailing love, mercy, and grace, Holy Father. I love You so much, God! Amen.

May 10
REJOICE IN THE LORD

Through the fig tree does not bud and there are no grapes on the vines, through the olive crop fails and the fields produce no food, through there are no sheep in the pen and no cattle in the stalls, yet I will rejoice in the LORD, I will be joyful in God my Savior.
Habakkuk 3:17-18 (NIV)

The fierce Babylonians came and enacted punishment on the Israelites for disobeying the Lord. Can you relate to Habakkuk? Habakkuk cried out to the Lord, feeling his prayers weren't answered. But in the end, Habakkuk's prayer was one of praise: *"Yet I will rejoice in the LORD, I will be joyful in God my Savior."*

Even though you may feel like you have lost everything dear to you, through tragic events that have swept through your life like a tornado, destroying everything in its path; call on the dependable name of the Lord, and he will surround you with songs of deliverance, and unfailing love like healing balm. Yes, the things that have happened to you are devastating; remember, the LORD your GOD, will be your light and salvation; your refuge and strength, when the storms of life invade your peace and serenity. You are not alone, for the LORD will never leave nor forsake you!

O MY LORD GOD, why won't You answer my prayer? I feel all alone in this devastating storm that has totally destroyed my life, Father God. Please hear me! I need You, LORD! I am in despair! But, I will rejoice in You, my LORD and SAVIOR. Amen.

May 11

THE SHELTER THAT CAN NEVER BE TORN DOWN

Turn Yourself to me, and have mercy on me, for I am desolate and afflicted. The troubles of my heart have enlarged; bring me out of this distress! Look on my afflictions and my pain…Let me not be ashamed, for I put my trust in You. Let integrity and uprightness preserve me, for I wait for You.
Psalm 25:16-18, 20-21 (NKJV)

The pain may be so bad, that you can't pray. Don't lose hope, because the Lord hears your silent prayers. He takes all the pain and suffering you are feeling, holds every tear inside of His heart, and cries for you.

The Lord is the shelter that can never be torn down. The shelter of the Lord will hold you securely when you are feeling *desolate and afflicted.* The Lord will remain with you for everlasting to everlasting. Everything in this world may fail you, but the Lord never will! He has your back every time.

O Lord, my God, when I am in pain You are the shelter that can never be torn down. Sometimes, I am in so much pain that I feel all alone in this world, Holy Father! But, as I cry out to You, even though I cry silently, You hear me, My Life Mate. You carry me, Lord, until I can walk again without falling. Thank You very much, God, for always loving me unconditionally. I can't make it without You, My Constant Companion. Amen.

May 12

HIS INHERITANCE

What joy for the nation whose God is the Lord, whose people he has chosen as his inheritance.
Psalm 33:12 (NLT)

Isn't the above Holy Word of God, amazing? You are *his inheritance!* The day that Jesus died for all of your sins, you were guaranteed a place in heaven beside Him forever. What a glorious gift you were given! The truly awesome thing is you didn't earn such as blessing, but God the Father gave it to you from His gracious heart. God's unfailing love and mercy for you can never, ever be taken away from you. It is like a gift that keeps on giving. Glory Hallelujah to the GREAT AND POWERFUL GOD ALMIGHTY!

I am so humbled with praises and hymns to the Prince of Peace, My Jesus! I am waiting in anticipation for that glorious day when You come to take me home, O Lord, with You forever. I am Your inheritance! I didn't deserve to be forgiven of my sins, Jesus, but You suffered tremendous pain on the cross because of Your unfailing love for me, Jesus. Thank You, thank You, thank You, the Lover of My Soul! Amen.

May 13
ABUNDANT BLESSINGS

From his abundance we have all received one gracious blessing after another. John 1:16 (NLT)

God is the wonderful and marvelous One! He is so generous and kind to His children. God delights in giving abundant blessings to you, especially as He sees you sharing the gifts He gave you with others.

God enjoys giving you *one gracious blessing after another*. You can never out give God. All God asks you to do is to take care of the people He sends to you. This is God's will for your life. If you do this for God, He will provide for all of your needs, and send you infinite blessings all the rest of your life.

Holy Father God, I will praise you always! I am so filled with gratitude for all the abundant blessings You have graciously given me, Lord. Your compassion and kindness towards me, Dear Friend, is so overwhelming! I delight in Your presence, Father God! Amen.

May 14

NO TURNING BACK

For since the world began, no ear has heard, no eye has seen a God like you, who works for those who wait for him. Isaiah 64:4 (NLT)

Can you say with assurance, no turning back, I am following Jesus? Be confident, that if you trust in Jesus with your whole being, He will work *for those who wait for him.* Even though the road may be rough at times, and you get distracted by the demands facing you, as you seek the mighty presence of Jesus you will never be lost.

My God of Hope, I will not turn back from following You. You are the truth and the way to a life filled with peace and joy, O Lord, My God! Nothing behind me is better than what awaits me with You by my side, Jesus. I anticipate the blessings You have for me up ahead, My Constant Companion! Amen.

May 15
I SAW THE LORD ALWAYS IN MY PRESENCE

I saw the Lord always in my presence; for he is at my right hand, so that I will not be shaken. Therefore my heart was glad and my tongue exulted; moreover my flesh also will live in hope; because you will not abandon my soul to Hades, nor allow your Holy One to undergo decay. Acts 2:25-27 (NASB)

The local news can be very frightening. But don't lose hope. The Lord is always will you. He would never abandon nor forsake you. Don't be afraid to walk in this dark, scary world in which you live. Be like King David and say, *"I saw the Lord always in my presence; for he is at my right hand, so that I will not be shaken."*

Concentrate more on the precious blessings God gives you. They may not be noticeable to you, but they are a delightful surprise from God. For instance; look up in the sky and see the fluffy white clouds greeting you, or the sun shining its warmth in your inner being on a dreary day in your soul, also the infinite stars which guide your steps in the night. The flowers are sending you a delightful fragrance which puts a joyful smile on your face.

Dear Heavenly Father, I can miss the presents You sent me to bring joy into my heart because I am worrying about the many atrocities I see on the local news. Please, O Lord, help me to see and appreciate all the blessings you bestow upon me. I want to be like King David and say, "I saw the Lord always in my presence; for he is at my right hand, so that I will not be shaken." I love You very much! You, O God, are always concerned with my needs. Thank You! Amen.

Sue Reidell

May 16

JESUS NEVER CHANGES

Jesus Christ is the same yesterday, today, and forever.
Hebrews 13:8 (NKJV)

Jesus never changes. He *is the same yesterday, today, and forever.* When you seek Jesus for comfort, He doesn't push you away and say He is too busy right now. Does He say come back later and maybe I will squeeze some time out for you? Jesus is always available when you come to Him. It doesn't matter the reason. Jesus just loves you with an unfailing love that will never leave you to fend for yourself. Jesus' promises all through His Holy Word that He will be there for you. So just call on the precious name of Jesus when you are in need of Him, and Jesus will come running to help you!

I am so very thankful, Jesus that You never change. I have the assurance all through You Holy Word, that You will never abandon me to fend for myself ever. What a truly marvelous blessing You have given me Lord. I know I disappoint You at times, Holy Father, but You still come running to help me when I need You. I will praise you Glorious Name forever! Amen.

May 17

GLORY TO THE ONE AND ONLY TRUE GOD

Oh, gives thanks to the LORD! Call upon His name; make known His deeds among the peoples! Sing to Him, sing psalms to Him; talk of all His wondrous works! Glory in His holy name; let the hearts of those rejoice who seek the LORD! Seek the LORD and his strength; seek his face forevermore!
1 Chronicles 16:8-11 (NKJV)

I will praise and honor your sacred name forever Lord! Glory to the one and only true God, throughout all the ages of time! You are the Great and Awesome Creator of all living things!

You humbled yourself in the form of an innocent baby who was dependent upon Mary and Joseph, your human parents, to care for all of your needs. When you became a man, you continued to humble yourself among the needy, comforting and healing them.

A lot of people became your disciples, but in the end when you were dying on the cross for their sins, not one remained by your side, Jesus. Instead, all abandoned you in your time of need. They were the ones crying out from the crowds, crucify him.

I cried, crucify you, Jesus, until I surrendered everything to you. Now I *give thanks to the LORD.... for His wonderful works! Glory in His Holy Name.* I love you so much!

Glory to the One and Only True God! The Marvelous God, who is always for me, and sees down deep into my soul. Praise and Honor, and Glory, are Your names! Amen.

May 18
NEVER GIVE UP

Never stop praying. Be thankful in all circumstances, for this is God's will for you who belong to Christ Jesus. I Thessalonians 5:17-18 (NLT)

The evil one would like nothing better than for you to throw up the white flag and surrender to him. But never give up! God is coming to you on a white horse to save you. The Mighty Warrior will reach down and sweep you up into His arms and rescue you from the enemy.

Never stop praying. Even if you feel totally defeated. Because when you seek the Lord, He will answer your prayers swiftly. God is your light and salvation in the darkness. He is the strong rock you can stand upon and never be destroyed by the enemy.

Precious Savior, I can always count on You to save me from the enemy. I will never give up! I may experience dark times, but I will always seek You, Lord, in prayer, Sometimes I am so wounded that I can't find the words to say to You, Father, but I will still come to You in prayer, and be thankful for all that You have graciously given me. I love You so much, My Warrior King! Amen.

May 19
THE UNPERISHABLE TREASURE

But we have this treasure in earthen vessels that the excellence of the power may be of God and not of us. We are hard-pressed on every side, yet not crushed; we are perplexed, but not in despair.
2 Corinthians 4:7-8 (NKJV)

When you go through painful circumstances in your life let others see that your faith in the Lord is strong and that you depend on Him to get you through this difficult problem. They will see the unperishable treasure of God's light inside of you. It is a testimony that no matter what happens to you in life, even though you *are pressed on every side, yet not crushed,* because you have been seeking the glorious presence of the Lord for your comfort and strength.

Oh Father God, I am so grateful and thankful for all that You do for me! I never, ever, have to walk alone unless I choose to Lord. You are the unperishable treasure inside of me, which gets me through the most painful and difficult circumstances in my life. Amen.

May 20
REAL LOVE

God showed how much he loved us by sending his one and only Son into the world so that we might have eternal life through him. This is real love—not that we loved God, but he loved us and sent his Son as a sacrifice to take away our sins. 1 John 4:9-10 (NLT)

God is your trusted friend, who enjoys hearing your voice. God delights in you! His unconditional love for you is unfailing! God waits patiently for you to come to Him with devotion and affection in your love for Him. Then God will go deep into your soul, placing kisses of unrelenting compassion and love to comfort each of your days.

This is real love—not that we loved God, but he loved us and sent his Son as a sacrifice to take away our sins. God wasn't concerned with Himself when He sent Jesus to die for your sins. God's love for you was all-consuming! He loved you so much that He was willing to give His Beloved Son, Jesus, to die in your place to atone for your transgressions against Him.

I come to You, O Love of My Life, uninhibited and freely surrendering all that I am to You. I have experienced real love in Your Glorious Presence, Beautiful and Awesome, Friend! I have never had any friend love me unconditionally like You, Father God. To give up Your Beloved Son, Jesus for me, is overwhelming! That is a love that is unfailing and forever available in my Life, O Lord! Amen.

May 21

GOD'S WILL IS ALWAYS PERFECT

And we know that in all things God works for the good of those who love him, and who have been called according to his purpose. Romans 8:28 (NIV)

When you go about your day, do you make a conscious thought of what God's will is for you? If you can remember that God's will is always perfect, you will be more aware of when you are doing your own will. *God works for the good of those who love him, and have been called according to his purpose.* It is pointless anyway to try to make your will fit into the plans God has for you. It never works out the way you planned without consulting God first. So seek God and watch Him take all your best laid plans and make them a perfect fit for many enjoyable blessings from God.

My Precious Counselor, You have taken my chaotic day, and turned it into a joyous day. I am so glad I have You God, in my life to help me when my plans go astray. You will is always perfect, God! Teach me to trust in You more Lord. Amen.

May 22
GOD IS SOVEREIGN OVER ALL CREATION

How great are His signs! And how mighty His wonders! His kingdom is an everlasting kingdom, and His dominion is from generation to generation.
Daniel 4:3 (AMP)

God is sovereign over all creation! He knows all things. No other god is capable of such omniscience! So be assured that as you seek the mighty presence of God, He has already taken care of what you need. He sees you, so he knows every detail about you. God will reach down from heaven on bended knees and surround you with a cocoon of everlasting love.

His kingdom is an everlasting kingdom, and His dominion is from generation to generation. His miracles are all around you. If you are still and wait upon the Lord, God will reveal Himself to you. Like a gentle wind kissing your cheeks, or feeling God's breath breathing healing into your wounded heart and soul, when you are in distress, the voice of God's Holy Spirit is directing you to the pathway of peace.

God, You are My Light and Salvation so I don't ever have to fear! You are My Strong Tower of Refuge and Strength, when I am weak! You are the Sovereign God over all creation! Your miracles, My God, are always there for me to see, if I am still before You. Thank You, Father God, for all the wonderful blessings You give me. Amen.

May 23

HOPE IS IN THE LIVING GOD

This is why we work hard and continue to struggle, for our hope is in the living God, who is the Savior of all the people and particularly of all believers.
1 Timothy 4:10 (NLT)

You need not fear when others who are not believers of God, tell you how to live your life. Don't allow them to take space up in your head. That is a bad neighborhood to get lost in! *Hope is in the living God, who is the Savior of all people and particularly all believers.* Seek the presence of the God, who knows you intimately, for the truth and let Him guide you through His Holy Word for the correct answers on how to conduct your life as a servant of the Lord.

I am glad I know my hope is in You, the living God. No one else can influence me to live their way, especially if they are not believers of You, Lord. I will continue to walk in Your Divine Presence, Father, even if challenges come my way. Because when I am faced with difficulties, this is when I am able to keep my eyes on You, O God, for help when my faith is tested. I love You! Amen.

May 24
DON'T FEAR

Put on the full armor of God, so that you can take your stand against the devil's schemes...Stand firm then with the belt of truth buckled around your waist, with the breastplate of righteousness in place, and with your feet fitted with the readiness that comes from the gospel of peace. In addition to all this, take up the shield of faith, with which you can extinguish all the flaming arrows of the evil one. Take the helmet of salvation and the sword of the Spirit, which is the word of God. And pray in the Spirit on all occasions with all kinds of prayers and requests.
Ephesians 6:10, 14-18 (NIV)

Don't fear when the devil irritates you. Stay focused on the mighty presence of the Lord. And remember, the devil doesn't bother you with his antics unless you are doing the will of God. The evil one wants to deter your work for the Lord by making you stumble on your faithful journey. Don't lose hope! Put on the full armor of God, so that you can take your stand against the devil's schemes. The devil has nothing original to use against you. He uses the same boring thing to cause discord in your life. When you call on the Glorious name of Jesus, the devil must flee. Stand strong under the everlasting arms of God the Father.

What a Glorious Lord You are! As I call on Your Precious Name, O God, the devil must flee! He can't continue to disturb me with his nonsense Lord, when I am strong in You. I don't have to fear the evil one's poor attempts at causing me to stumble and fall, as I continue on my journey in faith, knowing You My Holy Father are by my side. Amen.

May 25

HAPPINESS AND PEACE OF MIND

Rejoice in the Lord always; again I will say rejoice! Let your gentle spirit be known to all men. The Lord is near. Be anxious for nothing, but in everything by prayer and supplication with thanksgiving let your requests be made known to God. And the peace of God with surpasses all comprehension, will guard your hearts and minds in Christ Jesus.
Philippians 4:4-7 (NASB)

Nothing, absolutely nothing, can seriously upset you, when you look to the Lord for comfort and peace. The Lord is always right beside you. But, sometimes you don't see Him there. That is the reason you get so fearful and anxious. When you do this, you begin doubting the faithfulness of the Lord to walk with you through the problems in your life. In an instant, you allow the problems to become bigger than the Lord! But happiness and peace of mind is right beside you. *Be anxious for nothing, but in everything by prayer and supplication with thanksgiving let your requests be made known to God.* By doing this, you allow God to become bigger than the problems and they shrink to nothing right before your eyes.

I love You so much, Father God! When I allow You to have complete control over all my life You are my happiness and peace of mind, , O Lord. I need to keep reminding myself when problems invade my safe haven, You are right beside me, available, My Devoted Friend, to fight the problems for me. I need to say to the problems I face, "My God is bigger and mightier than you, so scram." In Your Precious Name, My God! Amen.

May 26

INTIMATELY FROM YOUR HEART

By day the Lord directs his love, at night his song is with me—a prayer to the God of my life.
Psalm 42:8 (NIV)

When you share intimately from your heart in communion with God, He is delighted with you, because He loves you very much, and desires a personal relationship with you. God is very excited to be with you. *By day the Lord directs his love, at night his song is with* you. So come to God immediately, and He will graciously reward you with unlimited blessings.

O Holy Father God, I am coming into Your beautiful presence, because I enjoy being with You! I am praying intimately from my heart to You, Lord. All I ask is that you never leave me, My Life Mate. I need You always with me God! I am overwhelmed at Your compassion and unfailing love for me, Devoted Friend. Amen.

May 27

GOD'S MASTERPIECE

For we are God's masterpiece. He has created us anew in Christ Jesus, so we can do the good things he planned for us long ago. Ephesians 2:10 (NLT)

You are God's masterpiece, created to be unique and precious; viewed by the world as the light of God, a servant entrusted with the duty, *he planned for* (you) *long ago,* to guide others to eternal life through His beloved Son, Jesus.

God will use your past as a vantage point that others will be drawn to, as they see you living your life for God, instead of living a life of sin. They will want what you have. Then you will be able to show them how to surrender their lives to God just like you did.

I never considered surrendering my life to You, O God, especially when I was following the ruler of the world. Until the day when I realized my life was empty and unfulfilled without You in it, Lord, I was so alone! The idols I worshipped never satisfied me, My God. Only when I humbled myself before You, Holy Father, and atoned for my sins, did I feel totally alive and free! Today I know I am a masterpiece You created, God, to lead the world to You through Your Son, Jesus. This is where I get total fulfillment. Amen.

May 28
LIGHT AFFLICTIONS

For momentary, light afflictions is producing for us an eternal weight of glory far beyond all comparison, while we look not at the things which are seen; for the things which are seen are temporal, but the things which are not seen are eternal.
2 Corinthians 4:17-18 (NASB)

When you experience light afflictions, God will surround you with a stream of comforting light which will take away all your anxiety and stress. God's light is like a gentle wave of the ocean that comes upon you while surfing on a warm summer day. It is *producing for* (you) *an eternal weight of glory far beyond all comparison,* for God is not seen; but you still have faith that He will take care of all your needs. You know you are never forsaken nor abandoned by God! He watches over you, and shelters you always.

Holy Father God, You are very precious to me! When I am faced with light afflictions, Heavenly Father, You are always there for me. When I seek your Glorious Presence, O Lord, I am secure in Your comforting light of warmth which surrounds me, and takes away all my stress and anxiety. I love You so much, Beautiful One! Amen.

May 29

RESTORE JOY AND PEACE

Now may God of hope fill you with all joy and peace in believing, that you may abound in hope by the power of the Holy Spirit. Romans 15:13 (NKJV)

As you go about your day things may distract you. You may even find your thoughts wondering haphazardly from one thing to another, never really being able to clearly define what you need to do. If you stop and pause for a moment and refocus your thoughts on the Lord, He will gladly help to restore joy and peace to your heart and soul *by the power of the Holy Spirit.* Then you can finish out the rest of your day with a song of happiness to the Lord, with praises of delight and thankfulness for His goodness always.

Precious Heavenly Father, I didn't know how to handle all the responsibilities of my day by myself. I was overwhelmed, O Lord, until I sought help from You. Only when I realized Your gentle presence beside me, God, did I feel You restore joy and peace back to my heart and soul. Thank You so much, My Prince of Peace, for Your unfailing love, that demands that You make me happy. Amen.

May 30
MISTAKES

Indeed, we all make many mistakes. For if we could control our tongues, we would be perfect and could also control ourselves in every other way.
James 3:2 (NLT)

Indeed we all make many mistakes. Don't beat yourself up when you make a mistake. God knew you would not be perfect in your humanness. That is why God is the only perfect One. If you could do all things perfect, what would be the need of God in your life?

Also, you tend to make errors of the tongue. Your first thought can be negative, especially when you are angry about something someone did or said. So even the words that come from your mouth you can't control at times. This is why it is important to have an intimate relationship with God. You can seek Him when you are upset, and He will calm you, so you can think clearly enough to apologize for the unkind words you said. No one is perfect!

I am so imperfect Lord! I have made many mistakes in my life, Father God, but You still love me unconditionally. You see me as your precious child, and comfort me, and help me correct my mistakes O Lord. You don't yell at me, or belittle me, ever. You are always a Loving Father to me! I am never afraid to come to You with anything! Amen.

May 31

YOU CAME AND SAVED ME

For this I will give thanks and extol You, O Lord, among the nations; I will sing praises to Your name.
2 Samuel 22:50 (AMP)

All the blessings I have in my life comes from you, O Lord. My life was worth nothing until you came and saved me, Lord, and made my life happy, joyous, and free. Every day when I arise, I will give you praises and thanks for making my life so good and fulfilled.

I will sing praises to Your name, my Glorious Redeemer! I was a filthy sinner, a nothing, with no hopes and dreams. Then you came and saved me, My Sacred Healer! Now my life is overflowing with blessings. You have given me more than I could have ever hoped or dreamed of receiving. All I can say is thank you so very much for your mercy and grace, Father God, which changed this broken person into a brand new miracle.

The above words are dedicated to You, My Life Mate! I just wanted to let You know how thankful I am that You are always beside me, My Devoted Companion, even when I don't feel worthy of Your love. But you came and saved me because of Your unfailing love for me. Thank You for the new life I have with You today, My Precious Lord! Amen.

June 1

FEARFULNESS AND TREMBLING

Fearfulness and trembling have come upon me, and horror has overcome me... As for me, I will call on God, and the Lord will save me. Psalm 55:5, 16 (NIV)

Have you ever felt *fearfulness come upon* you, because you were convinced God abandoned you to fend for yourself against a huge avalanche of problems. Were they going to come down and bury you under their onslaught? If you have ever felt this way, then you know how hopeless you felt. But to combat those feelings, say the precious name of Jesus, over and over again, until you feel all the fear just melt away. This is God holding you in His gentle, loving arms and comforting you.

Holy Father God, I am so afraid of the unknown! These problems I am facing have me fearful and trembling, Jesus. I need You to come right now! Where are You, Lord? There You are! I can feel You holding me now, Awesome Comforter. I am so blessed that You love me so much, Jesus! Amen.

June 2
TREASURES IN HEAVEN

Do not lay up for yourselves treasures on earth, where moth and rust destroy and where thieves break in and steal; but lay up for yourselves treasures in heaven, where neither moth nor rust destroys and where thieves do not break in and steal. For where your treasure is, there your heart will be also.
Matthew 6:19-21 (NKJV)

When you continually trust in God, it is like you are depositing money faithfully in a savings account. When a financial emergency occurs, you don't need to worry, but are secure. That is exactly what happens when your trust in God is strong. The storms of life may hit you, but you will not falter, because God will direct the stormy winds and rains around you to cease. A You will safely weather the storm uninjured.

You have invested in the treasures of heaven, by increasing your spiritual journey; developing perseverance through studying the Holy Word of God, where you get guidance in your journey of faith. For where your treasure is, there your heart will be also.

I am so grateful that I have treasures in heaven, O Lord! Each day I can be thankful for all the special, wonderful gifts I receive from You, Father. I will keep on trusting You each day, Lord God. Then when I am faced with the storms of Life, I will not fear, because I have a strong faith in You, Precious Friend, Amen.

June 3

WHAT IS THE LORD'S PURPOSE FOR YOU?

Then the word of the LORD came to me saying: "Before I formed you in the womb I knew you; before you were born I sanctified you; I ordained you a prophet to the nations." Jeremiah 1:4-5 (NKJV)

What is the Lord's purpose for you? He has instructed you through the Holy Spirit to use your talents that He gifted you with, before He *formed you in the womb*. The Lord might not have called you to be a prophet like Jeremiah, but He does expect you to use the gifts He gracious gave you wisely in service to others. Some examples are: artist, writer, health care professional, chef, teacher, janitor, waitress, waiter, and dishwasher, to name a few. The point is, whatever your gift is, don't be ashamed! Use it in dedication to your Awesome Creator

Each gift the Great Artisan gave to His children was specifically crafted by His masterful hands, uniquely imprinted on each soul that was formed to display His marvelous workmanship for others to gaze upon. So go out and 'WOW' the world with your special gift from the Lord!

I didn't even realize how special and unique I was to You, O Lord! But now, I will gladly display my talents to the world to see. I know I was lovingly created by You, the Great Artisan! I know my purpose is valuable to You, O Lord, for the world to observe, so I can bring them into Your holy light of healing for their broken souls. Thank You, My Father in heaven, for calling me to be Your trusted servant. Amen.

June 4

DO EVERYTHING TO GLORIFY THE LORD

If you search for good, you will find favor, but if you search for evil, it will find you. Proverbs 11:27 (NLT)

This life can be very hard! There is no question about that. Especially if you are a follower of Jesus Christ. This world in which you live is ruled by the king of evil. He doesn't like that you are devoted to Jesus Christ, and have given your life over to Him. The evil one will try to persuade you to come worship him. He is the great tempter of causing people to fall away from Christ.

Do everything to glorify the Lord, and don't *search for evil*, or the devil will send his minions to recruit you in their army of destruction, which leads to eternal death of your soul. The evil one can't do anything that the Lord isn't aware of. Jesus sees everything! So if you have strayed far away from the Lord, don't lose hope, because the Lord is waiting with loving arms, open wide to welcome you back to Him.

I am so ashamed for straying away from Your loving presence, Jesus! I got caught up in the temptations of the evil one, and I was lost for a time from You, O Lord. But I want to now do everything to glorify You, Lord. Please forgive me, and please use all of me, to benefit Your kingdom, Father. I want Your sunlight of the Holy Spirit to wash me clean again in Your sacred blood, Jesus. Amen.

June 5

DON'T WALK THE STEPS OF A FOOL

Guard your steps as you go to the house of God and draw near to listen rather than offer the sacrifice of fools; for they do not know they are doing evil.
Ecclesiastes 5:1 (NASB)

Don't walk the steps of a fool, *for they do not know they are doing evil.* When you make a promise to God, don't let it be an empty commitment. God knows what you are going to say and do, so you are only fooling yourself when you say to God, "I promise that I will quit doing this or that."

Some examples of transgressions against God are: Worshipping drugs, alcohol, and pornography, adultery, eating food, and gambling as idols. When you do these things, you have taken God out of your life, and only seek God when you are in trouble. So come back to God with all of your heart and soul, and sincerely ask for forgiveness, and God will restore your life to good standing with Him; making it better than it was before.

O Precious, Heavenly Father, I have been walking the steps of a fool! I am coming to You Lord with a devoted heart, asking for Your forgiveness for worshipping idols instead of worshipping You. I am truly repenting to You, God, of all of my sins against You. Please help me, Lord, to walk a life worthy of Your mercy and grace. I love You, Father God! Amen.

June 6

ENJOY THE SURPRISES

In the morning, O LORD, you hear my voice; in the morning I lay my requests before you and wait with expectation. Psalm 5:3 (NIV)

As you *laid* your requests before the Lord in the morning, enjoy the surprises the Lord has prepared for you, as you take a peaceful walk together. It is like you are taking a walk on a beautiful summer day with a Devoted Friend who enjoys walking beside you, and showing you all the beautiful things He has prepared for you. God delights in making your heart light up in enjoyment when He presents you with many gifts He has hidden along the pathway. As you continue your precious walk with the Lord, you are so awed by the many gifts along the way, like the breathtaking fragrance of the lilac bush blooming in a neighbor's yard, or the soft green grass between your bare toes, or the morning sun gliding with you, that brighten your day. And there is the peacefulness you feel for no other reason than you are walking hand-in-hand with your Best Friend.

I have enjoyed all the surprises, My Special Friend, You have given me today! As we walked, each gift was more magnificent than the last one, Devoted Friend! I find delight in being in Your Glorious Presence, Lord. The gifts that You gave me, made my heart sing with happiness. I love You, My Life Mate! Amen.

June 7

GOD IS MASTER OF ALL THINGS

For with God nothing will be impossible.
Luke 1:37 (NKJV)

Anything you set your mind on achieving, if it is God's will for your life, no obstacle in your path will prevent you from achieving your goal. God is the Master of all things! *For with God nothing will be impossible,* so don't give up! Cross the finish line and grab onto the goal you have earned with all your heart.

Thank You, O God, for believing in me. Without Your confidence in me, Sacred Counselor, I would have never had the courage to go after the goal I wanted. I am so grateful You are the Master of all things, My Lord! Nothing can delay my progress to the finish line with Your loving presence by my side, Holy Father! Amen.

June 8

GET RID OF SELFISH BEHAVIORS

Do nothing from selfish or empty conceit, but with humility of mind regard one another as more important than yourselves; do not merely look out for your own personal interests, but also for the interests of others. Philippians 2:3-4 (NASB)

When you are concerned with your own self-interests, you are not concerned with the *interests of others*. This selfish behavior is futile, and locks the door to your soul, where God can't enter without your permission.

Until you are ready to get rid of all your selfish behaviors, and open the door of your soul so God can enter, you will continue to live an unproductive life; traveling down a road that leads to a dead end. So submit yourself over into God's care, and travel down a different road with God. You will find many intersections that will lead you to unlimited blessings, as you serve others along the way.

Holy Father God, my life is filled with such peace and serenity! I am so thankful that my life belongs to You, O God. I enjoy helping others very much! Getting rid of all my selfish behaviors has been the best thing I ever did! Please continue to help me, Lord, to stay free of my own self-interests, especially when I am neglecting the interests of others. My life is only fulfilled when I am helping others, God. Amen.

June 9

NONE OF YOUR BUSINESS

And don't sin by letting anger control you, don't let the sun go down while you are still angry, for anger gives the devil a foothold. Ephesians 4:26 (NLT)

Don't allow others to cause you to explode with anger. Stay away from people like that. They don't have your best interest in their hearts. Instead, allow the Lord to take up residence inside of your heart and soul. Then you will be able to accept those that want to wound you with their words; it is none of your business to know what they say about you. Don't sin by letting *anger control you...for anger gives the devil a foothold.* Seek peace and serenity from the Lord as He comforts your heart and soul.

O Precious Healer, I am so wounded in my heart and soul because of what others are saying about me! Please surround me with your loving arms, O Lord, and send peace and contentment into my inner most being. You are My Safe Haven, where I can go and find rest when my heart and soul are weary! I love You, Prince of Peace! Amen.

June 10
SPIRTUAL ATTACKS

So be subject to God. Resist the devil [stand firm against him], and he will flee from you. Come close to God and He will come close to you. James 4:7-8 (AMP)

The devil is relentless in his spiritual attacks against you. The evil one will attack you over and over again. Don't allow him and his minions to crush you spiritually, mentally, or physically, with the huge, flaming arrows he and his minions are shooting at you.

The destroyer wants you to give up and quit. He doesn't want you to finish what you are doing for God. Don't submit to him! Instead, *[stand firm against him], and he will flee from you. Come close to God and He will come close to you.* The evil one may cause you to stumble and fall over the obstacles he put in your path. Take hold of God's righteous right hand, and God will be the Strong Rock upon which you stand.

I feel so crushed and weary down deep in my soul, My Constant Companion! The evil one will not give up on his spiritual attacks against me, O Lord. Please fight for me, My Mighty Warrior, I am very tired! I can't hold on much longer! Please comfort me, My Life Mate, and carry me until I can walk again! Amen.

June 11

SEEK THE GUIDANCE OF THE LORD

You will keep in perfect peace all who trust in you, all whose thoughts are fixed on you! Isaiah 26:3 (NLT)

You are worried about all you perceive is going to happen tomorrow, when all you have is today! Even today will not go smoothly unless you seek the guidance of the Lord. Then you will find *perfect peace,* as you take one step at a time with God. Along the path, God has hidden gifts of joy and happiness for you to unwrap and place inside of your heart and mind to savor anytime you choose.

Lord, when I seek Your guidance my day is very peaceful. When I try to control not only what's going to happen today, but tomorrow also, I get very worried and upset. This proves I don't know what's best for me, O God. You can have all of me, My Life Mate, to do what you want with me! I know it will be good! Amen.

June 12

YOUR LIFE IS NOT YOUR OWN

I have been crucified with Christ; it is no longer I who live, but Christ who lives in me; and the life which I now live in the flesh I live by faith in the Son of God, who loved me and gave Himself up for me.
Galatians 2:20 (NASB)

Your life is not your own. It belongs to Christ Jesus. By Jesus' mercy and grace, you were spared an eternal life in darkness. Christ Jesus gave Himself willing to be whipped, beaten, spit upon, nailed to a cross by His hands and feet, and upon His head was placed a crown of thorns. Then He was crucified to pay the penalty for your sins to His Father in heaven.

Do you *live by faith in the Son of God?* Do you consider it an honor when the Lord asked you to be His servant? Or do you moan and groan when Christ Jesus asks you to do something for Him? Christ Jesus paid too high a price to save your damaged soul! You can never fully repay Him for all He gave up for you. But you can gladly offer up worship to Christ Jesus, by the way you live your life for Him.

Precious Heavenly Father, I know my life is not my own! It belongs exclusively to you, Jesus. I want to honor and praise You, for saving me from the tormenting darkness of living forever with the evil one, Sacred Healer. I will live each day of my life in worship to You, by serving others. Amen.

June 13
GREATLY REJOICE

In this you greatly rejoice, though now for a little while, if need be, you have been grieved by various trials, that the genuineness of the your faith, being much more precious than gold that perishes, though it is tested by fire, may be found to praise, honor, and glory at the revelation of Jesus. 1 Peter 1:6-7 (NKJV)

Trials are definitely hard to go through. But, they can be used to glorify and honor God. For instance, if someone you care about uses all the pain and suffering you have been through in the past to help others who are going through, or have been through the same painful experiences as you, you may get angry at first. Once you have had time to process everything through God, you may greatly rejoice, because even though it greatly grieves you, what you shared with another was actually used in *praise, honor, and glory at the revelation of Jesus.* Another person came to trust Jesus with all their pain and suffering as you did.

For a while, O Lord, I was greatly grieved that what I shared with another was told to others. But, now, Precious Redeemer, I can see that other people have greatly benefited from what I suffered. I can also see my suffering brought great joy to others, as they came to know you, Jesus, and trust you with their lives. I greatly rejoice that I was used to glorify the kingdom of God! Amen.

June 14

A BETTER HOPE

For the law never made anything perfect. But now we have confidence in a better hope, through which we draw near to God. Hebrews 7:19 (NLT)

Two thousand years ago, the people of Israel didn't put much faith in God. They followed the laws that were written for them to obey by the priests they elected to follow. The law never washed their souls clean from their sins, like Jesus did.

Today, as you trust in God totally with your life, you *have confidence in a better hope*. He will take the messes that you still make today, and repair all the damage you have brought upon yourself, as you follow your own advice. God is like glue, He sticks to you, and can't even be pulled loose from you! His unfailing love forgives all your messes that you make.

Merciful and Gracious Father, please help me to depend on Your perfect guidance, instead of my own foolish wisdom. I know I can do nothing without You with me Lord! When I try to accomplish things on my own, I stumble and fall in my imperfections. I cause danger to follow wherever I go, without You, My Constant Companion by my side! I love You, so much, My Devoted Friend! Amen.

June 15

GOING ASTRAY

But if from there you seek the Lord your God, you will find him if you look for him with all your heart and with all your soul. Deuteronomy 4:29 (NIV)

When you wake up in the morning, humble yourself to God by hitting your knees in holy reverence to Him. When you surrender everything into the confident hands of the Lord, you are honoring Him, *with all your heart and with all your soul.* God deserves nothing less than total submission from you.

Don't go astray and convince yourself you don't need God in your life. That ridiculous thought was implanted in your mind by the devil and his minions. Imagine God looking over your shoulder and touching your mind, cleansing it from all impure thoughts that the devil put there. Then get back on your knees and ask for forgiveness for not trusting the Lord with your life!

I am sorry, O Lord, for going astray by not trusting You with my life. Sometimes I allow the devil to convince me I don't need You, Holy Father. When I do this, I have a fool as my companion! Thank You for your unconditional love that came after me and brought me home to You, Precious Father. Amen.

June 16
THINK BEFORE YOU SPEAK

Everyone enjoys a fitting reply; it is wonderful to say the right thing at the right time! Proverbs 15:23 (NLT)

When you are upset over what someone didn't do or say, your first thought will always be negative. Especially when you have set expectations for that person that they didn't live up to. So before you say anything out of anger, which will undoubtedly cause you to say things you don't mean, and will hurt the other person, think before you speak; take a time out and ask God to give you the words to say that will be a *fitting reply*, showing the other person love instead.

Sometimes I can be selfish and self-centered, demanding that others meet all my needs, Awesome Comforter! Please help me, My Wonderful Counselor, to come to You first before I put my foot in my mouth, and say something I am going to regret. Teach me to think before I speak, so I can say kind and loving words, instead of harsh words spoken out of anger, O Lord. Amen.

June 17

THE ENEMY IS PROWLING AROUND TO DEVOUR YOU

The eternal God is your refuge, and underneath are the everlasting arms, He will thrust out the enemy from before you, and will say, "Destroy!"
Deuteronomy 33:27 (NKJV)

Your past transgressions may pop up from time to time, like an electronic bulletin board flashing all your shame, remorse, and guilt, in your thoughts making you feel excruciating pain. As these memories flash in your mind, disconnect them, by praying to God, *your refuge, and underneath are the everlasting arms, which will* comfort you and hold you in His gentle embrace, making all your painful memories turn into joyous memories of a loving and faithful Servant who takes care of all your needs.

Also, when these memories torment you, the enemy is prowling around to devoir you like a lion. His only purpose is to satisfy his hunger by eating your entire soul. He wants to destroy you! He is a killer, an assassin who won't rest until He murders your heart and soul, and makes it his. Your Mighty God will destroy the devil, if you seek his help.

Holy Father God, I am in distress! My past is tormenting me, Lord! I know the enemy is prowling around to devour me. Please come and rescue me. Destroy the devil and his minions, Mighty Warrior. I need you to surround me with Your everlasting arms of comfort and peace. Amen.

June 18
BLESSED WITH STRENGTH AND PEACE

The Lord will give [unyielding and impenetrable] strength to His people; the Lord will bless His people with peace. Psalm 29:11 (AMP)

Each day, God showers you with compassion and unfailing love, because He adores you. He gets great enjoyment when He can put a smile upon your face and peace in your heart.

The Lord will give [unyielding and impenetrable] strength to His people; the Lord will bless His people with peace. Blessed with strength and peace, anything that comes your way, you will most assuredly be able to handle easily. This is only attainable because you have placed your trust in the Lord. Then the Lord will become a strong anchor in your life; grounded in solid faith that cannot be penetrated by the mightiest opposition. Peace, serenity, joy, and happiness will be present in your life every day.

I want to praise and honor You, Lord above all lords, and King above all kings! All the glory goes to You, My Everlasting Father, and Prince of Peace! I never thank You enough for giving me blessings of strength and peace in my life, Divine Healer of my heart and soul! I enjoy each day I spend in Your Sacred Presence, O Lord. I am so grateful You find delight in making me happy, My Devoted Friend. I love You! Amen.

June 19

YOU ARE VERY IMPORTANT TO GOD

Look at the birds of the air; they do not sow or reap or store away in barns, and yet your heavenly Father feeds them. Are you not more valuable then they? Can any one of you by worrying add a single hour to your life? Matthew 6:26-27 (NIV)

You are very important to God; He knows how many hairs you have on your head. You are unique! No one else has your exact DNA. When you were formed in the secret place, in the depths of the earth, God knew everything about you. You are *more valuable* to God then any of His other creations. God loves you so much and only wants the best for you. That is why He gave up His Only Son Jesus Christ to die on the cross at Calvary, so your sins would be scattered as far as the east is from the west; God has no memory of them.

Merciful and Gracious Father God, I am so overwhelmed at how wide and deep Your unfailing love is for me! I am so imperfect; sinning every day. But You still welcome me back, with arms held wide open, for me to seek comfort from You, O Lord. I am so humbled at the enormity of how important I am to You, God. To think I am more important than Your other creations, Perfect One, is just too much for me to comprehend! Thank You for never leaving me nor forsaking me, Wonderful Provider! I love You, My Soul Mate! Amen.

June 20
DO NOT JUDGE OTHERS

Do not judge others, and you will not be judged. Do not condemn and you will not be condemned. Forgive and you will be forgiven. Luke 6:37 (NLT)

God wants you to forgive others who have wronged you. He doesn't want you to hold a resentment toward them. When you continue to have a resentment toward another person, you are the one that suffers the most! It is like you have termites inside the walls of your soul, eating away the healthy spiritual part of yourself, until there is nothing left inside of your soul but a deep, dark abyss of hatred.

Do not judge others, and you will not be judged by God. God forgave you of all your sins. So how can you not forgive others who have sinned against you? In the long run, if you forgive others, you will find that you are the one set free from the chains of anger and resentment, which has held you prisoner way too long!

I praise You, God, for helping me see how bitter I had become, because I wouldn't forgive the person who wronged me. Now, I feel as light as a feather, Lord! I am finally free from my self-made prison of anger and rage. Thanks to Your loving and gentle voice, My Devoted Friend, that was the key that freed me. Please give me the willingness, Holy Father, to not judge others again. Amen.

June 21
THE HOLY ONE

And he was preaching, and saying, "After me One is coming who is mightier than I, and I am not fit to stoop down and untie the thong of His sandals. I baptized you with water; but He will baptize you with the Holy Spirit." Mark 1:7-8 (NASB)

John the Baptist was baptizing people and preaching to them about the coming of Jesus Christ, who was the Holy One, telling them that He was coming to baptize them *with the Holy Spirit.*

John's remarkable words of the revelation of Jesus Christ' miraculous coming is not too far off from happening again very soon. Is your own house in order? If today, Jesus would come to take you back home with Him, are you ready to go with Him? Is His baptism of blood that cleansed your soul from all sins, still active and alive inside of you today? If you live by the Holy Spirit of God, You will die into the Glorious Awakening where Jesus is waiting to receive you.

O Precious Heavenly Father, thank You for the glorious and miraculous blessing of your Holy One, Jesus Christ. Without His sacrifice on the cross, I would not be alive today in His cleansing blood, which healed my broken and damaged soul. I am forever grateful to You, God! I wasn't worthy enough to receive the gift of peace Jesus gave me, when He set me free, but You, God, found me to be worthy of Your Son's unfailing love for me. I love You, God, so much! Amen.

June 22

THE BIG JUMP

I have told you all this so that you may have peace in me. Here on earth you will have many trials and sorrows. But take heart, because I have overcome the world. John 16:33 (NLT)

You are not going to be able to avoid going through trials and tribulations in life. Especially since the world is under the dominion of the devil. He takes delight in making you squirm going through a difficult situation. Don't lose hope. God has *overcome the world.*

It is like when the devil tempted Jesus in Matthew 4:5-6. The devil wanted to torment Jesus, give Him troubles and rule God. That would certainly destroy any peace we could ever hope to have. Jesus gave the devil what for! 'You must not test the Lord your God.'

The devil tried other ways to give Jesus trouble, but Jesus' response is the same you should have during trials and tribulations. *"Get out of here, Satan."*

We need to tell the devil to get lost! Tell him 'Leave me alone.' When you do this, you will find your trials and tribulations are not mightier than God! That is when the Holy Spirit comes to get you out of those sticky situations.

God, You are my Strong Refuge and Strength through all the trials and tribulations of this world! I will not listen to the devil's temptations. Instead, I will not be afraid, O Lord. I will say just like You, my God and Strong Deliverer, "Get out of here, Satan." I trust and have confidence that You, My Devoted Friend, will take care of the problems which come into my life. Amen.

June 23

EVEN IN THE DARKNESS SHINES THE LIGHT OF JESUS

Light shines in the darkness for the godly. They are generous, compassionate, and righteous...They do not fear bad news; they confidently trust the LORD to care for them. Psalms 112:4, 7 (NLT)

If you are still struggling with problems, even though you know God is waiting for you to seek His presence to help you; even in the darkness shines the light of Jesus. The Lord will come and gladly rescue you, take you by His righteous right hand, and gently lead you into His loving haven. When you are willing, go with the Lord, and *confidently trust the LORD to care for* (you), He will rain blessings down into your heart and soul; which when opened will reveal peace and serenity that will gladly become your new best friends and trusting companions!

Gentle and Loving Father, thank You for coming to my rescue! I am very sorry for not trusting in You, Jesus. Because, even in the darkness shines Your light, Jesus! Let this be the day that I surrender all of my life over into Your care, O Lord. I pray that I will not take my problems back, Lord God, into my own hands. Please help me, My Wonderful Counselor, to every day surrender, in prayer, my life over into Your capable hands. I love You, Jesus, very much! Amen.

June 24

TRANSFIGURED INTO HIS VERY OWN IMAGE

And all of us, as with unveiled face, [because we] continued to behold [in the Word of God] as in a mirror the glory of the Lord, are constantly being transfigured into His very own image in ever increasing splendor and from one degree of glory to another; [for this comes] from the Lord [Who is] the Spirit. 2 Corinthians 3:18 (AMP)

As you continue to incorporate the Word of God in your life, you will be more aware of how you no longer want to be part of this evil, sinful world. The things you worshipped have been replaced with God.

You will be concerned with the world around you in a different manner. The people you see struggling around you, you will no longer forget about like you used to do. Instead you will stop to help them by telling them about the transformation that occurred in your life, once you surrendered your life to Jesus Christ. What a glorious awakening in God has come over your life, as seeping lava, the hot, rich blood of Jesus has come into your heart and soul! You have been *transfigured into His very own image in ever increasing splendor and from one degree of glory to another...from the Lord...the Spirit.*

Holy Father God, thank You for rescuing me from a life spent in bondage. I now have joy and happiness in my life, O Lord! I love the life I lead today, My Devoted Friend! I wouldn't trade this life for anything the world has to offer me, God. I find such excitement in being Your trusted servant! I love You! Amen.

June 25

GOD IS PROTECTING YOU BY HIS POWER

And through your faith, God is protecting you by his power until you receive this salvation, which is ready to be revealed on the last day for all to see.
1 Peter 1:5 (NLT)

Are you deeply excited, and waiting in anticipation to go home to be with Jesus forever? This earth is not your home! You are only one of millions of travelers on the road, as a servant of God. The experiences you find, and the peace and joy that comes into your heart, as you help others in the Glorious Name of your Lord, will be overwhelming to you; to comprehend that God loves you so much that He entrusted the care of His people to you.

Until you accepted God into your heart and soul, you were in a waste land, with garbage all around you. Until it stunk badly enough, did you get off your butt and admit your sins to God, and ask for forgiveness? *Through your faith, God is protecting you by his power,* as the evil one tries to take you off the pathway that leads to the Lord; as you walk the narrow road that leads to a crown of glory for being a good and faithful servant for God.

I am so excited to return home to You, My Glorious One! To spend eternity with You, Father God, will be a pleasure! There will be only peace and contentment, as I worship at the throne of God, with You, Jesus. You are My Savior and My Redeemer! I will live forever getting to look upon your beauty and grace forever! Amen.

June 26
SHOUT PRAISES TO THE LORD

The LORD is my strength and my defense; he has become my salvation. He is my God and I will praise him, my father's God, and I will exult him. The LORD is a warrior; the LORD is his name. Exodus 15:2-3 (NIV)

Shout praises to the Lord! He deserves to be praised! Tell everyone all that the Lord has done for you. How He willingly submitted Himself over to Pilate, to be put on trial and found guilty for crimes He did not commit. Then the Lord Jesus, died in your place, to honor His Father in heaven, so your debt could be cancelled forever. *The LORD is a warrior; the LORD is his name.* So shout loudly in praises and worship in celebration of the remarkable Lord, your God, whose unfailing love, mercy, and grace, is the reason your life is so blessed!

O what a friend I have in You, My Lord Jesus! O how I love You, Jesus! With Your dying breath, Lord, You gave me life! A life so wonderful and blessed, that I have to share it with everyone. I will shout praises to You, Lord God, with my hands lifted high to the heavens, dancing and singing with all my heart to the GREAT I AM! Amen.

June 27

THERE IS NO ONE HOLY LIKE THE LORD

My heart rejoices in the LORD...There is no one holy like the LORD; there is no one besides you; there is no Rock like our God. 1 Samuel 2:1-2 (NIV)

There is no one holy like the LORD. When you drink from the living water offered to you from the cup of the Lord, you are sealed by the blood of the covenant of the Lord, which can never be broken by God. It is a solid promise that provides an impenetrable shield of protection around you from all opposition. The sacred and binding covenant between you and the Lord, can only be broken by you continuously disobeying the commandments of God, written all through His Holy Word. But, if you admit your sins, and ask for forgiveness, the covenant between you and the Lord will be honored once again by Him.

Lord God, You are my Solid Rock and Shield of Protection! I need never fear anything, My Mighty God, as Your faithful promises which are sealed in the sacred covenant between us, follows me wherever I go. There is no one Holy like You, LORD. Your divine sovereignty is above all gods! You know everything that goes on in the world. The god of this evil world can only do what you allow him to do, Father God. So I feel secure in the knowledge and truth that the evil one can't hurt me, when I have You as My Protector. Amen.

June 28

GOOD DEEDS

In the same way, the good deeds of some people are obvious. And the good deeds done in secret will someday come to light. I Timothy 5:25 (NLT)

As you go through life, try not to make public the good deeds you do for others. Sometimes it can be hard to not toot your own horn. Always keep this in the back of your mind; a*nd the good deeds done in secret will someday come into the light.* You may not get praise and recognition for all your generosity to others until you go home to heaven, where God will say, *"Good job my faithful servant. You are rewarded the crown of glory today, for all your hard work done in my name."* Wouldn't that be well worth all the times you helped another, and didn't tell anyone about what you had done?

I am so grateful to be a good and faithful servant of Yours, Holy Father! I love doing good deeds for others. But, sometimes it can be hard for me to keep quiet, O Lord. Then I remember that some day when I come before You, God, you will say to me, "When I was hungry, you gave me something to eat. When I was thirsty, you gave me something to drink. When I needed clothes, you gave me some clothes to wear. When I was sick, you took care of me. When I was a stranger, you invited me in. When I was in prison, you visited me. Take your inheritance, My Precious Child." This will be all the reward I need! I love you so much, My Father! Amen.

June 29
THE STRONG HOOK

I have seen that fools may be successful for the moment, but then comes sudden disaster.
Job 5:3 (NLT)

There was this show on NBC Television called the *Gong Show*. It was an amateur talent show which had some of the worst talent ever seen. But the show would deal with the foolish talent by using a huge cane with a hook to pull them off the stage.

That is exactly what God does for you when you do foolish behaviors. He rescues you from the foolish behavior you have done, by taking you off this worst stage of your life by His strong hook of spiritual wisdom; God's Holy Spirt speaks to your innermost being, directing you from the *sudden disaster* you caused yourself and others in your life.

O Father God, I can't believe I was so foolish, that I would think what I did was acceptable to You. I need Your guidance and help, Lord, to direct all of my passages through life. I am so thankful, Wonderful Counselor, that You came to my rescue immediately. When Your strong hook, O Lord, wrapped around me, I felt the power of Your Holy Spirit guide me along the correct path that leads to peace and serenity. I love you! Amen.

June 30

FOR SUCH A TIME AS THIS

Then Mordecai told them to reply to Esther, "Do you imagine that you in the King's palace can escape any more than all the Jews. For if you remain silent at this time, relief and deliverance will arise for the Jews from another place and you and your Father's house will perish. And who knows whether you have not attained royalty for such a time as this?"
Esther 4:13-14 (NASB)

Esther was a strong Jewish woman who became King Ahasuerus' queen. But it was hidden from the King that Esther was Jewish. So when Haman, King Ahasuerus's top official, got the King to issue a decree that all the Jews be killed, Queen Esther came before King Ahasuerus and requested an audience, knowing she could be killed if he did not put up his golden scepter. As it was written in the book of Esther, she was granted an audience with the King. She bravely presented her case to King Ahasuerus and got the law vanquished. Esther and her people were saved.

What is God calling you to do like Esther? Do you have the courage to complete the task God wants you to do? Could it be that you were chosen by God, *for such a time as this?* You could be the only one able to get positive results. Trust in God to walk with you through this scary, difficult mission. At no time do you ever walk alone!

Holy Father, I am scared to do what You want me to do! Please walk with me through this, Lord. Give me the courage and strength for such a time as this, God. Amen.

July 1

WHEN YOU WALK THROUGH THE FIRE YOU WILL NOT BE BURNED

When you pass through the waters, I will be with you; and when you pass through the rivers, they will not sweep over you. When you walk through the fire, you will not be burned; the flames will not set you ablaze. For I am the LORD, your God, the Holy One of Israel, your Savior. Isaiah 43:2-3 (NIV)

Life is full of broken promises and heartache. But the Lord will never break your heart. He is always for you and never against you! When you are seeking God, no matter what happens in your life, you never need to be upset about anything. Because of your intimate relationship with God, He will always be there for you.

For instance, words can set your heart ablaze, if they were aimed to destroy you. But *when you walk through the fire, you will not be burned; the flames will not set you ablaze,* because the Lord, will cover you with healing waters that put the fire out before serious harm is done to your heart. He will take you in His comforting arms until you are able to walk unassisted.

O Lord, my heart is broken by careless words said to me. I am fading away fast, Lord! Why did they set my heart ablaze, with their scorching words, My Best Friend? I was good to them! I didn't deserve to be treated so badly, Lord. You said, "When I walk through the fire, I will not be burned." Well, my heart is certainly ablaze, God. Please put out the fire with your healing waters. Surround me with your peace, Father. Amen.

July 2

TRYING TO FIX WHAT ISN'T BROKEN

And we know that all things work together for good for those who love God, to those who are called according to His purpose. Romans 8:28 (NKJV)

Your whole life has been mapped out by God. He took a compass and drew a line through all the different places He was going to take you. He selected the most interesting place for you and Him to travel to. God spared no expense where you were concerned. He wanted to delight you with the most beautiful and luxurious places set aside just for His precious ones.

So why are you trying to fix what isn't broken? Do you think your life will be any better if you take control over it? Don't you feel that God is doing an excellent job with your life? You have everything you need! Not necessarily everything you wanted God to give you. But, when you think about all the blessings God gave you, which you didn't deserve, you are living in paradise! And the truth is: *And we know that all things work together for good for those who love God, to those who are called according to His purpose.* You are right where you are supposed to be in God's timing, not yours. So trust in God, He knows what He is doing!

My Precious Redeemer, I am so impatient at times! I don't like when troubles come my way, O Lord. So I try to fix them, but it isn't in Your timing for my life. I need to learn not to try to fix things that are not broken, Lord! Please help me to quit trying to control everything in my life, God, and remember You, My Life Mate have mapped my life out perfectly before I was in my mother's womb. I love You, My Savior! Amen.

July 3
FACED WITH DISTRACTIONS

Looking away [from all that will distract] to Jesus, Who is the Leader and the Source of our faith [giving the first incentive for our belief] and is also its Finisher [bringing it to maturity and perfection]. He, for the joy [of obtaining the prize] that was set before Him, endured the cross, despising and ignoring shame, and is now seated at the right hand of the throne of God.
Hebrews 12:2 (AMP)

You have distractions around you all day long. In this world in which you live, it is very hard not to be distracted from your goal, which is to live for the Lord Jesus Christ, dedicating your life to Him. The Lord knew you would be faced with distractions. That is why He is always present in your thoughts. But you don't always acknowledge His presence. So, *looking away [from all that will distract] to Jesus,* allow Him, the Director of Planning, to organize your activities in His electronic calendar. Then you can be guaranteed that all you have to do for the Lord will be accomplished productively.

Lord Jesus, I want to live my life for You, My Savior! This world in which I live can't satisfy me, like You can, O Lord! I want to continue on the path to completing the mission You sent me on, Christ Jesus. I am just faced with so many distractions, I lose sight of Your presence there with me. Please continue to help me meet all of my daily tasks given to me by You Jesus. Amen.

July 4
LET JOY WALK WITH YOU

But let all those who take refuge and put their trust in You rejoice; let them ever sing and shout for joy, because You make a covering over them and defend them; let those also who love Your name be joyful in You and be in high spirits. Psalms 5:11 (AMP)

When you have the Lord in your life, even though the stormy winds and torrential rains are beating down upon you, you can let joy walk with you. Because you know the Lord will get you safely through the storm.

The Lord will provide a glorious rainbow of magnificent colors in a spectacular display so amazing and delightfully entertaining; showering you with blessings that give pleasure to your heart. Allow the gift displayed to dazzle your innermost parts from the Lord. This is a treasured reward given to you from the Lord, because you put all your trust in Him. So, forever *sing and shout for joy,* and let the whole world know what a loving, compassionate God you have in your life, who never leaves you nor forsakes you in times of trouble.

O Glorious, Precious Father, I am so grateful to You, for coming to my rescue when the storms of life were raging around me. I knew, O Lord, You would come and save me. This is why I can let joy walk with me through the storms, God. I have confidence in Your unfailing love for me, My Constant Companion. Amen.

July 5

THE SOVEREIGN LORD IS YOUR STRENGTH

The Sovereign Lord is my strength; he makes my feet like the feet of a deer, he enables me to go to the heights. Habakkuk 3:19 (NIV)

Hallelujah, hallelujah, praise the Lord God Almighty, Creator of heaven and Earth! He is worthy to be praised and worshipped! Get on bended knee, and glorify the Lord for all He has done for you! Thank the Lord, over and over again for the blessed life you have. It is a life filled with peace and contentment because the Lord sacrificed Himself for you. Praise, honor, and glory, to the GREAT I AM!

When you are weary, *the Sovereign LORD is (your) strength.* He provides shelter for you, so you can rest from your enemies. God is also your Sanctuary when you need peace and serenity, to ease away your worries. The Lord is also your Powerful Enforcer when you think you are in control. He makes you as weak as a baby, needing Him to provide for all of your needs. Finally, the Lord is a Pride Breaker, making you fall to your knees in humble submission to Him.

I praise and honor Your Glorious Name, above all names, My Life Mate! You are the Sovereign LORD over all of creation! I would not be alive today, Lord, without You giving permission for my heart to still beat. I am very thankful to You, God, for knowing what I need at all times! When I am weak, You are Strong. When I try to control my life, You make me surrender to your will. Lord, I praise and humble myself to you, Glorious Father, on bended knee. Amen.

July 6

SHOW THE LORD YOU LOVE HIM

And you must love the LORD your God with all your heart, all your soul, and all your strength.
Deuteronomy 6:5 (NLT)

Don't come into the Lord's presence with nonsense telling the Lord what you are going to do in the coming months. Instead, why don't you ask the Lord what He wants you to do for today? Quit thinking about your own selfish needs and work tirelessly at pleasing God!

The most obvious way you can please God is to be His willing servant. When you can demonstrate to the Lord, by your actions in obeying His commands, you will show the Lord you love Him. Only then will you understand what humility means: by serving others first, and yourself last you will *love the LORD your God with all your heart, all your soul, and all your strength.*

You are so very special to me, O Lord! I love You so very much! I know I sometimes, Precious Master of My Destiny, don't treat You with respect. Especially when I tell You what I am going to do, instead of asking You, Lord, what You want me to do for You! I am so sorry for disrespecting You. From now on I want to honor and worship You, God, by being Your devoted servant. I want to show You how much I love You, Lord. Actions speak louder than words! Amen.

July 7
ADMIT DEFEAT

I can do all things through Christ who strengthens me.
Philippians 4:13 (NKJV)

When you have had nothing but huge problems come your way, and you feel despair settle down deep into your heart and soul; also you feel weak and weary from struggling to find a solution all by yourself; admit defeat, gain confidence, and be assured that you *can do all things through Christ who strengthens* you, when you and the Lord solve the problems together.

I praise You, Lord, for easing my anxiety and worry! These huge problems came and surrounded me. I was trapped, with no way of escape, God. As they held me in their strong grips of steel, I became weaker and weaker, as they crushed my heart and soul! But I refused to admit defeat and asked You to save me, O God. You came rushing in with Your powerful, strong arms and ripped the steel claws of the problems off of me, and gave me peace and serenity. Thank You very much for helping me, My Devoted Friend! Amen.

July 8

IN PLAIN SIGHT

Trust in the LORD with all your heart; do not depend on your own understanding. Seek His will in all you do, and He will show you which path to take.
Proverbs 3:5-6 (NLT)

When you seek other things to comfort you instead of seeking comfort from the Lord, you are headed down a wide path that will lead you to total self-destruction.

The reality is in plain sight for you to see. But you may not be seeing all the evidence presented before you. *Trust in the LORD with all your heart; do not depend on your own understanding.* The roads marked with good intentions are never the way you should travel. Pause before going alone on your journey, and take time to talk to the Lord. You will find you are doing your own thing, instead of seeking after God's will for you. But this is Amen.dable! Go back to the Lord, and see His arms open wide, ready to comfort you.

I don't know why, O Lord, that I don't immediately seek Your presence for my life? I guess the most logical answer is God, I think I can handle everything by myself! This, of course, is when I get overwhelmed and seek other things to comfort me. It is in plain sight, marked on the road I am travelling, "<u>YOU ARE DOING YOUR OWN WILL.</u>", but I choose not to see it! Lord, HELP ME PLEASE GOD! I am a mess, Holy Father! I desperately need You, My Life Mate! I am coming to you for comfort now, Father God. I love You! Amen.

July 9

O GOD, LOVER OF MY HEART AND SOUL

How precious is your unfailing love, O God! All humanity finds shelter in the shadow of your wings.
Psalm 36:7 (NLT)

O God, lover of My Heart and Soul, I praise and honor you for *your unfailing love* that saved a filthy sinner like me! I always have unlimited shelter in your arms, Lord, forever.

No matter what is occurring in my life, I know I can find peace and contentment flowing into me, as I breathe your powerful essence of sweet nectar down deep into my innermost being. You are My Precious Friend who delights in giving me joy, happiness, and serenity, all the rest of my days in your beautiful and glorious presence.

O God, lover of My Heart and Soul, I love You, so very, very much! I am lifting my hands up to You in worship and praise, for saving a wretched sinner like me, O Lord! I am deeply humbled with gratitude to You, Holy Father, for Your unfailing love which grants me blessings of unlimited mercy and grace, from the bottom of Your heart. Praise, Honor, and Glory, Lord, are your precious names! Amen.

July 10

THE POTTER AND THE CLAY

My frame was not hidden from you when I was made in the secret place, when I was woven together in the depths of the earth. Your eyes saw my unformed body; all the days ordained for me were written in your book before one of them came to be.
Psalms 139:15-16 (NIV)

What a marvelous revelation to know that you are very precious to God. He didn't just throw your body together any haphazard way. He took precious time molding and shaping you *in the secret place,* deep in the earth. As God began shaping your body into His own image, God perfected a masterpiece of unique craftsmanship so spectacular, that you are a one-of-a kind creation.

The potter and the clay; excellent in skill and quality, made a pattern out of the dirt of the earth, and created a body with a soul that is very precious to Him. There is no price tag that could be offered for you that would describe how valuable you are to God.

O Holy Father, I am so very grateful that You love me unconditionally! You are the Master Potter, who took the clay, then shaped and molded me into Your Perfect Creation. You made me, God, a little lower than the angels. Thank You for getting to know me intimately before I was born. You know everything about me, Lord. That gives me great comfort! Amen.

July 11

I AM THE VINE; YOUR ARE THE BRANCHES

Yes, I am the vine; you are the branches. Those who remain in me, and I in them, will produce much fruit. Apart from me you can do nothing. John 15:5 (NLT)

Why do you even try to do anything without God? Maybe you think to yourself, "I don't want to bother God with this problem. He is too busy. I can handle this little problem on my own". Really? How did it work out for you? Do you know what is so ridiculous about your thinking? God always knows what is going on in your life. Like Jesus said, *"Yes, I am the vine; you are the branches. Those who remain in me, and I in them, will produce much fruit. Apart from me you can do nothing."*

The Lord is the expert gardener of your soul. He prunes away all the bad fruit of your soul, until only the most beautiful fruit remains. Wait patiently for the Lord to direct your path, then peace and serenity will enter your soul, followed by happiness and joy for all of your days.

Hallelujah, hallelujah, praise the Lord, who sees me! You know everything about me, God. So why do I think I can handle anything alone? All I do when I go apart from You Jesus, is make a mess of things. Like You said, "I am the vine; you are the branches." For all that I do to go smoothly I need to have You be a major part of my life Lord! Amen.

July 12

UNLIMITED SUPPLY

May mercy and peace and love be multiplied to you.
Jude 1:2 (NASB)

Lean not on your own understanding, but lean on the understanding of your Father in heaven. He has an unlimited supply of *mercy and peace and love*, which God will give to you, if you put your faith totally in Him. Your life will take on epic portions of contentment and joyous wonder, when you surrender everything to the Lord.

All the Lord requires of you is to believe in Him and accept that He has the best intentions for your life. When your faith is strong in the Lord, you can make it through all the trials and tribulations that try to render you helpless. If you seek the presence of the Lord, waves will sweep over all the trials and tribulations that are disturbing you, and bury them down deep in the depths of the sea, where they will remain forever.

What can I say to My God, who has everything in my life under His control? I am speechless, Lord, about how much You love me! I can't comprehend why You, Holy Father, would still take me under Your mighty wing of protection every time I call for help? I turn away from You, O Lord, and do my own will, but still You welcome me back with open arms. How can this be? I know that if I lean on Your understanding for my life, and not on my own understanding, God, You have an unlimited supply of mercy and peace and love waiting for me to receive from You. I love You, so very, very much, Father God! Amen.

July 13

THE LORD GRACIOUSLY GIVES YOU BLESSINGS

The Lord bless you and keep you; the Lord make His face shine upon you, and be gracious to you; the Lord lift up His countenance upon you, and give you peace.
Numbers 6:24-26 (NKJV)

The Lord is an awesome God! He never thinks about His own needs, but is always thinking about how He can serve you better, and take care of you. He is your Glorious King, who put His royal title behind Him, and humbled Himself as your devoted servant! He graciously gives you blessings all the time. Even though you sin against the Lord many times in a day, He still (lifts) *up His countenance upon you,* and sings a song of deliverance around you, forgiving you of all your sins, and kissing away all the shame, remorse, and guilt from your heart and soul.

I am so grateful You forgive all of my sins against You, Holy Father God! I don't know how You can keep forgiving me time after time, Lord? I am so sorry for sinning, O God. You are a gracious Lord, who gives me blessings all the time! What is so amazing is how You are My Devoted Servant. I want to humbly praise You, O Lord on my knees. You are worthy to be praised! Amen.

July 14
MORE THAN CONQUERORS

Yet in all these things we are more than conquerors through Him who loved us. For I am persuaded that neither death nor life, nor angels nor principalities, nor powers, nor things present nor things to come, nor height nor depth, nor any other created thing, shall be able to separate us from the love of God which is in Christ Jesus our Lord.
Romans 8:37-39 (NKJV)

We are more than conquerors through Him who loved us. God will supply you with all you need to defend yourself against your fierce opponents. When you are given a strong blow, and knocked down, you will be able to get up to fight and win the battle. The strength of God will come upon you so your enemies will have to flee from your presence, especially when you are vigilant with your pursuit of the Lord.

O Mighty Warrior, You are always in the battle with me! Never do I have to fear the giants who come to do me harm, because as I walk together with You, Lord, nothing can hurt me. Thank You, Father God, for never leaving me nor forsaking me. I love You, with all my heart and soul, My Constant Companion! Amen.

July 15

LOVE THE UNLOVEABLE

A new commandment I give to you: Love one another. As I have loved you, so you must love one another.
John 13:34 (NIV)

It is very hard to love someone who has wronged you! Your first response is probably anger at that person, especially when they have no remorse for what they have done to you. But God calls you to, *"love one another, as I have loved you."*

Forgiveness can be very hard. People who have done something to hurt you, sometimes don't consider your feelings. But if you can love the unlovable, in spite of what they have done to you, God will rejoice and blessings will be found, just like the most precious diamonds, shined and refined by the Lord, along the pathways of peace with Him.

What a glorious life I have experienced with my walk with You, Lord! My life now is filled with peace most of the time, Father. But, sometimes, I get very upset when people hurt me, O Lord, especially those who have no regard for my feelings what- so- ever. I get so angry and disgusted with them that I find myself, Holy Father, saying things that I regret saying. It is hard to love the unlovable, God, but I will try, with Your help. Thank You! Amen.

July 16

LET EVERYTHING YOU DO BE WORTHY OF THE LORD

And whatever you do, whether in word or deed, do it all in the name of the Lord Jesus, giving thanks to God the Father through him. Colossians 3:17 (NIV)

You represent God wherever you go. Let everything you do be worthy of the Lord. People are looking to see how you react to life. If they know you are a Christian, they will not want to follow you out of the darkness and into the light where Jesus can be found if they witness you acting like the world. So *whatever you do, whether in word or deed,* show others that you are obeying the commandments that the Lord has written for you in the Holy Word of God. Then they will gladly want to live for Jesus!

O Father God, I have again worshipped idols of this world. I am so very sorry for disappointing You, O Precious Redeemer! Please forgive me. I am on my knees asking for help in my daily walk, Lord. I surrender all of myself to You. I want everything I do to be worthy of You, Lord. How can I lead others out of the darkness and into the light where Jesus is, if I still walk in the darkness? Take all of me, and do an overhaul of my innermost being, God! I need a remodeling of my heart and soul, where Jesus is the most important thing to me! Amen.

July 17

THE LORD IS A SAFE REFUGE AND STRONG TOWER

From the ends of the earth, I cry to you for help when my heart is overwhelmed. Lead me to the towering rock of safety, for you are my safe refuge, a fortress where my enemies cannot reach me.
Psalm 61:2-3 (NLT)

The Lord is a safe refuge and strong tower when you are overwhelmed, anxious, and faint in your heart, because you tried to take on too many things on at once. It is like you are swirling in a tornado and carried away by the force of the winds, unable to fight yourself free. You know you are going to die, but you are too weak to struggle against the onslaught of the storm that is destroying you.

When you allow yourself to be desolate in your heart and spirit, and can't go on anymore, fall to your knees in complete exhaustion, seeking the presence of the Lord. He is your *fortress,* and sanctuary where you can shut out the problems of the world around you. Bask in the gentle arms of the Lord, and let Him hold you and comfort you until you feel serenity seep into your heart and spirit.

Lord Jesus, I am so overwhelmed and exhausted from trying to handle all the problems that are surrounding me. They are too numerous for me to handle without Your help, Lord. Please be my safe refuge and strong tower so that I can lean upon. I love You! Amen.

July 18

WAITING ON GOD

But those who trust in the LORD will find new strength. They will soar on wings like eagles. They will run and now grow weary. They will walk and not be faint. Isaiah 40:31 (NLT)

You want everything yesterday! But the Lord's timing is not your timing. His is perfect! The Lord knows if He gave you everything you needed, it would bring disaster to your life. So, you may have to wait for what you ask the Lord for. Remember, you will only get what you asked for, if it is in His plan for your life.

Waiting on God can be frustrating. *But those who trust in the LORD will find new strength.* The renewing of your strength can be compared to lifting 10 pound weights at first when you start training at a gym. But, after you put some time into working hard at strengthening your muscles through day to day dedication of lifting the weights, your now find your endurance allows you to lift 100 pound weights.

When you endure day to day struggles, your faith gets strengthened in God, and you are able to wait on Him to take care of your requests. This is only possible by becoming spiritually fit through increasing time in God's presence. You are training your heart and soul to seek God faithfully through good and bad days.

Glory, glory, hallelujah to the ONE AND ONLY TRUE GOD! You are faithful to take care of all my needs, Lord. You give me what I need, not what I want. Praise You for that, Lord. As I wait on You, Lord, to answer my prayers, my spiritual well- being gets strengthened, God, as I continue to seek your presence. Amen.

July 19

PULL BACK THE SHADES

The hearing ear and the seeing eyes, the LORD has made them both. Proverbs 20:12 (NKJV)

Be vigilant in dedication to honoring the Lord, in how you live your life. It is not OK to do what you want, and think the Lord will look the other way. When you surrendered your life over to the care of God, He gained complete control over your life, and expects you to glorify Him by doing His will, instead of your own will. When you continue to do your will, it is like slapping God in the face with your disrespecting heart. Don't look forward to a life filled with blessing from God. The only thing you can expect is discord and distress.

Open your eyes and pull back the shades that have led you to be unconscionable. You know right from wrong, but you have chosen willingly to entertain doing wrong more than you accepted good behavior to rule your heart. *The hearing ear and the seeing eyes, the LORD has made them both.* Look around you and see how messed up your life is. Go back to God, and start over again, surrendering everything to God, and watch the blessings multiply in your life. Peace and contentment can be present in your life every day.

Lord God, I am asking for forgiveness for living my life apart from You. I want to pull back the shades off of my eyes which have led me to be unconstitutionally honest with myself, O Lord. I now have a mess to clean up, Father! Please be with me always, and direct my paths, God, to a fulfilled and happy life spent in your wonderful presence. Amen.

July 20
FOCUS ON JESUS

...fixing our eyes on Jesus, the author and perfecter of faith, who for the joy set before for Him endured the cross, despising the shame, and has sat down at the right hand of the throne of God. Hebrews 12:2 (NASB)

If you want to have happiness and joy take over your day, focus on Jesus, *who for the joy set before Him endured the cross,* for you, so you wouldn't have to. If Jesus, out of unfailing love for you, paid the penalty for your sins, He will gladly take all that disturbs you upon Himself delightfully, pleasing you with gifts of spiritual sunlight for your soul. He will shine pleasurable paintings of colors on you; decorating the walls of your soul, making your heart shout with pleasure to the Perfect Provider of your happiness.

O Lover of My Soul, I am so delighted to know You love me so much! No one has ever showed me such compassion and kindness before, Lord. You take pleasure in making me happy and filled with joy, Jesus. If I focus on You first, Jesus, before I start my day, everything that needed to be done would go smoothly. I love You with all of my heart, Lord! Amen.

July 21
ALL OF A SUDDEN

When people are saying, All is well and secure, and there is peace and safety, then in a moment unforeseen destruction (ruin and death) will come upon them as suddenly as labor pains come upon a woman with child; and they shall by no means escape, for there will be no escape.
1 Thessalonians 5:3 (AMP)

All of a sudden there will be *no means for escape, for there will be no escape,* for anyone who chooses to follow the evil one of this world. Especially when they have had warnings from others who have studied the Holy Word of God and know the only way for salvation is to surrender their lives and repent of their sins.

Don't be unprepared for the second coming of Jesus. If your life isn't right with God, seek His presence, and ask for forgiveness for transgressions against Him. Surrender yourself to His will for your life. If you have already given yourself totally, rejoice and praise the Lord, with gratitude and thankfulness for an inheritance you don't deserve. Because of the sacrificial blood of the Lamb, you will live forever worshipping beside Jesus before the throne of God.

Praise, Honor and Glory are the glorified names of the One true Lamb of God. He took away my sins, by dying on the cross at Calvary! I bow in worship to You, Jesus, for the mercy and grace that saved a wretched sinner like me. All of a sudden, in the blink of an eye, You will come and take me home to heaven with You. I hope I have lived a life worthy enough to please You, because I can't live apart from Your presence, Jesus! I love You too much! Amen.

July 22
ALL GLORY TO GOD

Now all glory to God, who is able, through his mighty power at work within us, to accomplish infinitely more than we might ask or think. Ephesians 3:20 (NLT)

Life can suck at times! You can be having a wonderful day when all of a sudden, problems come and bury you underneath their heavy weight. Don't get so exhausted and overwhelmed trying to figure out a way to remove the mighty problems that are trapping you. Instead, seek the presence of the Lord to help you. His added strength combined with yours will be enough to throw the problems off of you, and give you a reprieve from your heavy load pf anguish…. All the glory to God, who is able, through his mighty power at work within (you), to accomplish infinitely more than you could ever accomplish on your own.

I praise You, God, for taking care of me today, when I was so overwhelmed by problems that caused me extreme anxiety. I didn't know what to do Lord, so I called on Your beautiful name to help me. Thank You for coming to my rescue, Lord. I feel such a load lifted off of me! I am peaceful once again because of Your tender mercies, Father God! Amen.

July 23

PUTTING ON THE RITZ

"Do not be afraid. I am the First, and the Last. I am the Living One; I was dead, and behold I am alive for ever and ever! And I hold the keys of death and Hades." Revelations 1:17 (NIV)

When is the last time you prayed, or had any communication with God? Don't just act like you know God, when your soul is undernourished. You are spiritually bankrupt! Remember God said, *"I hold the keys of death and Hades."* Where do you want to go when you die?

To your family, friends, and co-workers, you act like your life is really good, but you are dead inside. It is like you are putting on the Ritz: dressing your outsides up very fashionably, when your insides have huge holes of brokenness that can only be stitched up and made brand new by the Great Physician. Come back to the Lord, and receive forgiveness and everlasting life.

Gracious Heavenly Father, I have not prayed in a long time to You, but I am praying now. Please forgive me for turning my back on You Lord. I was so obsessed with putting on the Ritz, that I lost what was most precious to me, You, Jesus! I know You patiently waited for me to seek You again, O Lord. I missed You so very much God! I need You desperately to be a part of my life again Lord! Amen.

July 24
WHO IS YOUR ALLIANCE TO?

So they said, "believe on the Lord Jesus Christ, and you will be saved, you and your household."
Acts 16:31 (NKJV)

You were given free will from God to choose how you were going to live your life. God will not force you to *believe on the Lord Jesus Christ*. The question is, who is your alliance to?

If you believe in the god of this world, your life will be empty and void of any true happiness. You will have no hope for the afterlife, because your death will be spent forever with the devil and his minions.

If you believe in the *Lord Jesus Christ,* you will have a prosperous life, filled with unlimited blessings. Hope, faith, love, compassion, kindness, happiness, and joy, will fill all of your days in the presence of the Lord.

Holy Father God, I am so blessed by You! Never did I imagine I could live a life so filled with joy and happiness, O Lord. I have hope of everlasting life in Your presence, Jesus. Thank You for pulling me out of this world where I worshipped the evil one. My alliance is with You, Father God. I will to live all of my days in your beautiful presence! Amen.

July 25
ON THE SOLID ROCK

He lifted me out of the pit of despair, out of the mud and the mire, He set my feet on solid ground and steadied me as I walked along. Psalm 40:2 (NLT)

Up out of the valleys of despair you come into the presence of the Lord, and travel to the mountain tops, where your feet are placed on the solid rock of God. He is behind you, beside you, and before you, protecting you from all the obstacles that hindered your passage with Him.

God took you *out of the pit of despair, out of the mud and mire,* and celebrated the faithful journey you had walked with Him, and threw a party in your honor with His Father and the angels among you, cheering your success in following Jesus all the way to glory! Imagine this being the reward you will receive for your faithful servitude to the Lord through trials and tribulations, where you never gave up!

All glory and honor, worship and praise go to the One True God, Who was always there for me! When trials and tribulations came, I never had to fear, because I knew You would never leave me nor forsake me, God. You always put my feet on the solid rock of Your faithful presence, Father God. I want to continue on my journey with You, until I am taken into glory with You, My Devoted Companion. Amen.

July 26
GOD IS YOUR ONE AND ONLY COMFORTER

I will ask the Father, and He will give you another helper, that He may be with you forever; that is the Spirit of truth, whom the world cannot receive, because it does not see Him or know Him, but you know Him because He abides in you and will be in you. John 14:16-17 (NASB)

When you have a lot on your plate to digest, do not lose hope, because the living hope which is inside of you will not let your plate overflow. He will instead take all the excess waste that is left and turn it into spiritual food for your soul.

God is your One and Only Comforter when you are traveling on the desolate pathway filled with despair and anguish! He is the *Spirit of truth….He abides in you and will be in you* forever. The Lord will reach out His righteous right hand and lead you to the end of the road where peace and serenity is waiting for you.

O Precious Comforter, You are my One and Only God, who I can depend on for help when I am overwhelmed with everything! I need You so much to be a Constant Companion for me. I love You, My Life Mate! You are all that I need! Amen.

July 27

FRIEND OF GOD

And so it happened just as the Scriptures say: "Abraham believed God, and God counted him as righteous because of his faith." He was even called the friend of God. So you see, we are shown to be right with God by what we do, not faith alone.
James 2:23-24 (NIV)

The world around you is so negative. It is easy to fall into the patterns of this world. By trusting and believing in God, you can make a new pattern by weaving a spiritual design on your heart and soul. As you turn to God more and more through prayer, mediation, and applying His Holy Word into your life, the colors of the spiritual pattern you have designed will transcend all understanding; through faith that God is the truth and the way for a life filled with harmony and joy.

When you trust in the Lord exclusively no matter what happens to try to make you fall away from Him, you will be *called a friend of God. So you see,* (you) *are shown to be right with God,* by the actions you take to be righteous in God's sight. Living a Godly life is very hard, but well worth the blessing you get in simply knowing God is everything to you. Without Him you will have no good thing in your life!

O what a friend I have in God. Where I walk, You walk Lord. No matter what I do You are forever by my side, My Devoted Comforter! I am assured when I arise, You are there beside me. As I go through my day with trust in my heart, O Father God, nothing can seriously upset me. This world is negative God, but I chose to be peaceful and calm in Your Glorious Presence. Amen.

July 28

TUG OF WAR

*The LORD is my rock, my fortress, and my savior;
my God is my rock, in whom I find protection.
He is my shield, the power that saves me.
2 Samuel 22:2-3 (NLT)*

Quit playing tug of war with your problems! You are always going to end up with the short end of the rope. Call on God for help, and watch your problems be defeated one by one, as you and the Lord whip their butts. How does it feel to have the long end of the rope? Never again do you have to try to defeat any of your problems by yourself, because *God is* (your) *fortress, and* (your) *savior.*

You are my salvation when my problems take control over me, Lord! Why I play tug of war with my problems, Father God, I don't know. I never win the battle, God, over my problems, when I allow them to gain victory over me. Only when I call on You, O Lord, do my problems get defeated. Thank You for always coming to save me! Amen.

July 29
CENTER YOURSELF IN CHRIST JESUS

Come to me, all you who are weary and burdened, and I will give you rest. Take my yoke upon you and learn from me, for I am gentle and humble in heart, and you will find rest for your souls. For my yoke is easy and my burden is light. Matthew 11:28-30 (NIV)

When you have good days, enjoy them, because you know that soon you will experience bad days filled with trials and tribulations. It is sometimes no comfort to you to know that God has control over the good and bad days in your life. But if you center yourself in Christ Jesus, you will find that He will instantly take your burdens upon Himself, *and give you rest.* Think of Jesus as a favorite stuffed animal that you had as a child which comforted you every time you held it in your arms and helped you fall asleep.

Praise be to Jesus who always gives me peace and comfort! When I center myself in You, Christ Jesus, when my day is bad, You take all my burdens upon Yourself, and give me rest for my soul! Thank You, O Lord, for never leaving me nor forsaking me to fend for myself. I don't know what I would do without You in my life, Holy Father? I am so grateful that You hold my right hand and guide me through all of my days, My Devoted Friend! Amen.

July 30

UNFAILING LOVE

I prayed to the LORD my God and confessed: "O lord, you are a great and awesome God! You always fulfill your covenant and keep your promises of unfailing love to those who love and obey your covenant.
Daniel 9:4 (NLT)

There cannot be any other example of unfailing love, than God giving up His Only beloved Son to pay the penalty for your sins, so your slate would be wiped clean. God did not require you to be whipped, mocked, spit upon, nailed to the cross by your hands and feet, dying in humiliation and shame for your sins. Jesus Christ took that responsibility away from you.

"O lord, you are a great and awesome God!" Your unfailing love washes over me and purifies my wounded soul with mercy and grace, Lord. You are My God, and I will worship and praise You for having arms spread wide in joy when I seek Your

The words from my mouth could never praise and honor You enough, O Lord. It is the actions I take that honors You, Holy Father! I have to live for You! This is the only way I can show true thankfulness to You, Jesus, for dying in my place on the Old Rugged Cross of Calvary. Your unfailing love for me, My Life Mate is more than I feel I deserve. But, You find me precious in You sight, God, and keep blessing me anyway. I love You! Amen.

July 31
EXPLODING FIREWORKS

Light is sown for the righteous, and gladness for the upright heart. Psalm 97:11 (NKJV)

When you are doing the will of God, it is like exploding fireworks in your soul. The brightness of the multiple colors shines forth from your soul, as you walk *righteous* in the Lord. The colors are brilliantly displayed for others to seek. They tell a marvelous story of an *upright heart* witnessing the glory of the God, How can others come to know God, if they have never seen God? Keep shinning your bright light so others can be led out of the darkness into the loving arms of Jesus.

O Holy Father God, I thank You for allowing me to be Your servant. I gladly praise You Glorious Name, every time I shine my light, so others can be led out of the darkness to You, Lord. The exploding fireworks that I graciously display, God, is a truly remarkable blessing! I am deeply amazed at how many people have been saved because of me walking in You footsteps, Jesus! Amen.

August 1
OVERFLOWING WITH BLESSINGS

The thief comes only in order to steal and kill and destroy. I came that they may have and enjoy life, and have it in abundance (to the full, till it overflows).
John 10:10 (AMP)

Is your life overflowing with blessings from God? If it is, then you should be thanking and praising God for giving you more than you deserve. Because you really deserve nothing from God!

God is faithful in providing for His precious children. No matter how many times you disappoint God, He still will forgive you over and over again, when you admit your shortcomings to Him. It is like God keeps drawing from His storehouse of blessings; the most expensive riches He has there, so that you can *have and enjoy life, and have it in abundance.*

Beautiful and Precious Lord, I love You so much! I cannot remember a time when You were not looking out for me, Devoted Friend! You are always with me, Lord, even when I do not recognize You walking beside me. I want to repent of my selfishness to You right now, Father God. I don't deserve to be overflowing with blessings in my life! Too many times I have not even been concerned with seeking an intimate relationship with You, God. But still You delight in giving me blessings each day. What a remarkable God I serve! Amen.

August 2
THE BROKEN PIECES

The Lord is my light and my salvation-so why should I be afraid? The Lord is my fortress, protecting me from danger, so why should I tremble? Psalm 27:1 (NLT)

Have you ever cried out to God screaming, "Where are you?" And then when He still didn't answer you cried out again, "Why have you abandoned me God, in my time of trouble?" Only to discover God has already helped you. You just didn't know it yet.

When you start falling apart at the seams, God will sew the broken pieces of yourself back together again, better than you were before. Next time you want to go alone on a difficult journey, where everything dangerous surrounds you, remember the Lord is *protecting* (you) *from danger*. He goes in front and behind you keeping you safe. Don't fret and fall to pieces, because the Lord is there with you!

In my foolishness, O Lord, I try to handle all of my problems alone. But it leaves me feeling downcast in my heart and soul. Then I start falling apart at the seams, Father God. That is when I need You to sew my broken pieces back together again, Lord. I find I am much better than I was before, because you are always surrounding me, my Constant Companion, and protecting me from danger. Amen.

August 3

THE POORLY LIT MIRROR

For now we see in a mirror, dimly, but then face to face. Now I know in part, but then I shall know just as I am known. 1 Corinthians 13:12 (NKJV)

God loves you so much! He is disappointed greatly by your constant disregard for His needs. You don't share an intimate relationship with Him often. In fact, you think you can control every aspect of your life by yourself!

You have been looking at your reflection in a poorly lit mirror. Once you leave the mirror you forget who you are; which will always be a child of God. *Now I know in part, but then I shall know just am I have known.* If you really knew God, you would know He is crying for you. He loves you, but you don't return that love. What is stopping you from seeking God? Whatever it is, give it up, because you are worshipping an idol, instead of worshipping God!

Holy Father God, I have been lax in my relationship with You. In fact, I have avoided You, Father. Please could You save me from myself, Lord? I can't be away from You anymore, My Life Mate. I need You to light up my spirit again with Your Holy Spirit directing my path. I love You God, and am so sorry for neglecting You! Amen.

August 4

WAIT QUIETLY FOR SALVATION FROM THE LORD

Great is his faithfulness; his mercies begin afresh every morning...The LORD is good to those who depend on him, for those who search for him. So it is good to sit quietly for salvation from the LORD. LAmen.tations 3:23, 25-26 (NLT)

When your back is hunched over because you carried too many problems upon your shoulders, *sit quietly for salvation from the LORD,* and He will be your Heating Pad which eases all the tension out of your back and shoulders.

When you think you can go alone on the journey through life; getting into huge messes along the way, the Lord sweeps up all the garbage accumulated around you, purifying your heart and soul. When you are weak the Lord is strong. When you are prideful, the Lord teaches you humility.

O Daddy, I need You so much! I have made a huge mess of my life! Now all these problems are preventing me from walking along the pathway You set for me, Lord. Come quickly and save me please, My Strong Rock of Strength. I will wait quietly for Your salvation Lord. Amen.

August 5
THE DEVIL MADE ME DO IT!

No temptation have overtaken you but such as is common to man; and God is faithful, who will not allow you to be tempted beyond what you are able, but with the temptation will provide the way of escape also, so that you will be able to endure it.
1 Corinthians 10:13 (NASB)

If someone tells you to jump off a 60 foot bridge with them, are you going to jump? Then why would you allow the devil to make you do anything you did not want to do? The most common statement used is, "The devil made me do it!" The devil cannot make you do anything! He can only tempt you. *God is faithful, who will not allow you to be tempted beyond what you are able* to endure on your own. The devil is not a good enough excuse to use when you sin against God. You sin because you like to sin, plain and simple! So seek the wonderful presence of God, and He will keep you safe and secure in His loving embrace, where you can resist the devil.

O Precious Heavenly Father, I am a sinner! I sin every day, Lord, against you. Like Your Holy Word says, "All have sinned and fall short of the glory of God." (Romans 3: 23) Please forgive me for sinning against You, My Redeemer! The devil made me do it, is only an excuse I use when I do not want to admit I sinned, Lord. I love You! Amen.

August 6
GLORY TO THE ONE TRUE GOD

His divine power has given us everything we need for a godly life through our knowledge of him who called us by his own glory and goodness. Through these he has given us his very great and precious promises, so that through them you may participate in the divine nature, having escaped the corruption in the world caused by evil desires. 2 Peter 1:3-4 (NIV)

What a precious life God gave you to enjoy! He took you out of the filthy gutter of despair, where sin was surrounding you, and had you trapped in its empty promises of a fulfilling life, if you just worshipped it. But the reality is, no matter how many times you followed in the footsteps of sin, you were left lagging behind it; your expectations of a happy, fulfilled life unmet.

So worship Your LORD, and shout to the heavens: Glory to the One True God, praising Him for *having escaped the corruption in the world caused by evil desires.* Whatever you participated in and worshipped instead of God, You are now set free to live a glorious and fulfilled life in the presence of God the Holy Father. Sin now longer has a hold on you!

I praise and honor Your Glorious Name above all Names, Holy Father! You are the only God I need that can satisfy all of my needs! The world left me empty and unfilled, O Lord. Glory to the One True God who gracious gave me everything I need to be contented and fulfilled! My Life, Lord, is so blessed with You being a special part of it! I need You always, My Life Mate! Amen.

August 7

UNABLE TO GET OUT OF THE DARKNESS

Do not rejoice over me, my enemy; when I fall, I will arise; when I sit in darkness, the LORD will be a light for me. Micah 7:7 (NKJV)

Anger will destroy you! Its main purpose is death to your soul! Anger takes ahold of you with its steel claws and tries to squeeze the life out of you. Defeat anger by calling on the Lord, your Mighty Warrior, when you are unable to get out of the darkness where anger is holding you prisoner. *The LORD will be a light* guiding you out of the darkness to where peace, serenity, joy, and happiness are waiting for you.

Anger has ahold of me Lord, and I can't break free from its steel grip of death. I am crying out to You, My Savior, to come and rescue me. I am unable to get out of the darkness where anger is holding me prisoner, O God. Be my shining light of salvation, My Life Mate, and lead me to where peace, serenity, joy, and happiness are waiting for me. I can't stand on my own, Father God. Thank You, thank You, My Awesome Comforter for holding me in You gentle arms and giving me healing balm for my soul! Amen.

August 8
HEART ON FIRE

In all your ways acknowledge Him, and He will make your paths straight. Proverbs 3:6 (NASB)

Do not regret your past. The Lord will use all the bad things that have happened to you to help other people. You have a wonderful testimony to tell others about how God took the bad experiences in your past and turned them all into blessings.

When you have a heart on fire for the Lord, you will be carrying around a flame thrower of love that will scorch the hearts and souls of those in bondage to sin. In an essence, *when you acknowledge* the bad things that happened in the past, and how God has completely healed you soul, by giving you treasures money cannot buy, such as a peaceful mind, and joy shining out of your eyes; you are the radiant fire that destroys their shackles of self-pity, anger, shame, and guilt, and shows them the way to freedom in Jesus.

My heart is on fire for You, My Lord of lords, and King of kings! Hallelujah to the Lord God Almighty, Maker of heaven and Earth! I am so blessed by the bad experiences I went through in my past, O Lord, because I can tell others what happened to me, and set them free in the unfailing love of Jesus. And see the blessings unfold in their lives, by surrendering everything to You, God. Amen.

August 9

THE HOLE

You will keep in perfect peace all who trust in you, all whose thoughts are fixed on you! Trust in the LORD always, for the LORD GOD is the eternal Rock.
Isaiah 26:3-4 (NLT)

When you let pride and arrogance take control over you heart and soul, you end up in the hole of self-pity. No matter how many times you walk down different roads, you still are going to fall into the hole of self-pity. Why? Simply put, when you became self-sufficient, your expectations are high. When things go wrong, your attitude becomes one of anger, because you put everything on yourself to take care of. Which is not very realistic to accomplish without the help of the Lord. Trust in the LORD always, for the LORD God is the eternal Rock. Focus your thoughts on Him, instead of focusing on your own self-importance, and the Lord will make all that you do prosperous!

Lover of My Heart and Soul, I need Your perfect peace right now. I have made a mess of things without You helping me, O Lord! You are My Divine Helper always, Father God. I can do nothing right without You by my side, God. I keep falling into the hole, because of my self-pity, when things do not go as I planned. I need to follow Your plans for my life, My Wonderful Counselor! Amen.

August 10

FREE ME FROM MY ANGUISH

The troubles of my heart have multiplied; free me from my anguish. Psalm 25:17 (NIV)

Life is not always fair. It can be really hard at times to escape the feelings that are surrounding you. For instance, when anger, mistrust, fear, disbelief, and loneliness, capture you and bind you up in chains of anxiety because someone you trusted broke their promise to you, seek the beautiful presence of the Lord, and cry out to Him, *"Free me from my anguish, O Lord,"* and the Lord will cut the chains that bound your heart with His wire cutters of comfort. And once again, peace, serenity, happiness, and joy will reside in your heart.

I knew that I needed to come into Your Glorious Presence, O Lord, immediately for comfort. Free me from my anguish, Prince of Peace. I can't stand how I am feeling, Father God! These feelings of anger, fear, mistrust, disbelief, and loneliness have captured my heart, and I cannot get free from the heart-retching pain I am feeling, O Precious One. How could they hurt me so? I trusted them, Awesome Comforter, but they callously broke my trust! Please, My Devoted Friend, hold me in Your gentle arms and restore peace, serenity, joy, and happiness back into my heart. Amen.

August 11

SETTING YOUR SOUL FREE FROM SIN

It is for freedom that Christ has set us free. Stand firm then and do not let yourselves be burdened again by the yoke of slavery. Galatians 5:1 (NIV)

Jesus Christ died a horrendous death, setting your soul free from sin. He wore a crown of blood; thrones piercing His head. His hands and feet had holes in them form the nails that were hammered viciously into them. There Jesus hung on a cross of death, for you, willingly, your devoted servant, sacrificing Himself to be your atonement and salvation that freed you forever from your sins. Jesus paid the penalty of death, so you could live!`

Let the above paragraph be forever hung on the walls of your soul. Gaze upon it every day, and as you look at it, praise God, for sending His only Son, Jesus to die in your place. Then make a commitment to being a servant for others who do not know Jesus. Tell them that, *it is for freedom that Christ has set us free.* If they would surrender their lives over to Jesus, they can be set free from their sins, and come out of the darkness of despair, remorse, and guilt, and have joy, and peace in the light of the Lord for eternity.

Thank You, Jesus, for setting my soul free from sin. I cry every time I think about You dying on the cross, a horrible death, so my sins could be wiped clean from the slate of God forever. I love You so much Jesus, for the sacrifice of Your life, so I could live forever free from sin. I want to be You faithful servant Lord, for the people who are lost in the darkness, and bring them into the light of Your Holy Spirit. Amen.

August 12

GOD IS MERCIFUL AND FORGIVING

But the Lord our God is merciful and forgiving, even though we have rebelled against him. Daniel 9:9 (NLT)

God will never turn you away and say, *"I cannot be bothered now because I am packing My suitcase and going on a vacation."* God is always waiting with arms open wide to hold you tightly with unconditional love, when you come to Him and repent of your sins. *God is merciful and forgiving.* His unfailing love extends grace to you every time you ask for forgiveness when you sin against Him. God is slow to anger and abounding in love!

What an Awesome God I have in my life! You are My Devoted Friend, who is always concerned with making me happy. You are a merciful and forgiving God, seeing into my heart with unfailing love and delight. You wait for me, O Lord, with a smile on Your face, and gentle arms of comfort when I repent of my sins. I love You so much, Father God! Thank You for forgiving me once again of my transgressions against You, Lord. Amen.

August 13

WHY DO YOU PERMIT FEAR TO RULE OVER YOUR HEART?

There is no fear in love; but perfect love casts out fear, because fear involves torment. Because he who fears has not been made perfect in love. 1 John 4:18 (NKJV)

You cannot have both fear and love residing in your heart at the same time. *Perfect love cast out fear.* You pray because you have faith that God will take care of all your needs. So why do you permit fear to rule over your heart?

Fear comes from the devil, who is shooting darts at your heart, trying to convince you that you are walking alone through the mighty storm that is raging all around you. Do not listen to the evil one, and cry out to God, and He will calm the winds and stop the torrential rains, so you can walk unharmed through the storm.

My God, You are the strong shield of protection which surrounds me when the storms of life try to harm me. I will not allow the devil to convince me that I walk alone through the storm. You would never leave me or forsake me, O Lord. So I will not permit fear to rule over my heart! Amen.

August 14

NOTHING WORTHWHILE CAN BE ACCOMPLISHED WITHOUT GOD

We are assured and know that [God being a partner in their labor] all things work together and are [fitting into a plan] for good to those who love God and are called according to [His] design and purpose.
Romans 8:28 (AMP)

All things work together and are [fitting into a plan] for good to those who love God and are called according to [His] design and purpose. Nothing worthwhile can be accomplished without God being a part of the plans for your life. For instance, if you go and find a job that looks like it came from God, you will eventually find that God didn't guide you to this job. Either you will become dissatisfied, and go looking for a more fulfilling job, or you will end up getting laid off or fired. Either way, God's hand will be obvious to you. You will only be contented at where you are employed when you ask God to be in the planning.

When you have an intimate relationship with God, you will be more attuned to the guidance of His Holy Spirit inside of you. This is an absolute, totally trust in the Lord to plan your life. You will be amazed at the blessings the Lord will reward you with. He will give up more than you ever dreamed of having!

Hallelujah, hallelujah, praise and honor and glory to the Lord God Almighty! You are the GREAT I AM, who is sovereign over all of my life! There is nothing worthwhile that can be accomplished without You guiding me, O Lord. I love You very much, Precious Father, for You unconditionally love for me. Amen.

August 15

UNITED IN THE SPIRIT

Make every effort to keep yourselves united in the Spirit, binding yourselves together with peace. For there is one body and one Spirit, just as you have been called to one glorious hope for the future.
Ephesians 4:3-4 (NLT)

Everywhere you are, you will find others who you can lead to Jesus Christ. When you are *united in the Spirit;* there is unity in reflecting on the unfailing love of God present in your lives. A blessed and redeemed life that is fully restored in the realm of sanity leads to a *glorious hope for the future.* It is not lost in the insanity of this world that believes in worshipping idols to receive joy and happiness. Your real joy and happiness comes from the true knowledge that someday soon, you will live for eternity with Jesus Christ you Savior.

Precious Holy Father God, You took a lost soul and made me into a beautiful tapestry of unlimited value. I am a prized possession of Yours, Lord, that is very valuable to You. Your unfailing love covers all of me with never-ending blessings of peace and serenity, that brings joy every day into my life. I am so honored to be able to tell others about Your glorious promise of eternity with You Jesus. We then become united in Spirit together. Amen.

August 16
THANK YOU! THANK YOU LORD!

O give thanks to the LORD, for He is good;
for His lovingkindness is everlasting.
1 Chronicles 16:34 (NASB)

Thank You! Thank You, Lord, for all that You lovingly do for me. I am so grateful to You, Lord, for all the blessings I receive daily from You. When I am angry, You give me peace, Lord. When I am sad, Lord, you sing a happy song of deliverance, which surrounds me with joy. When I am weak from trying to handle every problem alone without You, Lord, You give me strength and comfort in Your glorious presence. When I needed a Savior to redeem my soul from the pits of hell, You came Lord and rescued me, cleansed my soul with Your blood, and made it white as snow. Your *lovingkindness is everlasting,* Lord!

Thank You! Thank You, Lord! I am so humbled by Your unfailing love for me. I want to praise Your goodness, O Lord, every day of my life! Every blessing You graciously give me, Father God, I will forever worship You by telling others how much You delight in making my life joyous and fulfilled. I love You, God! Amen.

August 17

QUIT TRYING TO CONTROL YOUR OWN DESTINY

You will be accepted if you do what is right. But if you refuse to do what is right, then watch out! Sin is crouching at the door, eager to control you. But you must subdue it and be its master. Genesis 4:7 (NLT)

God has everything taken care of. He doesn't need your help. But, when you take matters into your own hands without consulting God first, it is like you are the one running the show yourself. All the Director (God) requires you to do is to do your part accurately. He doesn't require you to assist Him in any way, shape, or form. God is the one in control of your destiny, quit trying to control your own destiny.

If you refuse to do what is right, you are sinning against God, especially when you permitted pride and E.G.O. (easing God out) to control everything you did. As a result, all you found along the way on your journey through life was obstacles blocking your passage. Allowing sin to enter, invited the evil one to direct your paths instead of God.

O Precious Comforter, I am in distress! I tried to control my destiny Lord. Now I have made such a mess out of everything I touched! Please help me to quit trying to control my own destiny Holy Father. I need You so much right now, to help repair the damage I made along the passage through life, O God. I humbly surrender everything to you, My Devoted Companion. I know You were there through the mess I created, My Life Mate. I just chose not to acknowledge Your presence. I repent of my sins against You, O Lord. Amen.

August 18
MY HEART IS CONFIDENT IN YOU O GOD

My heart is confident in you, O God; my heart is confident. No wonder I can sing your praises!
Psalm 57:7 (NLT)

Do you realize now that God is the One totally in control of your life. Of course, God gives you free will to do whatever you want, especially when you shut the Holy Spirit of God, out of your heart. It is like you have closed the door and placed a security system on it which only you know the codes to. So submit to the will of God and say to Him, *"My heart is confident in you, O God; my heart is confident. No wonder I can sing praises!"* The Lord is good! He only wants the very best for you. It hurts Him greatly when you do your own will, instead of obeying His perfect will for your life. At any time God could have made you do His will, but He wants you to come to Him freely, trusting Him with your life.

Perfect Creator of my life, I want to humbly apologize to You, giving my self-will over to You, O Wonderful Healer of my heart! I know I am placing my heart in confident hands, Lord. My heart is confident in You, God. I am lifting my hands up to Your Holy hands, so You can take ahold of my sinful hands, and reaffirm a covenant between us, Jesus, My Glorious Savior! I truly, truly, love You so much, Lord God! Make a clean heart in me! Amen.

August 19

HOLD ON TO THE RIGHTEOUS RIGHT HAND OF THE LORD

Who is wise? He will realize these things. Who is discerning? He will understand them. The ways of the LORD are right; the righteous walk in them, but the rebellious stumble in them. Hosea 14:9 (NIV)

Life can be a slick con-artist, hypnotizing you into automatically doing all it programs you to do, and you don't even realize you have been duped. For instance, the media will have you believe if you buy their beauty products, you can magically transform yourself into looking like their models. Or if you just buy their diet meals or diet pills you can be skinny and fit again. The point I am trying to make is, they are talking about fixing up your outsides so you look good, when God is more concerned with repairing your innermost parts.

It is healthy to be fit and look good. I am not debating that. What I am trying to get across is to be happy with who you are first. Too many times you can put yourself down by trying to conform to the world's standards, when you need to conform to God's. When you hold on to the righteous hand of the Lord, you will find *the ways of the LORD are right* for your life. This is where you find peace and contentment. The Lord sees the real you! So walk with the Lord, and He will purify your insides, so your outsides can be renewed also.

Gracious Heavenly Father, I want to hold on to Your righteous right hand because I need healthy guidance for my life. You know the perfected gifts I need to repair my innermost part so my exterior will be healthy also. I will trust in You, O Lord with my life. Amen.

August 20
THE END OF DAYS

Therefore, prepare your minds for action; be self-controlled; set your hope fully on the grace to be given you when Christ Jesus is revealed.
1 Peter 1:13 (NIV)

The end of days are here! The world is getting more evil each day. People are following the devil, instead of Christ Jesus. Don't allow the world to corrupt you into following their leader, the evil one. *Be self-controlled; set your hope fully on the grace to be given you when Christ Jesus is revealed.* Be alert! Jesus is coming back for you. It will not be long when you hear that trumpet sound, and you will be called by name to meet Jesus in the clouds. What a glorious day that will be!

These are the end of days, Father God! I can see how this world is getting more evil each day. But, I will not fear because I will do my best to follow Your commands for my life, O Lord. I can't wait to that glorious days, when I will see You again appearing on the white fluffy clouds of rapture for my soul. Then You, will take me up to heaven to live in everlasting peace, Jesus, worshipping Your Holy Father forever and forever! Amen.

August 21

JESUS WILL ALWAYS INTERCEDE ON YOUR BEHALF

Therefore He is also able to save to the uttermost those who come to God through Him, since He always lives to make intercession for them.
Hebrews 7:25 (NKJV)

Jesus knew what it meant to be tempted by the devil, but He was without sin. So don't fear, thinking you can't come to Jesus *to make intercession* for you with His Father. Jesus will always intercede on your behalf. He doesn't judge you like the world judges you. When you come to Him with your problems, He will be a trusting lawyer that will plead for you to the Great Judge over all creation. And the verdict will be community service to those in need, telling them about how Jesus saved you from a life in prison, setting you free from your sins.

I feel so comfortable talking to You Jesus, my friend, about anything. Even when I sin, I know I can come to You, Lord, and always feel like I am comforted and forgiven. You always intercede on my behalf with Your Father, Jesus! Thank You for showing me compassion and kindness when I am upset. I know there is no condemnation when I repent of my sins, Lord. You just hold me and comfort me in Your gentle arms, and show me mercy and grace. Amen.

August 22
HOPE AND SECURITY IS FOUND IN THE LORD

Let us hold tightly without wavering to the hope we affirm, for God can be trusted to keep his promise.
Hebrews 10:23 (NLT)

When your mind is disturbed by things you have no control over, hope and security can be found in the Lord. God is like a trusted guard dog that protects the house of your mind where your thoughts are stored. If you think of the Lord when you are confused, He will take all the confusing thoughts you are holding on to, and calm the strong turbulence that is shaking you apart, and rescue you as you hold on to His gentle arms of unfailing love. *Hold on tightly without wavering to the hope for God* will tenderly care for all your needs if you seek Him when you are in emotional distress.

Holy Father God, my hope and security is found in you, Lord. Take ahold of me, and comfort me with your gentle arms. I am so upset about everything I have to do today, Lord. My thoughts are racing out of control like an Indianapolis 500 car. I can see the bend coming up, but I can't stop my thoughts from crashing, My Precious Comforter. Amen.

August 23

DEEP AGONIZING SORROW

Be gracious to me, O Lord, for I am in distress; my eye is wasted away from grief, my soul and my body also.
Psalm 31:9 (NASB)

When you lose a child, you can be angry at God for taking that child away from you. But you can think of it as God taking all the pain and suffering from your child, giving them a glorified body free of pain and suffering. As you cry out to the Lord, *"Be gracious to me, O Lord, for I am in distress; my eye is worried away from grief, my soul and my body also,"* it may make it easier to endure. Your deep agonizing sorrow with be replaced with comfort knowing God has your child snuggly wrapped in His arms and held tightly and entwined with unfailing love.

Precious Father, I am so angry at You. Why did You take my child from me? Please answer me, Lord. I am crying deep agonizing sorrow. Please, O Lord, I need You to help me deal with this grief I am feeling. I pray that my child is with You now, and not suffering anymore. Take care of my child until I can be with them again, Precious Comforter. Amen.

August 24
THE INTERIOR DECORATOR

Blessed are you who are poor, for yours is the kingdom of God. Blessed are you who hunger now, for you will be satisfied. Blessed are you who weep now, for you will laugh. Blessed are you when men hate you, when they exclude you and insult you and reject your name as evil because of the Son of Man.
Luke 6:20-22 (NIV)

God is the Interior Decorator of the innermost being of your soul. It is like you were selected to receive a new soul built for free. You won the biggest prize of your life! God will decorate your soul with springs of living water which flow continuously through you, refreshing you with the fragrance of light that replaces darkness. This fills your soul with new beginnings of spring freshness of unfailing love!

Don't be upset when others shun you, because you know God has given you the ultimate prize of all prizes. He gave you eternal salvation when you gave yourself completely to Him. Your new self is free. You receive peace that brings happiness, joy, contentment, serenity, unfailing love, grace, mercy, compassion, and kindness when you seek the presence of the Lord.

O Holy Spirit of my soul. I delight in the fresh scents of your glorious love for me. You are the only Interior Decorator that can satisfy my soul. I delight in the newness that never disappears. Especially when I have given up self and been set free in Your beautiful presence forever. The springs of living water you graciously gave me, refresh my soul with the fragrance of Your unfailing love for me. I am complete only in Your presence, Lord. Amen.

August 25

KEEP DOING GOD'S WILL

We work wearily with our own hands to earn a living. We bless those who abuse us. We appeal gently when evil things are said about us. Yet we are treated like the world's garbage, like everybody's trash---right up to the present moment. 1 Corinthians 4:12-13 (NLT)

As Christians, we are abused by the world. Even our families treat us bad sometimes. Most often it is when we try to change a behavior that is harmful to them. But, don't give up, and keep doing God's will. Because in the end, you will be thankful that you persevered with continued faith and belief in God for the outcome. Even though you could not see the results, your blind faith in God will bring about a miraculous change in the person you are helping.

When you *are treated like the world's garbage, like everyone's trash,* which is thrown out on garbage day and easily ground up in the trash compactor; no longer of value to the world, they are angry and resentful at the blessed righteousness of God in your life. Do not be hurt or angry at them. Even if it is a family member. Pray for them in the precious name of the Lord, and trust Him for the care of that person.

O Holy One, blessed assurance, given in Your Divine Name, will take miraculous affect in changing a life through me. I just need to not give up and keep doing Your will, Glorious Lord over my life! Even if that person curses me in anger, God, I will keep praying for them in faith, and I am confident You will effect a blessed change; a miracle in them. Amen.

August 26

SLIPPERY PATCHES

He will feed His flock like a shepherd: He will gather the lambs in His arm, He will carry them in His bosom and will gently lead those that have their young.
Isaiah 40:11 (AMP)

As you walk wearily through the mist of chaos and mayhem alone, you find only slippery patches that you can't cross. Every time you try to get over a patch, you fall flat on your knees. While you are down on your knees, call to the Great *shepherd, He will gather* (You) *....in His arm* and carry you to a sweet patch of grass, where you can find nourishment for you deprived soul. As your soul becomes alive with the refreshing peace and unfailing love from the heart of the Shepherd King; softly feel the rejuvenating, cleansing beats of His heart free you from the disturbances within; breathing deep breathes of calmness into your soul.

I am so thankful to You, My Shepherd King, for coming and rescuing me from the slippery patches that prevented me from getting free from chaos and mayhem. As I remain in Your arms My Savior, I feel calmness and serenity chase out the disturbing feelings that held me trapped in darkness for so long. I love You so much, O Lord God Almighty, for the unfailing love that brings mercy and grace to me, and helps me flee from the darkness within. Amen.

August 27
WANDERING THROUGH THE DESERT

For the LORD your God has blessed you in everything you have done. He has watched your every step through the great wilderness. During these forty years, the LORD your God has been with you, and you have lacked nothing. Deuteronomy 2:7 (NLT)

Your weakness in your inability to be able to control anything is a blessing. When you are overcome with grief, and the tears are falling from your eyes, and you are aimlessly wandering through the desert, your tears making you stumble, and your feet unsteady, and you don't know your whereabouts; the sun beating down on you relentlessly, and the sand is furiously blowing in your eyes; look in front of you and behind you, and see *the LORD your God has been with you, and you have lacked nothing.* In your weakness the Lord has been strong. He has held you up, when you stumbled through the wasteland of despair. Never did God leave you or forsake you.

O LORD GOD, REDEEMER OF MY TEARS! I have cried a flood of tears, but they still keep coming, Wonderful Comforter. I am in distress! I keep wandering through the desert aimlessly, tears of grieve making me stumble, and my feet unsteady, I looked behind me and before me, and saw You, My Friend with me; tears falling from Your eyes, because You love me. You came, My Life Mate and gathered me in Your gentle arms and held me, comforting me until my tears subsided. I praise You My Lord God; hands and voice lifted up, humbling in gratitude for Your unfailing love that was upon me always. Amen.

August 28

MIGHTY POWER OF GOD

So humble yourselves under the mighty power of God, and at the right time he will lift you up in honor. Give all your worries and cares to God, for he cares for you.
1 Peter 5:6-7 (NLT)

The days to follow are not something you should be concerned about. Don't worry about what you cannot possibly see. Get off the merry-go-round of worry. Trust *the mighty power of God…Give all your worries and cares to God, for he cares for you.* God is reaching His righteous right hand for you to hold on to, so He can help you off of the merry-go-round; stimulating your senses to the warm, rejuvenating, heating pad of peace, serenity, joy, and happiness.

O My Prince of Peace, I cannot quit worrying about what is going to happen tomorrow. I am calling out to You, My Awesome Comforter to hold me in Your strong and gentle arms. I know that You will see deep inside of me, and wash all the worries out of my thoughts, with your cleansing kisses of unfailing love for me. I know that Your mighty power, God, is the healing balm for all the worries that trouble me. I love You! Amen.

August 29
I WILL NOT LEAVE YOU OR FORSAKE YOU

No man shall be able to stand before you all the days of your life; as I was with Moses, so I will be with you. I will not leave you nor forsake you. Joshua 1:5 (NKJV)

Moses demanded in the name of the Lord His God that Pharaoh release the Israelites from captivity. When Pharaoh refused, the Lord called down all forms of plagues against Egypt. When the Israelites were set free they were blessed by the Lord further, as the Egyptians chased them to the Red Sea, the Lord their God, opened the Red Sea, with the waters standing side to side so the Israelites could cross safety to the other side. He closed the Red Sea up, and drowned Pharaoh's army as they chased after the Israelites. What more blessing can the Lord your God give to you, if you trust Him explicitly with your life?

Most often, you may think that the Lord will not help you in your time of need. The crazy thinking that you envision of the Lord is so not true! Did you think the Lord doesn't already know what you are going through? He planned your life, like He did the Israelites before you were born. Like the Israelites, He will take care of all your needs, if you faithfully trust the Lord to provide for you. He will be your Strong Tower of Refuge and Strength. He will not *leave you or forsake you!* Praise God, and shout hallelujah for His faithfulness!

O Lord, My God, You will not leave me or forsake me! I trust in Your goodness and faithfulness in providing for all my needs. Praise and honor and glory, to the One and Only Lord over my life! Amen.

August 30

GET LOST IN THE SHUFFLE

Come to me all who are weary and heavy-laden and I will give you rest. Matthew 11:28 (NASB)

As life moves from day to day, you can get lost in the shuffle of going to and fro, in this crazy monotony of fitting into a tight space of time; draining you spiritually, physically, and mentally. What you desperately need when this happens is time away with Jesus so He can weave an intricate pattern; a mosaic of oiled stones that will loosen up the tight areas of your body and *give you rest.* When you awaken, you will feel young and healthy again. But you must remain in Jesus, and He in you, so you can stay energized with His Holy Spirit guiding you forever.

Jesus, You keep me feeling spectacular all the time! But the secret is simple, I must call Your Holy Spirit to guide my life. My body belongs to You, Lord! If I give You full access to my body, Jesus, I will not be lost in the shuffle of this world. I am tired of being beat down day by day, God! I surrender every part of my body to You. Amen.

August 31

BEING IN LOVE WITH THE LORD

He answered, "Love the Lord your God will all your heart and with all your soul and with all your strength and with all your mind, love your neighbor as yourself." Luke 10:27 (NIV)

Being in love with the LORD is the most wonderful feeling of all! It makes everything good or bad that you go through into a praise offering to the Lord. It tells you that you are still alive and well, because God is forever in love with you.

There will be those very difficult and heart wrenching moments where the only thing that keeps you from totally falling apart into a million pieces is being in love with Jesus and Him with you. That all-consuming love will get you through anything, even what you thought you could never get through! *Love the Lord your God with all your heart and with all your soul and with all your strength and with all your mind.* Even when you don't feel Jesus is there with you, He will be there, loving you, like you never have been loved before. Jesus will never, ever leave your side. Matter of fact, His loving arms are around you now!

Loving Father God, Your devotion and love for me is the only thing that has kept me strong through this most difficult, heart wrenching time. I felt like all the demons of hell where tearing me apart, limb by limb. But there You were at the very bottom, Jesus, holding me and keeping me whole and strong in your gentle arms. Being in love with You, Lord, is the greatest pleasure of all. Praise I sing to the LORD GOD ALMIGHTY! You love me and I love You, hallelujah, hallelujah. Amen.

September 1
ECHO OF VOICES

You, God, are awesome in your sanctuary; the God of Israel gives power and strength to his people. Praise be to God! Psalm 8:35 (NIV)

Without the power of God with you, you cannot successfully do anything! It is like you have an echo of voices bouncing off of your mind vying for your attention. The voices get louder and louder, the closer you come to making a bad decision. Turn around, God has been patiently waiting to help you. *The God of Israel gives power and strength to his people*, when they ask for it.

Praise You, O God! Glory hallelujah to the God of excellent advice. When I seek You, O Lord, before I try to solve anything on my own, You are there immediately to help me. Instead of going half-cocked, taking control away from you, God. This is when I find explosive voices echoing in my mind, firing questions at me from every direction. I become desolate and lost in my own self needs to dominate our relationship, My Life Mate. I am saying then, "I know better than you," when I desperately need your powerful guidance to direct my paths! Amen.

September 2

LIVE ABUNDANTLY

Seeing then that we have a great High Priest who has passed through the heavens, Jesus the Son of God, let us hold fast our confession. For we do not have a High Priest who cannot sympathize with our weaknesses, but was in all points tempted as we are, yet without sin. Let us therefore come boldly to the throne of grace that we may obtain mercy and find grace to help in time of need. Hebrews 4:14-16 (NIV)

Life is too short to regret anything you have done. You cannot change what you did, but you can come to Jesus, *to the throne of grace, that* (you) *may obtain mercy and find grace to help in time of need.* Quit beating yourself up with hammers of shame, remorse, and guilt. Let the Lord relieve the pressure by putting love, compassion and kindness upon your wound and repair the damage you caused.

Enjoy the life the Lord has graciously given you to savor. Our Father God takes the best fruits from the garden of heaven and places them around you. Be consciously aware of them, and take them as you need them. Some examples are: peace, contentment, happiness, songs of joy, faith, unfailing love, comfort, kindness, compassion, and hope. These satisfying fruits are available when you seek the Holy Spirit.

Praise your glorious presence, O Lord! You continue to give me delightful blessings from your precious garden of Spiritual Healing for my wounded heart. I can see I need to be thankful for what You have blessed me with today, and quit looking backwards to what I lost. Because I certainly lost the power to change anything in the past, Jesus. I love You! Amen.

September 3

I AM OUT OF CONTROL AND LOVING IT

In that day the people will proclaim, "This is our God! We trusted him, and he saved us! This is the LORD, in whom we trusted. Let us rejoice in the salvation that he brings!" Isaiah 25:9 (NLT)

Do you think you have control of your life? It's a simple question, with a complicated answer! You may not even realize you are taking control of your life. You may still think you have surrendered everything to God. It is hard to see the truth, when you are looking for it. Denial (De-Nile) is a river in Egypt! Either God has total control of your life, or you choose by your own free-will to hide away in a huge compartment the things you do not want to share with God.

The greatest moment will be when you can shout from the mountain tops, "I am out of control and loving it! The Lord has set me free! There is nothing hidden from the Lord. I *trusted in him,* and gave Him free access to my life."

I praise the Name above all names. You are a Glorious and Beautiful God! I gladly give You control, O Lord, over my life. I want to do Your will for me, God. I am out of control, and loving it! Amen.

September 4

SERVE GOD ACCEPTABLY WITH REVERENCE AND GODLY FEAR

Therefore since we are receiving a kingdom which cannot be shaken, let us have grace, by which we may serve God acceptably with reverence and godly fear. For God is a consuming fire. Hebrews 12:28-29 (NKJV)

Anger and fear can be present in your thoughts, when you are overwhelmed by stressful situations beyond your control. The stressful nuisances can cause deep emotional wounds which will fester and split open; oozing emotional poison that, if not dealt with, can make you spiritually dead to the guidance of the Holy Spirit. Anger can be healthy if dealt with properly. God can make you spiritually alive again. Only when you are still before God, and willing to have God disperse healing water over your wounds, will you be healed emotionally.

The Holy Spirit inside of you is patient and will wait for you to seek Him for guidance. When you *serve God acceptably with reverence and Godly fear,* you will accept His leading without reservation. He will be the main center of your life, the strong Cornerstone that will never collapse when trials and tribulations forcibly attack you, making you weak and vulnerable.

God, I serve you with reverence and godly fear. I am walking where You lead me. The guidance of Your Holy Spirit is what I need. I am so filled with sadness, which has caused anger and fear to dominate my thoughts. The wounds are festering with blisters of spiritual darkness. I am lying face down, submitting to Your authority for my life, Lord. I love You! Amen.

September 5

IN THE HANDS OF GOD

The LORD is good to those who wait for Him, to the person who seeks Him. LAmen.tations 3:25 (NASB)

Wear each day like your favorite piece of clothing. Enjoy how it looks and feels on you. The pleasure you receive from it is well worth the cost you paid for it! And the older it gets, the more comfortable it becomes!

No matter what happens in your day, you can learn valuable lessons from it. You can learn *that the LORD is good to those who wait for Him.* When you place your day in the hands of God, it goes smoothly and fits comfortably into your agenda. When you attempt to fit too many things into your day, you get a schedule that makes you depleted and worn out. You realize your day looks and feels good, when you call on your Old Buddy and Pal to help you.

This is the day You have made, Lord, I will rejoice and be glad in it! I will place my day in yours hands, God, and wear it like a loose garment; making it comfortable so I can enjoy it. I am done trying to do my day without You Lord in it. I love You! Amen.

September 6

GOD'S AWESOME PLAN FOR YOU

He has saved us and called us to a holy life—not because of anything we have done but because of his own purpose and grace. This grace was given us in Christ Jesus before the beginning of time.
2 Timothy 1:9 (NIV)

Jesus Christ gave up His seat at the Royal Throne of God in heaven, to come to earth as a human and also God, supernaturally conceived in Mary by His Father. Jesus knew He was destined to die a criminal's death; whipped, beaten, spit upon, mocked, a crown of thrones placed upon His head, nailed to the cross by His hands and feet. His unfailing love for you was given in His death, for the atonement of your sins. Jesus paid for that in full by the shedding of His royal blood on the cross to set you free from your sins!

God's awesome plan for you *was given before time* to His One and Only Son in fulfillment of the Holy Word of God so you could be born again by the mercy and grace of Jesus. Without grace and mercy, which redeemed you by the sacrifice of Jesus's blood, you would have been lost forever to suffer the fires of hell. Through Jesus you have access to the Holy mansion of God, where a room is prepared for you.

Holy Father God, I was a sinner that was redeemed and forgiven by the shedding of Jesus's blood on the cross. I didn't deserve mercy and grace; my sins were many, O Lord, but Your unfailing love saved a wretch like me! This was Your awesome plan for me before I was even formed in the depths of the earth, My Perfect Creator. I was fearfully and wonderfully made! Amen.

September 7
BE STILL

I pray that out of his glorious riches he may strengthen you with power through the Spirit in your inner being, so that Christ may dwell in your hearts through faith. Ephesians 3:16-17 (NLT)

Even though everyone is betting you are going to fail big-time, do not give up on your dreams. The Lord has confidence in you! He has placed the biggest bet on your success. God saved your life when you were lost to sin. He knew that you were going to do great things someday. Be still, and *through faith* believe that the Lord is right there beside you, cheering you on. With a huge smile on His face, God is shouting, *"You did it my child. I am very proud of you."*

How hopeless life can seem at times, Lord! Especially when everyone is telling me, I am a failure. But, as I strengthen my faith in You God, I have hope, because You are right beside me cheering me on to the finish line. As I cross the finish line, another dream has been fulfilled, all due to Your unfailing love for me! It is because I was still before You, Lord, and believed You will give me all that I ask for, pertaining to Your will for my life. You are a Glorious Lord. Amen.

September 8

OH HAPPY DAY

May the Lord lead your hearts into a full understanding and expression of the love of God and the patient endurance that comes from Christ.
2 Thessalonians 3:5 (NLT)

Oh happy day, it is time to rejoice! *The love of God is all around you.* He understands all that you have gone through today. God has a listening ear, ready to hear all about your miserable day, without interrupting you. God will empathize with you. He will never judge you in a harsh way. He will be ready to bounce ideas back and forth between the two of you, until you are able to catch the one idea that will be the best solution to solve the worrisome problem that is bothering you.

Praise the Lord! I have your complete attention, Wonderful Counselor! You will never tell me I am bothering you, O Lord. You will listen to every word I share with you. You patient endurance helps me to find a solution to the dilemma I am struggling with Lord. I wish I would have sought you right away instead of causing myself a lot of needless agony. I humbly submit myself before Your Holy Throne, in reverence and love, to honor You above all gods! Amen.

September 9
AUTHOR OF CONFUSION

For God is not the author of confusion but of peace, as in all the churches of the saints.
I Corinthians 14:33 (NKJV)

The one that thrives in causing confusion is the devil. The evil one is the father of lies! He will keep rehashing over and over again in your thoughts, how worthless you are. He will produce corroborating evidence from your past to prove to you that you are a despicable person. Don't believe the author of confusion. He is only harassing you to keep you away from where God is waiting for you. Rebuke the devil in God's name and He will flee from you.

For God is not the author of confusion but peace. God is just around the bend in the road. Keep walking on the path you are traveling until you reach your Strong Tower of Refuge and Strength. Inside of His heart, you will find a haven of security and love for your troubled spirit. Reach out and take hold of God's hand, and let Him lift you up into His arms of comfort.

O My God, I am so troubled in my heart and soul! I keep seeing visions of my past sins, flashing over and over again in my mind. I am hurting very bad! I need Your arms to surround me, Lord, and give me comfort or my weary thoughts. My enemy is harassing me, and telling me lies. He says I am a worthless and despicable person for doing the things I did in my past. I am fighting my way free from the devil's clutches in Your Glorious Name Lord, and coming straight to Your open arms of peace. I will not listen to the author of confusion anymore! Amen.

September 10

HUMBLE LIKE JESUS

Therefore [because He stooped so low] God has highly exalted Him and freely bestowed on Him the name that is above every name, that in (at) the name of Jesus every knee should (must) bow, in heaven and on earth and under the earth, and every tongue [frankly and openly] confess and acknowledge that Jesus Christ is Lord, to the glory of God the Father.
Philippians 2:9-11 (AMP)

What greater treasure do you have more precious than Jesus? He humbled Himself and obediently died on the Cross for you. You cannot put a price tag on the mercy and grace you received the day of Jesus' death. Christ's unfailing love for you is beyond value!

Can you be humble like Jesus? What would it take to give your life up for someone else? It does not have to be a physical death, but a spiritual awakening to open your eyes and see people around you. The time is now for you to not only pray and talk about helping others, but to go out and do something. People cannot find Jesus if they are not told about Him!

Precious Heavenly Father, I cannot wear blinders over my eyes anymore. I must go out and save the suffering, who are lost in the dark, and bring them out into the light where You are, Lord Jesus. Teach me to be humble like You through reading the Holy Word of God, and applying it to my daily life. I have to live it before I can walk in faith with You, Jesus, and be Your grateful servant to others in need. I want to humble myself like You did Jesus. I love You! Amen.

September 11
ENJOYMENT OF LIFE

So I say commend the enjoyment of life, because there is nothing better for a person under the sun than to eat and drink and be glad. Then joy will accompany them in their toil all the days of the life God has given them under the sun.
Ecclesiastes 8:15 (NIV)

Enjoyment of life is to be savored! You don't know what tomorrow will bring. But you can be assured that the Lord has every day under His control. If you are enjoying the day that the Lord has given you, then relish the blessings that the Lord has set before you.

Right around the corner can be hard times just waiting to pounce on you. So keep your focus on the Lord at all times, so God can keep you from being straddled and held down against you will. The more you are in sync with the Lord the brighter and happier your days with be because the sunlight of God's Spirit will be your escort wherever you go.

Keeper of blessings, I graciously thank you for giving me this day to enjoy! I know every day I wake up is a blessing to be savored. Enjoyment of life is an appetizing, sweet melody of gladness for my heart and soul; erupting in praise and worship to My Delightful Companion who makes me laugh even in the darkest days! Amen.

September 12

TASTE AND SEE THAT THE LORD IS GOOD

Taste and see that the LORD is good. Oh the joys of those who take refuge in him! Psalm 34:8 (NLT)

When you trust in the Lord completely, the calmness that will be present in your life is one of the greatest blessings you will receive! No more worries or fears. No more anxiousness or feelings of powerless will plague you. Instead of having all these pests invading and destroying your spiritual immune system, the Lord will construct a protective barrier that they will not be able to penetrate; sealed with His unconditional love for the continued growth of your soul. *Taste and see that the Lord is good. Oh the joys of those who take refuge in him!* Go to the Lord frequently to for a spiritual refill when you are tired and weak to give you the energy needed to live well.

What great rewards I receive in your loving and compassionate arms, o Lord! I am able to reboot and find sustaining power to throw of the weakness and replace it with strength to endure when I seek Your loving presence, My Prince of Peace! What a joy it is to taste and see that You are good all the time, and faithful in providing for all of my needs, My Life Mate. Amen.

September 13

BEYOND SPIRIT POWERLESSNESS

Therefore there is now no condemnation for those who are in Christ Jesus. Romans 8:1 (NASB)

God wants your full attention. When you place other things before Him, your attention is distracted. All your mind and thoughts can focus on is the huge mound of things that you surrender your time to, which takes you away from a relationship with God. All your spirit power is deleted, so you feel spirit powerlessness surround you.

Do not continue to feel spirit powerlessness. Go beyond spirit powerless, and break the hold it has on you. *Therefore there is now no condemnation for those who are in Christ Jesus.* When you ask for forgiveness from your Best Friend for neglecting your relationship with Him, there is an abundance of unfailing love and pride, comforting you on the difficult journey you made to escape the throne of spiritual powerlessness, and humbly bow down before the throne of God.

I am so sorry, My Best Friend, for choosing to entertain spiritual powerlessness, over seeking Your caring presence, O Lord Jesus. You have never let me down when I sought Your counsel, My Constant Companion! You were always willing to guide me beyond spiritual powerlessness, and gain power through surrendering everything to You. I love You so much, O Lord, for being my dependable partner through thick and thin! Amen.

September 14

EVERLASTING MERCY

In all their suffering he also suffered, and he personally rescued them. In his love and mercy he redeemed them. He lifted them up and carried them through all the years. Isaiah 63:9 (NLT)

When God has to punish you, He suffers! The tears that God sheds has to be many. But, thank God you receive everlasting mercy each day. For instance, there are sins you would not necessarily think is a sin. You may say, "I am just enjoying myself, when I play video games on my smart phone. Or I get such pleasure out of eating those chocolate chips cookies." But how much do you spend time on playing games on your smart phone? And do those chocolate chip cookie have you addicted to them? Ask yourself, how much time do these idols interfere with your relationship with God? *In all their suffering he also suffered.* The punishment you receive is a broken relationship with God. When you are broken, you are separated by a chasm that breaks your connection with God. You are in a dark abyss, where the Holy Spirit cannot reach you. Devote all your time in communion with God, and He will shine His light down into the blackness where you are trapped, and pull you free into His loving arms of grace.

Your everlasting mercy comforts my soul, O God! I am wrapped snuggly in the comfort of Your unfailing love for me. I know that no matter how far I get away from Your presence, Lord, You will be waiting for me with open arms of acceptance and forgiveness. I love You! Amen.

September 15

WHAT DO YOU THIRST FOR?

As the deer pants for streams of water, so my soul pants for you, my God. My soul thirsts for God, for the living God. When can I go and meet with God?
Psalms 42:1-2 (NIV)

My soul thirsts for God, for the living God. What do you thirst for? Do you thirst for the next job to make you happy? Or will the next relationship make you happy? What about the next drug, or the next drink. Will you be happy then? The point is, only God can satisfy all your needs. When you are sanctified in God, then you will be truly happy. All that God desires for you will be revealed when you wait patiently in trust for Him to direct your passage through life.

Hallelujah, hallelujah, praise to the Lord God Almighty! I thirst for the living God that has been my salvation through every aspect of my life. I have tried every worldly thing to satisfy me, Lord, but have found that my life was empty and unfilled without Your beautiful presence beside me, My God. What do I thirst for? I thirst for You, O Lord, to be the living water that satisfied me, Precious Father! Amen.

September 16

RIGHTEOUS WITHOUT WORKING FOR IT

Oh, what joy for those who disobedience is forgiven, whose sins are put out of sight. Yes, what joy for those whose record the Lord has cleared of sin.
Romans 4:6 (NLT)

Oh, God, You are a good and awesome Provider! You take care of all my needs, even when I don't ask You to. I praise You, for everlasting to everlasting! Mt heart is filled with joyous wonderful for all the continued blessings I receive everyday by your loving hands of mercy and grace.

"Oh, what joy for those who disobedience is forgiven, whose sins are put out of sight." I was given righteousness without working for it! I can't take any credit for the life I live today. All the credit goes to You, THE GREAT I AM! You have taken a worthless piece of garbage, and turned me into a sparkling gem, which you polished and refined with your redeeming blood of unfailing love, mercy, and grace. Hallelujah, hallelujah, praise, and honor, and glory, I shout on bended knee to the Holiest of Holiest!

Holy Father, I received righteousness without working for it! What a miracle I was given by Your Precious blood that was given as a mercy offering for my despicable life that I was living in worship to the god of this world. I praise You, O Lord, with all of my heart and soul; the healing chant of a devoted servant, thanking My Master for a joyous and blessed life. He has provided for me! Amen.

September 17

ALLURING LOVE OF JESUS

For God so loved the world that He gave His only begotten Son, that whoever believes in Him should not perish but have everlasting life." John 3:16 (NKJV)

Why are you wearing your grave clothes? They are dirty, and filthy rags that need to be replaced with the alluring love of Jesus; perfected and refined to fit all damaged souls. Instead you mope around, acting like your life has no meaning. You don't seek Jesus at all. You just go about your day living on the world's guidance for your life. The world doesn't have an intimate relationship with Jesus. They are just as lost as you are. Don't seek their counsel. Seek the proficient counsel of Jesus. He will guide you with His unfailing love, tender mercies, and unlimited grace. "That whoever believes in Him should not perish but have everlasting life."

Your alluring love, Jesus, set my soul free from the grave of death. There is an empty de-fouled tomb of my past mistakes waiting there for me to come back to at any time. If I seek my old habits and take up with my dirty and filthy rags of alcohol, drugs, food, gambling, pornography, and clothes to wear, because I feel I don't deserve to wear the perfect clothes of Your unfailing love, tender mercies, and unlimited grace, O Lord, I will be lost to the invading stink of the tomb of death. Amen.

September 18

THE LORD IS THE ONLY NAME THAT CAN SAVE YOU

Be silent before the LORD, all humanity, for he is springing into action from his holy dwelling.
Zechariah 2:13 (NLT)

God is your Rock of Salvation. The Lord is the Only Name that can save you! When you can *be silent before the LORD,* you are able rest and absorb His love that transcends all understanding, giving you freedom from disturbances which have taken away your tranquility. God is a peaceful and quiet haven you can run to when everything is closing in on you from all sides. Enjoy completely His everlasting, compassionate, and sturdy arms of love holding your tenderly, easing all you worries and cares; permeating to all the cells of your body.

Lord, you are the Only Name that can save me from myself. I get so caught up in the day to day worries, God. When all I need to do is give everything to You. You have told me over and over again God, "that You do not need my help." You have more than capable hands to handle the most difficult problems, My Omnipotent God of unlimited power and strength. I love You very much Lord! Amen.

September 19
ON A CLOUDY DAY

You will seek Me and find Me when you search for Me with all your heart. Jeremiah 29:13 (NASB)

On a cloudy day, everything from your view point may seem dreary and drab. Although the landscape of your heart appears colorless. It actually is producing a glowing light, illuminated by the presence of the Holy Spirit of the Lord.

The Lord provides top quality blessings for you! Take your heart that seems gray and redundant, and give it to God. As He says, *"You will seek Me and find Me when you search for Me with all your heart."* The Father of Delightful Surprises, will pierce your heart with the healing light of His Holy Spirit; His glorious gift of joy!

My Precious Heavenly Father, You always amaze me! When I am downcast in my heart, You provide a brilliant kaleidoscope of blessings so dazzling, that on a cloudy day of my heart, joy erupts jubilantly in singing and rejoicing to the Reviver of My Heart! The landscapes that seemed so dark and drab inside of me are now bursting with sparkling waterfalls of cleansing light of Your Holy Spirit. Amen.

September 20

CONFESS TO HIM HONESTLY

But if we confess our sins to him, he is faithful and just to forgive us our sins and to cleanse us from all wickedness. 1 John 1:9 (NLT)

God is not waiting to strike you down with a bolt of lightning when you sin. He already knows all your sins. The Lord just wants you to confess to Him honestly, with a contrite heart. *He is faithful and just to forgive* you of all your sins. You have a loving God that is slow to anger and abounding in unfailing love for you. If He was a tyrant, you would be dead to your sins without a pardon. But God has scattered your sins as far as the east is from the west!

Amazing grace which saved a wretch like me! I once was lost, but You found me, O Lord, and saved me. My sins have all have been forgiven, by the grace of Your unfailing love for me, My Soul Mate! When I confessed honestly to You, Lord Jesus, Your life sustaining water covered my sins and wiped me clean as new fallen snow! I love You! Amen.

September 21
TRAPPED IN A UPS BOX

Where can I go from your Spirit? Where can I flee from your presence? If I go up to the heavens, you are there; if I make my bed in the depths., you are there.
Psalm 139:7-8 (NIV)

When you are trapped in a UPS box of life, with no way of escape; destination uncertain. Don't fear! The Lord has your destination marked: PACKAGE TO BE DELIVERED IN THE HANDS OF YOUR COMFORTER. As your box is gently opened by Your Compassionate Friend, seek His face. Look into His sensitive eyes; tears of empathy falling down His cheeks, understanding in every tear that He cries. God's arms are reaching to lift you out of the UPS box, so He can hold you in His gentle and comforting arms of love. As you are resting your head on the Lord's shoulder, you can feel the tension leaving your body, as you relax in consoling arms of Your Precious Friend. Before you fall into a peaceful sleep, mediate on these Holy Words from the God: *Where can I go from your Spirit? Where can I flee from your presence?*

I am so, so, very grateful that You love me, Lord! I cannot be far from Your Relaxing Presence, My Gentle Comforter. Trapped in the UPS box of life, had me so fearful and distressed! When I cried out for help, O Lord, You came immediately and rescued me. I am humbly hitting my knees in praise to My Devoted Friend and My Life Companion. I love you! Amen.

September 22

DESTRUCTION IS AT THE DOOR OF YOUR HEART

Pride goes before destruction, and a haughty spirit before a fall. Proverbs 16:18 (NKJV)

Are you choking on your prideful attitude, yet? Can anything be accomplished effectively when you are full of pride? Pride falsely permits you to believe you know everything. If you know everything then you do not need anyone's help, especially from God! Remember, *pride goes before destruction.* Destruction is at the door of your heart, knocking for you to let it in. If you do not allow God to use the Heimlich maneuver to dislodge the pride that is corrupting your heart, you will be buried under the destructive forces of the enemy. God is waiting and willing to save your life from being damaged beyond repair. Humbly submit yourself under the complete control of God and He will take the broken pieces of your life and make all things brand new.

O My God, I have been so very prideful! I wasn't willing to see that my life was out-of-control. All I could see was my need to be right, My Dependable Helper! Destruction is at the door of my heart, forcibly demanding entrance. Please come and save me, My Mighty Warrior, and crush the enemy underneath your feet. Amen.

September 23
THE SELF-VICTIMIZED TUNNEL

Have not I commanded you? Be strong, vigorous, and very courageous. Be not afraid, neither be dismayed, for the Lord your God is with you wherever you go.
Joshua 1:9 (AMP)

Do you follow your own advice that you give to others? Or do find yourself in the self-victimizing tunnel, where denial cuts you with its razor, until you bleed from every part of your body, insecure and helpless over a life decision? You don't have to remain in the darkness that has covered your soul with hopelessness. But, you will never get rid of the fear attached to your heart until you surrender your powerlessness to the Lord. Or you can remain stuck in the manure of self-pity. It's your choice!

God wants to remove you from your self-victimizing tunnel, but it isn't possible for Him to do so until you take action to help yourself. The Lord is your Solid Protection! As He has made absolutely clear, *"Have I not commanded you? Be strong, vigorous, and very courageous….for the Lord your God is with you wherever you go."* He is there amongst the decaying matter of your heart. Just reach out to your Light and Salvation, and surrender the darkness you are trapped in; letting the Lord free you and give you hope again.

Heavenly Father, I am thankful and appreciative You never leave me to clean up the messes of life. The self-victimizing tunnel I have erected is not protecting me. Instead, it is burying me. I am ready to surrender my messes to You! As I grab Your hand of strength, I am set free, where I find hope in Your Presence. Amen.

September 24

SUFFERING PRODUCES PERSEVERANCE

Therefore, since we have been justified through faith, we have peace with God through our Lord Jesus Christ, through whom we have gained access by faith into this grace in which we now stand. And we boast in hope of the glory of God. Not only so, but we also glory in our sufferings, because we know that suffering produces perseverance; perseverance, character; and character, hope. Romans 5:1-4 (NIV)

Be strong in the Lord and His mighty power! Do not allow your enemy, the devil to cause you one moment of sadness. Don't give him the power to torment you. He is a despicable excuse for a ruler! The evil one can only do what God allows him to do. Be bold and confident, because armies of angels are fighting in heavenly realms in God's Holy name for you.

Have peace with God through our Lord Jesus Christ...because we know that suffering produces perseverance; perseverance, character; and character, hope. The devil cannot give you hope. He only brings confusion, ruling over your thoughts, making you fatigued and unable to find God anywhere. Don't despair, the protection of God has gone ahead of you, behind you, and is hovering over you.

Why can't I find You, God? I am crying out to You, My Strong Tower of Refuge and Strength, come help me! I am desperate to be in your gentle arms. The enemy is attacking me with doubts and fears; telling me I am unworthy of Your love, Father. But I know that Your Holy Word says, "Suffering produces perseverance." I trust Your Word with all my heart! I am confident that You, My Comforter, are with me now. Amen.

September 25
JOY IN THE DAY

Nehemiah said, "Go and enjoy choice food and sweet drinks, and send some of those who have nothing prepared. This day is holy to our Lord. Do not grieve, for the joy of the LORD is our strength."
Nehemiah 8:10 (NIV)

Nehemiah was distressed when Hanani, one of his brothers, informed him the Israelites who survived the exile were in trouble and the walls of Jerusalem were broken down and the gates burned with fire. Nehemiah took his grief to the Lord and asked for direction on what to do. Nehemiah admitted he was powerless and got strength from the Lord to approach King Artaxerxes to ask to go to Judah to repair the walls. The king listened and honored each request.

The example of Nehemiah is a great testimony of tremendous faith in the Lord, to grant strength when you are experiencing fear over any situation in your life. It takes faithful confidence in the Lord's availability to handle your problems, especially when you can't see Him. Faith will take your exhaustion and defeat and give you the blessing of joy in your day. Just accept compassion and tenderness from the Lover of Your Heart and Soul, to care for all your needs. Stop fighting the Lord, hand over your control to him. Do not grieve, *"for the joy of the LORD is our strength."*

How I love thee, My Precious Creator! I feel joy in my day, because I gave up the fight of trying to control everything. I am coming into Your passionate embrace, Special Friend, and finding liberation for my heart and soul. I will sing songs of praise to You, My Life Mate. The feeling of exuberance excites my spirit. Amen.

September 26

THE OLD PERSON INSIDE OF YOU

Therefore, if anyone is in Christ, the new creation has come: The old has gone, the new is here! 2 Corinthians 5:17 (NIV)

After a person gets renewed in the redeeming blood of Jesus Christ, they can still revert back to the same old pattern of negative behaviors. It is like a pattern that is cut out perfectly to be made into a special gift for a precious friend, but the finished product ends up being the most hideous thing that has ever been seen!

How can this happen? The old person inside of you sneaks out when you are distracted by day to day activities, and do not take the time to pray to God, and ask for guidance. Now everything in your life is out of control. You are frustrated and angry. Stress has become your worst enemy! Invite God to come visit you. He will persuade the old you with His unfailing love and devotion to return back through the dark portal from which it came. *The old is gone,* by the powerful, unconditional love of the Lord. Your old self can stay gone, if you permit Christ to live permanently in your heart.

I know that I need You to live permanently inside of my heart, O Lord! But I treat You like an unwanted house guest, Father, by throwing You out of my heart. If I would faithfully pray to You, Jesus, I would always be victorious over all of life's problems. The old person inside of me would never get the chance to sneak out again. Amen.

September 27

THE ROYAL KING OF THE UNIVERSE

Rejoice always; pray without ceasing; give thanks; for this is God's will for you in Christ Jesus. 1 Thessalonians 5:6-17 (NASB)

God loves you so much! He uniquely created you in His perfect image. You are fearfully and wonderfully made by the Lord. As such, God delights in you! You are exceptional in His eyes! Your whole life was fashioned by the Master Artisan's gifted hands. He foresaw the entire scope of your life. Nothing in His line of vision was out of place. God blessed every area of your life. *Give thanks; this is God's will for you in Christ Jesus.* All that you have gone through was officially approved by the Royal King of the universe. So rest assured! The King always takes care of His devoted servants.

I am so honored to be the devoted servant of the Royal King of the universe! I am so very grateful, My Lord, for being trusted with all Your special treasures. I know that each and every one of Your valuable treasures has a special place in Your heart, God. I will sing Your praises, Sacred Father, to the world. I love You! Amen.

September 28

RIVERS OF LIVING WATER

Anyone who believes in me may come and drink! For the Scriptures declare, 'Rivers of living water will flow from his heart.' John 7:38 (NLT)

As your troubled heart is beating erratically from excessive worrying about things you cannot control. It is like you heart is expelled from your body, causing lifelessness to invade your soul. It feels real, like you are suspended above a body that you do not recognize. As you look down upon this person lying there, you see eyes that are blood-shot from uncontrollable weeping. Sunken cheeks deprived of nourishment. And bluest lips that are in shock; paralyzed from fear. When you come closer to the body lying prone on its back, you realize that brokenhearted soul is you. Immediately, seek the Great Physician whose *"Rivers of living water will flow from his heart,"* to yours. Your soul has been revived with the spiritual nourishment of unfailing love and acceptance from the Lord. When in surrender completely to God, the electrical waves of atonement will comfort your soul with peace and serenity.

I am so head-strung, that I find controlling things actually comforting to me, O Lord! Then I come to my senses and realize You are the Only Comfort I need, Holy Father. I am feeling very warm and cozy, as your rivers of living water flow through my heart and soul! I love You, Blessed Redeemer for taking this weary soul inside of me, and giving it abundance life, in your healing hands of everlasting grace, Lord! Amen.

September 29

A PRICELESS TRESURE

But, you, LORD, are a shield around me, my glory, the One who lifts my head high. Psalm 3:3 (NIV)

The Lord is your priceless treasure! As a prospector explores an area for gold and discovers the mother lode, God is your Mother Lode; valuable in abundant grace and mercy; *the One who lifts (your) head high, when* you are *feeling shame, remorse,* and guilt, because you feel you have once again let Him down! But, the Father God comes after you, and wraps His compassionate arms around you; unconditional love, soothingly rubbing all the regrets you have out through the pores of your skin. You are forgiven! Freedom feels so good when you are in the glorious presence of your Constant Provider!

O Gracious Heavenly Father, You are my priceless treasure! A shield of mercy and grace setting me free from my self-inflicted chains of shame, remorse, and guilt. Thank You, Lord, for being my Valuable Gold Bar of Atonement! Amen.

September 30

JOY IN THE MORNING

But the fruit of the Spirit is love, joy, peace, longsuffering, kindness, goodness, faithfulness, gentleness, self-control... If we live in the Spirit, let us also walk in the Spirit. Galatians 5:22, 27 (NKJV)

Quit going into the storage box of negative thinking. Make a healthy choice to honor the Spirit of God with the God-box of love, peace, longsuffering, kindness, goodness, faithfulness, gentleness, self-control. The devil is the enemy of God. All whom God loves are going to be under attack. That is a fact you can read about through the Holy Word of God. This is why you keep going back to the storage box in your mind, and pulling out negative feelings.

If you want to have joy in the morning, make sure your spiritual condition is fit. You can do this by not letting the distractions of the world get in the way of your intimate communication with God. Make it a good habit to be in reverence to Him, Your best friend. Humbly thank God by devoting each day to Him. Without God's permission, you can do nothing.

I am down on my knees surrendering, humbly, this day to You, O Lord of My Heart. My Precious, loving God, I am so very, very blessed by Your loving-kindness, especially when I allow the world's distraction to pull me apart from You. I am deeply contrite about hurting You, Devoted Friend. I don't deserve You, but You pursue me relentlessly, because You don't want me to be parted from You Holy Spirit. Only when I am totally devoted to worshipping Your Divine Presence, O Lord, will I be able to discover joy in the morning! Amen.

October 1

HOW IS IT THAT YOU HAVE NO FAITH?

Then He arose and rebuked the wind, and said, "Peace, be still!" And the wind ceased and there was a great calm. But he said to them, "Why are you fearful? How is it that you have no faith?"
Mark 4:39-40 (NKJV)

The Disciples were afraid when a mighty storm came upon them while Jesus was asleep in boat. They approached Him in fear, doubting He could save them.

Isn't this how you approach Jesus, in fear, skeptical and convinced He doesn't care about what you are going through? The reason is you become frantic in your own power to find a solution to your problem. You come to Jesus, like a disobedient child approaches a parent with hesitant steps; panicked, nervous, and frightened of the consequences of the wayward behavior they participated, willingly in. But as you come into the presence of the Lord, He says to you, *"Why are you fearful? How is it that you have no faith?"* No yelling at you or condemning you for not seeking Him first. Just understanding and compassion.

Lord God, You are the Only One that can ease my fears when I am terrified! Why is every step I take towards Your Loving Presence filled with apprehension and panic? You have always been my strength and confidence, Father, when I came to You for help. You never chastised me for being afraid. You gently asked, "After everything we have been through, how is it you have no faith in me to take care of your life? My unfailing love for you will never cease." I feel peace in these words Jesus lovingly says to me. Amen.

October 2

THE MIND SET ON THE SPIRIT IS LIFE AND PEACE

For the mind set on the flesh is death, because the mind set on the Spirit is life and peace, the mind set on the flesh is hostile toward God; because it does not subject itself to the law of God, for it is not even able to do so, and those who are in the flesh cannot please God. Romans 8:6-8 (NASB)

To live in chaos and mayhem every day is death to the spirit. It is an unremitting path through life unwilling to follow the will of God. It is like continuing to jay walk immediately after being discharged from the hospital with a broken arm and leg, believing you have learned your lesson this time.

The same concept can be applied to following the will of God faithfully. The mind set on the Spirit is life and peace. Even though things keep going wrong in your life, you relentlessly study the word of God, mediating on it; eyes focused on the path the Lord has set before you. As you continue to rely on the guidance of the Father, you have built a strong foundation for your life. One that is infallible, no matter what tries to destroy it.

Hallelujah, hallelujah, I praise Your Glorious Name above all names! You are the Lord God Almighty! The GREAT I AM! I promise to follow You to the ends of the ages, My Beloved Redeemer! You are the One True God; that through Your Guiding Spirit, I can find life and peace each day. Amen.

October 3

GO UP TO THE MOUNTAIN OF THE MOST HIGH

...great and marvelous are your works. O Lord God, the Almighty. Just and true are your ways. O King of nations. Revelations 15:3 (NLT)

When you are feeling like life is too much to handle, and you just need to break away from the repetitious monotony of the earthy world, go up to the mountains of the Most High; *King of the nations.* As you enter His holy temple, relax in the calming, sweet, fragrance of incense; burning the aroma of tranquility and peace and serenity throughout your innermost being.

Oh how I love thee, Beautiful Savior and Light of the world! You gladly take all of my darkest days, and burn the calming, sweet, fragrance of incense into my innermost being healing my troubled areas with the aroma of peace, serenity, and tranquility. When You invite me to come up to Your sacred mountain, Most High, King of the nations, I leave my soiled shoes of sin outside Your Holy Temple, My Wonderful Counselor. I don't want to contaminate Your Blessed Sanctuary! Amen.

October 4

BLESS THOSE WHO WRONG YOU

Bless those who curse you. Pray for those who hurt you. Luke 6:28 (NLT)

Continue to pray for *those who hurt you.* They need prayer the most. It is easy to pray for those who have not harmed you! As you continue to ask the Lord in prayer to bless those who wronged you you have learned a valuable truth. Forgiveness is the bounty hunter, who has caught the number one killer of your heart and soul - resentment! The reward you receive for surrendering resentment to the recovery agent is the valuable gift of unfailing love, to heal your broken heart and soul from Your Wonderful Comforter

Oh Giver of the most luxurious gifts, I am overjoyed with the rich, pleasurable feeling of unfailing love, leaping for joy in my heart and soul! I have held so much anger and resentment in my heart for so long, My Prince of Peace! It was way over due for me to finally forgive the person who wronged me, like You forgave me, Jesus. Blessing the person who wronged me, Lord of My Heart, was hard at first. But the more I prayed to You, Father God, and asked for blessings for them, I was able to replace anger with love. Praise the Lord! Amen.

October 5

HOPE IS FAITHFUL TRUST IN GOD

But if we hope for what we do not yet have, we wait for it patiently. Romans 8:25 (NIV)

There is a lot of things to hope for in this worldly life. One example is, hoping you will win the 50 million dollar jackpot. You keep buying lottery tickets, hoping you will be set for life. Even if you do win the 50 million dollars and can buy all the materials possessions you think you need in your life, you will never be able to buy enough things to truly make you happy and fulfilled. Hope is faithful trust in God, to satisfy all your needs. Only then, will you be truly happy!

Hope is always fulfilled in your life by the Lord, if you put Him first above all else. Then anything that comes in your life will be good, because you surrendered your life to God. Listen quietly for the Lord to reveal His plans for your life. *Wait for it patiently,* in anticipation for the gifts you can unwrap as you playfully romp through the passages of the Great Artisan's heart; hope for true happiness as each gift reveals the daily plans of your life, holding onto the righteous right hand of Your Faithful Guide.

I have dreamed the wrong dreams, My Delightful Dream Maker! I fantasized about winning the lottery, so I could be able to buy all the worldly possessions I wanted to obtain happiness. When true happiness can only be found in You, O Lord! To be happy, I need to faithfully trust you, God, to find hope. Hope and happiness go hand in hand with You, My Precious Friend! Amen.

October 6

DO NOT BE FRIGHTENED

But even if you should suffer for what is right, you are blessed. "Do not fear what they fear; do not be frightened." But in your hearts set apart Christ as Lord... 1 Peter 3:14-15 (NIV)

Do not be frightened by situations beyond your control. You are not powerful enough to control these situations, but you are not powerless over your actions. When you surrender all your weaknesses to God, you gain power when you *set apart Christ as Lord* in your heart. For instance, you have no control over what another person chooses to do. Christ gave them free will. For example, if they choose to use drugs, alcohol, pornography, gambling, etc. One of these things just mentioned can cause you to feel paralyzed with fear; immobilized in your mind, like a magnetic force that propels your thoughts into a suspended illusion of hopelessness. You are not hopeless, because God has you. You need to remember that no matter what you suggest a person needs to do to help themselves, they may choose to disregard your suggestions. This is when God will bless you with peacefulness despite your preoccupation in trying to fix the situation on your own. God's way is always the right way, the way to tranquility and lightheartedness.

You are good all the time! All the time You are good, Lord! I will not be deterred by anything that disrupts my relationship with You, Father God. I am not frightened as long as I have You with me everywhere I go. You are my Devoted Friend and Helper through life's storms. I love You for being such an Awesome Counselor to me! Amen.

October 7

WALK ERECT, NO LONGER A SLAVE

I am the Lord your God, Who brought you forth out of the land of Egypt, that you should no more be slaves; and I have broken the bars of your yoke and make you walk erect [as free men] Leviticus 26:13 (AMP)

Just as the Israelites were physically taken out of Egypt by God where they were enslaved to Pharaoh, you are living in similar circumstances. Every day you walk through this evil, sinful world. It is your choice to either bow down to the enslaver, which is the devil, or hold on to the righteous right hand of God, and *walk erect,* no longer a slave to sin.

Heavenly Father, I get all my direction from You for living my life. Your Holy Word takes me by Your righteous right hand and safely helps me live in this sinful, evil world, spiritually fit in You, Lord! I am no longer a slave to sin! I know I sin every day, but, as I come to You obediently, and confess my sins, You keep me on the right path of mercy and grace, Beloved Healer! Amen.

October 8

MY STRONG TOWER OF REFUGE AND STRENGTH

Taste and see that the Lord is good. Oh, the joys of those who take refuge in him! Psalm 34:8 (NLT)

You can be beat down and pinned to the ground with the heavy burdens that are placed on your shoulders when you submit to the circumstances in your life. You may feel like there is no use going on! Your legs will not support the heavy weight you are carrying. You tumble to the ground, fatigued in your soul; no energy left to care what happens to you. With your last breath, whisper, "My Strong Tower of Refuge and Strength, I need your mighty power to save me."

On the wings of an eagle, God soars in and lifts you up in His powerful arms, and takes you to His safe haven of refuge. It is there your downcast soul can heal from the wounds inflicted by the heavy burdens that tore the exterior of your soul. *Taste and see the Lord is good,* as He shares His sweet nectar of empathy; the gentle touch upon your soul. His compassionate tears fall on your wounds, taking all your heavy burdens upon Himself, restoring happiness and joy to your soul, restoring His cherished temple!

I glorify the Mighty King of kings, the Lord above all Lords! I worship and praise your Holy Name, Father God! You are My Strong Tower of Refuge and Strength, when life beats me down with its heavy burdens placed upon my soul. I have confidence and faith in My Mighty Warrior King to come and save me from my many enemies who want to harm me. I love You, Awesome One, who never left me or forsake me! Amen.

October 9

WHO DO YOU GIVE YOUR TOTAL LOYALTY TO?

Fear of the Lord is the foundation of wisdom. Knowledge of the Holy One results in good judgement. Proverbs 9:10 (NLT)

God is all knowing! To think that you can hide anything from God is plain lunacy! He knew everything that you would experience in life before you were born. The Lord is the One true God, who walks in front and behind you.

Who do you give your total loyalty to? Is your total loyalty given to your friends imitating them, even if you know that your actions are wrong and displeasing to God? Or do you give your total loyalty to God? *Fear of the Lord is the foundation of wisdom.* Knowing you disobey God when you commit a sin against Him should make you sad, and frightened, because you should be setting your vision on Jesus, who is the only entrance to heaven.

Father God, You complete me! I was lost and desolate, going through each day without a purpose, O Lord. I was an empty shell without any substantial importance! I was rotting away from the inside out, until you came and made me a brand new creation, upon the old rugged cross of Calvary, where my sins are wiped clean with your atoning blood! My total loyalty belongs to You, My Constant Companion. Amen.

October 10

PRAISE THE LORD, O MY SOUL

Praise the Lord! Praise the Lord, O my soul! I will praise the Lord while I live; I will sing praises to my God while I have my being. Psalm 146:1-2 (NASB)

O Mighty King, I love you so much! I am your precious child who desires a moment of Your time, O Anointed One! I have come to bow down and praise You before the holy throne of God. *Praise the LORD, O my soul.*

All the angels of God bring the harp and lyre, the tambourine and flute. Let's sing hymns and psalms to honor and praise the King of Glory; THE GREAT I AM; The light that makes those in heaven and on earth, and in hell, fall to their knees in holy reverence and fear.

Praise the LORD, O my soul! I want to dance and shout, for the King of Glory has come to live inside of my heart and soul. Hallelujah, hallelujah! Amen. and Amen.!

October 11

JESUS ASCENDED INTO HEAVEN

In my distress I called to the LORD; I cried to my God for help. From his temple he heard my voice; my cry came before him, into his ears. Psalm 18:6 (NIV)

Jesus came in the form of an innocent baby. God trusted Mary and Joseph, His earthly parents to care for all His needs. As a young boy, Jesus began preaching the Holy Word of God in His Father's temple. When Jesus became a man, He went from town to town with His disciples, preaching to all those who needed a Savior. Christ brought the willing into His Father's kingdom in heaven.

God the Father of Jesus, heard the distressful cries of the people on Earth: "Please help me, *my God*." The Perfect Creator of all the nations was saddened that His people were dying to their sinful natures. He sent His One and Only Son, Beloved Jesus to earth to save all His people from their sins. Christ Jesus willingly gave up His life; a sacrificial Lamb, who poured out His righteous blood in atonement for your sins. Three days later after His death Jesus ascended into heaven, so your soul could be healed from your spiritual sickness, and be born again by the purifying blood of Christ.

O Gracious Heavenly Father, I am so sad that You had to sacrifice Your One and Only, Beloved Son, Jesus, to save a filthy sinner like me. I didn't deserve such unfailing love that redeemed me by Your mercy and grace, O Lord! My soul was covered with blisters, oozing black puss filled with all my sins! Thank You, thank You, for the precious gift of salvation, Holy Father! I love You! Amen.

October 12
WORRY CANNOT HELP YOU!

Can all the worries add a single moment to your life? And if worry can't accomplish a single thing like that, what's the use of worrying over bigger things?
Luke 12:25-26 (NLT)

Worry is the most useless feeling you can experience! Worry cannot help you! Worry only causes anxiety and fear to be your worst enemies. They feed on every beat of your heart, until your heart is racing out of control. The Expert Exterminator will come into your heart, and use a pest repellant to get rid of the pest, worry, that laid the eggs of anxiety and fear inside the walls of your heart. *Can all your worries add a single moment to your life?*

I know worry cannot help me, Awesome Counselor! When I seek your lovely presence, Lord, I feel contentment wash over my heart. My heart beats the simultaneous pitches of harmony and peace, as You, My Efficient Exterminator sweep Your pesticide over the pests of worry, that has invaded my heart, and laid eggs of anxiety and worry inside of its walls. Thank You very much, My Life Mate! Amen.

October 13

WHY, WHY, WHY?

...If God is for us, who [can be] against us? [Who can be our foe, if God is on our side?] Romans 8:31 (AMP)

Just when you think your life is as full as you can handle, something else gets put on your plate. You have already had enough! Your life is already beyond what you can handle. You have prayed to God without ceasing, read the Holy Word of God for life answers to problems, and talked to other Christians for advice and prayer, but nothing seems to alleviate the problems.

You scream at God, "WHY, WHY, WHY, GOD, ISN'T ANYTHING GETTING BETTER IN MY LIFE?" You remind Him, "GOD, I HAVE TRUSTED YOU TO HANDLE MY PROBLEMS. MY LIFE PLATE IS OVERFLOWING. WHEN ONE PROBLEM DISAPPERS, THREE PROBLEMS APPEAR ON THE PLATE. WHERE ARE YOU? DO YOU HEAR ME, GOD?" God hears you! His timing is perfect! *If God is for us, [who can be] against us?* Exactly! Keep seeking the presence of God. He will reassure you through intimate conversations with Him, *"You are exactly where you are meant to be. Everything that is happening in your life is leading you to face some important changes you need to make for yourself. You can only learn life lessons, through life experiences. I am with you. I will not leave you, nor forsake you, My Precious Child."*

What an awesome Creator you are God! You not only made me, but You don't leave me to fend for myself through any of life's challenges. I was very upset when I screamed at you, O Lord, WHY, WHY, WHY! It is frustrating waiting for You, My God, to take care of my problems! But, I surrender! Amen.

October 14

YOU CAN'T COMFORT ANYONE UNTIL YOU ALLOW GOD TO COMFORT YOU

Praise be to God and father of our Lord Jesus Christ, the Father of compassion and the God of all comfort, who comforts us in all our troubles, so that we can comfort those in any trouble with the comfort we ourselves have received from God.
2 Corinthians 1:3-4 (NIV)

You can't comfort anyone until you have allowed God to comfort you. Too many times you have gone head first into an empty pool, expecting to find water of comfort and healing, but you always came up sad and disconnected from God. You couldn't see God, because you were consumed with the idolatry of the world. When your attention is on fixing yourself with things other than God, you are in a web spun with deceit and confusion from the evil one.

Are you tired of giving the devil free rent in your mind? Stand up to the deceiver and rebuke him. He has to leave when you call on the Name of God. As you allow God to serve you with His unfailing love and devotion, you will be ready to help others by having the Lord speak words of comfort and healing over them in prayer. Prayer will free them from the darkness of evil and into the light were Jesus Christ is waiting for them.

Holy Father, thank you for comforting me in unfailing love and devotion. I am grateful You always save me from the darkness of the devil. I desire to be Your devoted servant, but I have to allow You to comfort me first, when I am in trouble. Then I am ready to comfort others, the way You comforted me! Amen.

October 15

THE WHOLE PICTURE

Give thanks to the LORD, for he is good! His faithful love endures forever. 1 Chronicles 16:4 (NLT)

Before you start your day, hit your knees and *give thanks to the LORD, for he is good! His faithful love endures forever.* It is right to give thanks to the Lord, because He never lets you down! He provides for you, even when you don't realize you need provision. He sees the whole picture of your life. You only see a small piece of the picture. The rest of the picture of your life is hidden from your view. The Lord knows you wouldn't be able to handle seeing your whole life flash before your eyes. Praise God for protecting you from the unavoidable grief that tomorrow brings. You are very important to the Lord! He loves you very much!

Lord, You are always looking out for me! No matter where I go, You faithfully go with me. You are My Protective Shield that surrounds me on all sides from my enemies. I am glad You see the whole picture of my life, and I can see a small piece of the picture, My Great Artisan! Your perfect painting of my life will unfold when You feel I am ready to see it in all its glory. I love You, for the unique and special Friend You are to me! Amen.

October 16

YOUR FULL PROOF SECURITY SYSTEM

Now to Him who is able to keep you from stumbling, and to present you faultless before the presence of His glory with exceeding joy. Jude 1:24 (NKJV)

As many times as you fall in your imperfections, God will pick you up each time and hold you and comfort you in His Perfect Presence. God's holiness will *present you faultless before the presence of His glory and exceeding joy.* He is your full proof security system that sets off an alarm in your eternal soul, which notifies God that the blemish of sin has tried to break in and invade your holy dwelling, defiling it with its vile presence.

I have fallen a lot in my imperfections, but You have been there each time to catch me, My Strong Tower of Protection. I was made in Your precious image, My Perfect Maker, but when sin entered me I became an imperfect being! You are my full proof security system, Holy Father, that detects the slightest hint of sin trying to crack the code of Your protective armor surrounding my soul. I love You, My life Mate! Amen.

October 17

RETURN TO THE LORD YOUR GOD

Rend your hearts and not your garments. Return to the LORD your God, he is gracious and compassionate, slow to anger and abounding in love, and he relents from sending calamity. Joel 2:13 (NIV)

When you do things on your own without consulting the advice of the Lord first, you have the companionship of a nitwit, a stupid and silly person. It is like you are trying to get free from the valleys of affliction, but each attempt you make to escape your circumstances and rise to the top of the mountain is met with opposition from the evil one, who jumps on the opportunity you presented him. In your vulnerable state, you are fair game for the devil to pick you off with his arrows of indecision, frustration, and defeat. *Return to the LORD your God, he is gracious and compassionate,* His unfailing love is infinite! God will be your intercessor, and fight your battle with the deceiver. But you need to back down from the fight, and submit to the authority of God, letting Him reign on your behalf.

O Mighty King of Glory, I submit to Your sovereignty over my life. When I can fully concede defeat, and return the reins to You, My Amazing Lord of Mercy, Your unfailing will seep into my innermost being, restoring peace to my soul, as I return to You LORD, My God! Amen.

October 18
I DON'T WANT TO GO!

O Sovereign LORD," I said, "I can't speak for you! I'm too young!" The LORD replied, 'Don't say I'm too young,' because you must go wherever I send you and say whatever I tell you. And don't be afraid of the people, I will be with you and protect you. I, the LORD, have spoken! Jeremiah 1:6-8 (NLT)

Have you ever, out of fear, uttered to the Lord, "I don't want to go! *I can't speak for you!* Please Lord, send someone else." Then you speak to the Lord again and say, "You got to be kidding me! I am not equipped to be your spokesperson for these people!"

It is shocking when you become aware that God knows exactly what He is doing! If He sent you to speak on His behalf to a lost and broken world, who has never heard the name of Jesus, God will go with you and give you the words to witness to people. But if you keep silent and never speak, you are sentencing them to imprisonment: the death of their souls to sin. Don't be afraid. God is with you.

You have called me, O God, to speak on your behalf to people who have never heard about Your Only Son, Jesus. Why do I have to go? I don't know what to say to Your people Lord! I don't speak well! Please send someone else better equipped than me at speaking. I don't want to go! What? You want me to go, Lord! I have no choice! Alright I will go, but I am telling You Lord, You are making a big mistake in sending me! I want to honor You, Precious Father! Please go with me, and give me the words to say to Your people, to lead them to the Your kingdom where Jesus is at. Amen.

October 19
A SPECIAL BLESSING

But as for me, I will watch expectantly for the LORD; I will wait for the God of my salvation. My God will hear me. Micah 7:7 (NASB)

Why are you back in yesterday and all its blunders that can never be changed? What happened yesterday is gone forever. Why beat yourself up with what-ifs and what you should have done differently! You are powerless to change a thing that occurred in the past.

Today is a special blessing from God! You can do anything you want with this day. Every moment should be spent enjoying what you are given by the merciful grace of the Lord. Go out and look at the spectacular gift of the sky; the white clouds soar above you, like angels floating on them, relaxing in blissful peace. *Watch expectantly for the LORD.* He has many more blessings for you to savor. Offer up a sweet incense of praise to the Lord God Almighty, thanking Him for the gifts around you because He delights in you!

Gracious Heavenly Father, my praise and honor and glory are shouting up to Your royal throne of mercy and grace! Today is a special blessing for Your Precious Child to enjoy. I am sorry for disrespecting my majestic, unfailing lover of my soul; my salvation and redemption for the freedom I have just for today. The sins of yesterday are gone from Your sight forever! The Holy Waters of refreshing beauty are bursting from my heart in everlasting joy for the beauty of the day. When the earth is no more, You, My Glorious Prince, will still give me presents; gifts to unwrap and savor to my heart's content! I love You so much! Amen.

October 20

PRAY IN THE SPIRT AT ALL TIMES AND ON EVERY OCCASION

Pray in the Spirit at all times and on every occasion. Stay alert and be persistent in your prayers for all believers everywhere. Ephesians 6:18 (NLT)

The devil and his minions are ruling the world! But don't have an attitude of fear. The evil one's time is running out. God will put closure on his delusions of power. In a very short time the devil and his minions will be locked up in the abyss forever!

Jesus is the Prince of Peace, and Monarch over His faithful servants! The Lord is protecting you with His legions of angels that are surrounding you with an impenetrable shield that the enemy cannot pass through to harm you. *Pray in the Spirit at all times and on every occasion. Stay alert and be persistent in your prayers for all the believers everywhere.* Prayers for other Christians is essential in this evil world, which is only getting worse each day. Prayer will hold you steadfast in your faith in God, until Jesus comes back and rescues you, and takes you up to Heaven with all your brothers and sisters in faith.

I am so ready to leave this earthly home, and return to heaven, which is my permanent home, with You God, Your Son Jesus, and the Holy Spirit, as well as all the faithful angels who have guarded me and kept me safe on earth from the devil and his minions. I will not cease in hitting my knees in worship to You, O Lord! I will pray in the Spirit at all times and on every occasion for my brothers and sisters in the faith. I love You, Jesus! Amen.

October 21
DEPEND UPON THE LORD

For David says in regard to Him, I saw the Lord constantly before me, for He is at my right hand that I may not be shaken or overthrown or cast down [from my secure and happy state]. Acts 2:25 (AMP)

Look at everything as coming from the Lord. Be grateful in good and bad times. Both will be life lessons from the Great Teacher of Spirituality! When you have a good day, you can rejoice and praise the Lord for getting your through the difficult paths on your journey through life. When a bad day occurs, the lesson you learned was that the Lord was holding on to your *right hand* [so you] *may not be shaken or overthrown or cast down,* as you depended upon the Lord through prayer and meditation; making your spiritual connection with the Lord very strong, so no negative static could interrupt your communication with Him!

I enjoy our special times together, O Lord. You are My Best Friend! I can depend upon You Lord, to come immediately when I need You. I am so grateful that I have a Wonderful Teacher, who teaches me by example. You are My Role Model in life, Lord! You walk the talk, Jesus! When You said in Your Holy Word that You would never leave me nor forsake me, You are faithful in keeping Your promises Father God. In good and bad times, You are always, always, there by my side! I love You, My Constant Helper, for being so good to me! Amen.

October 22

THE LORD MAKES EVERYTHING POSSIBLE

For everyone who asks receives; the one who seeks finds; and to the one who knocks, the door will be opened. Matthew 7:8 (NIV)

The Lord makes everything possible for you. There are no excuses that you can give for not obtaining the goals you have set for yourself! If your plans coincide with the Lord's plans for your life, the world is at your disposal. *For anyone who asks receives.* When you ask for what you need God will guide you along the right path where blessings can be found as you travel to help you successfully achieve your goals.

Lord God, I come to You, asking for help to successfully achieve my goals. I know what I want to do, I just don't know how to figure out how to do it. Please come and save me from my own folly, My Perfect Planner for my life! Nothing is impossible, O Lord, when I have You guiding all of my paths through life! Amen.

October 23

TRANSFORMING POWER OF GRACE

Then He said, "I will make all my goodness pass before you, and I will proclaim the name of the LORD before you. I will be gracious to whom I will be gracious, and I will have compassion on whom I have compassion." Exodus 20:19 (NKJV)

The Lord went before the Israelites in a pillar of cloud by day to lead the way, and a pillar of fire by night to give them light as they traveled through the wilderness.

Just like the Lord was with the Israelites. The Lord will be with you as you travel through the uninhibited wastelands of life. Though you feel you have trudged through the desolate, inhospitable regions, where discouragement, anguish, and desperation have formed a strong barrier around you, the transforming power of grace from the Lord will break through your horrible circumstances of life that have you trapped. *Proclaim the name of the LORD before you,* destroying the strongholds. Claim victory for His chosen one!

How soon I forget about You My Powerful Savior, when life's circumstances trap me in despondency. The fear cripples me Lord, and I am left helpless in unfamiliar territory, unable to fend for myself. Then I remember My Best friend will come and save me! The transforming power of Your grace, Jesus, breaks all the strongholds and sets me free. I love You Lord God! Amen.

October 24

AWAKE SLEEPER

For you know quite well that the day of the Lord's return will come unexpectedly like a thief in the night.
1 Thessalonians 5:2 (NLT)

Be prepared, making sure the Master's house is in order for His return. You don't know at what hour the Master of the house is going to be returning. Awake sleeper! Your Master will punish you severely, throwing you out on the street to be eaten up by wild dogs. *The Lord's return will come like a thief in the night.* Have a light turned on in the house, welcoming Him home, and you will be rewarded for your faithful service!

I try so hard to be a faithful servant, O Lord and Master of My Soul! The house of my soul I pray, God, meets your expectations! I have tried to follow Your orders Jesus, and keep everything clean and tidy. I know I am not perfect and sin every day Lord, but my light is shining in my soul, anxiously waiting for Your return. I love You so much and want to do a good job for You Father. Amen.

October 25

I SING PRAISES TO YOU, LORD ALL DAY LONG

Cause me to hear your loving-kindness in the morning, for on You do I lean and in You do I trust. Cause me to know the way wherein I should walk, for I lift up my inner self to You. Psalms 143:8 (AMP)

What would I do without You Lord? I sing praises to You Lord all day long, because You are My Glorious Redeemer! *Your loving-kindness Lord,* comforts me. Throughout the day, My loving and devoted Healer, I feel Your gracious hands of righteousness gently touch my troubled thoughts with the salve of tranquility. I am so blessed that You are My Life Mate into eternity!

Hallelujah, hallelujah, I praise My Everlasting Father, who is My Prince of Peace! I exult You Holy King of Glory! I will sing praises to You Lord, all day long, because You delight in providing for all of my needs. I am so thankful to You, My Constant Companion, for Your priceless gems of peacefulness when my heart is overwhelmed with everything around me. I will tell everyone how My Wonderful Counselor took wonderful care of me! Amen.

October 26

LIVING IN GOD'S WORLD IS NOT GOING TO BE EASY

"For My thoughts are not your thoughts, nor are my ways your ways," says the Lord. "For as the heavens are higher than the earth, so are my ways higher than your ways, and My thoughts than your thoughts.
Isaiah 55:8-9 (NKJV)

To be in obedience to God, you have to be subservient to Him. That means not questioning the Lord when He directs you to do something. You will be expected to depart from your comfort zone.

Living in God's world is not going to be easy, especially if you are holding on to old thoughts which lead you from Gods path. As the Lord says, *"For My thoughts are not your thoughts…For as the heavens are higher than the earth, so are my ways higher than your ways."* You can't possibly compete with the Maker of the Universe. He created everything, and is in everything! God is omniscient and knows all things. Your thoughts are only mediocre and His are supreme. Only when you are in vigilant prayer and meditate daily can you quiet your thoughts to be in tune with God's will for your life.

Graciously Heavenly Father, I want to be in tune to your will for my life. My ways can sometimes be chaotic. I need to communicate with You daily Lord, to be still and listen for your voice guiding me along the right path to where You are waiting patiently for me. I know that living in Your world God is not going to be easy, but as I follow Your footsteps for my life, I will find abounding joy in every day. Amen.

October 27

WATERS OF UNFAILING LOVE WASHES OVER YOU

I am the Lord; that is my name! I will not give my glory to another or my praise to idols. See, the former things have taken place, and new things I declare; before they spring into being I announce them to you.
Isaiah 42:8-9 (NIV)

What idols are you worshipping? The Lord didn't sanction you worshipping anything but Him. All idols are fake gods! There is no exception to this fact. Whether it is food, alcohol, drugs, gambling, pornography, clothes, a person, church, work, music, etc., all are bad when you excessively use any of them.

God's presence washes over you and sweeps away all that disturbs you. But, first, you have to make a healthy choice to come to God, instead of worshipping false gods. As God clearly states in His Holy Word: *"See, the former things have taken place, and new things I declare; before they spring into being I announce to you."* God blesses you continually when you submit control of your life to Him. It may be as simple as you day going calmer in the midst of problems. The problems may still be there, but you are content in the arms of God, as He carries you through each one!

O Father God, I want to surrender my life into Your more than capable hands. I can't do this anymore! I am tired of beating my head against the wall Lord. Please, please, My Prince of Peace, I need Your waters of unfailing love to wash over me, and sweep away all that disturbs me right now until only the peace of your Spirit remains inside of me. Amen.

October 28

A LIGHTNING BOLT OF REFUGE

The LORD is good, a refuge in times of trouble. He cares for those who trust in Him. Nahum 1:7 (NLT)

The LORD is good, a refuge in times of trouble. He will send a lightning bolt of refuge to strike down all you enemies. No weapon formed against you will prosper when you have God fighting for you. Do not fear! Keep your faith strong. Fear and faith cannot occupy the same space in your heart! Put on the shield of faith to stop the flaming arrows of the devil and he will be forced to run as God comes to whip his butt!

My Mighty Warrior King, thank you for fighting my enemies for me. Your lightning bolt of refuge struck down all my enemies, with the electrical bolt of Your powerful Holy Word, which erupted from Your sacred Mouth. My Protector, the devil didn't stand a chance against Your powerful mercy and grace, My Savior. I love you! Amen.

October 29

THE LORD IS YOUR STRENGTH AND SALVATION

The LORD will give strength to His people: The LORD will bless his people with peace. Psalm 29:11

The Lord's righteous right hand will hold onto your hand as you walk through your days, unmolested from life. Life isn't for the faint of heart! It certainly can be very draining, depleting all of your energy. It is like you are in a huge wind tunnel, trying to fight your way through, but you keep getting pushed back against the wind force of the tunnel; the force holding you captive in its powerful strength. Every day belongs to the Lord. His days are sanctions for you when you were being formed in the bowels of the earth. The Lord is your strength and salvation. *The LORD will bless* you with heavenly joy; more powerful than the earth can hold, if you continue to remain in the compassionate, kind, and patient presence of the LORD.

Your unfailing love is amazing, My Lord of Salvation! When life gets me down, by draining me physically and emotionally, Lord you are my strength and salvation; my compassion, unfailing love, and gentleness. I seek Your presence to reboot my energy, and give me incredible joy, as your gentle arms hold me tight, safe, and secure! Amen.

October 30

YOUR PARTNER IN CRIME

If we confess our sins, He is faithful and righteous to forgive us our sins and cleanse us from all unrighteousness. 1 John 1:9 (NASB)

Sin is a daily occurrence for all human beings. No man is found righteous by their own merit. Only God can call His people righteous. That is why God's children need Him to *cleanse us from all unrighteousness.* God knows that His special creations are broken. Therefore, His mercy and grace covers the sins of man each day.

You are one of God's broken creations. You have fallen head first into the decay of sin. The blessing is that, your "Partner in Crime", is always beside you, waiting for you to quit your foolishness and recognize your defiant behavior. He is waiting for you to get down on your knees in humble submission before His glorious presence, and ask for forgiveness. God will never withhold His mercy and grace from you, when you confess your sins to Him with a sincere heart.

I am so regretful, O God, that I didn't come to You first and ask for help. Instead I acted out foolishly in anger because another person didn't meet my expectations. My actions were plain stupid, My Friend! I allowed my pride to get in the way and I tried to control the situation, when I should have lifted my hands up to You God, in total defeat. You have always been my trusting "Partner in Crime", who waits patiently for me to turn to You and ask for help. Your ways are the better ways, the perfect ways for my life to run smoothly, My Sufficient and Dependable Helper! Amen.

October 31

QUIT TRYING TO BE PERFECT

And whatever you do in word or deed, do it all in the name of the Lord Jesus, giving thanks to God the Father through Him. Colossians 3:17 (NKJV)

God already knew when He created you that you were going to make many mistakes in your life. So quit trying to be perfect! What are you accomplishing by your actions? *Whatever you do in word or deed, do it all in the name of the Lord Jesus,* in thankfulness, so your actions please God greatly, and your gentleness will be evident to all. They too will worship God, thanking Him for all the blessings they have received from Him.

God can claim perfection! He never makes a mistake. He sees everything, and is in everything in your life. You are God's exquisite gem; very precious and delicate in His hands. Only God is allowed to run your life. The Father knows perfectly what His child needs!

I am hard pressed on every side to be perfect, Lord Jesus! This world demands perfection! I get so upset, O God, when I watch the commercials on TV, or read the magazines in the stores. No matter how hard I try, I don't measure up to the world's expectations of perfection. I will never look like those people, or be as rich as they are. As I read Your Holy Word Father, I find true perfection in Your Son, Jesus, whose unfailing love is my reward each day! In His unfailing love, I have found peace for I am fearfully and wonderfully made by the Great Artisan, who doesn't make anything He doesn't cherish with all His heart! Amen.

November 1

WHAT A FRIEND YOU HAVE IN JESUS

Look! I stand at the door and knock. If you hear my voice and open the door, I will come in, and we will share a meal together as friends.
Revelations 3:20 (NLT)

What a friend you have in Jesus! He gives you space when you need to be alone. He lets you decide when you want to spend time with Him. He will never push Himself on you. Jesus gave you free will. Jesus will *stand at the door and knock.* He is a gentleman! He will not enter your soul until you say, "Come in, Jesus." When you asked Jesus to enter, He comes in with a delightful smile on His face, love shining in His eyes for you. What an amazing, awesome blessing it is! It doesn't matter how long you make Jesus wait outside of the exterior of your soul, He will never give up on you! Let Jesus in to nourish your soul, right now with the spiritual food of His body. Enjoy His blood of eternal salvation, which is the entrance to heaven.

What a friend I have in You Jesus! I give myself to Thee! I open the door to my heart and soul to You Lord. Please come in and heal my weary soul with Your sacred body and the drink offering of Your blood of atonement. I have been struggling for so long, My Forever Friend. I acknowledge and decree my control of my life to You Lord God. Do with my life what You will! Amen.

November 2
WHAT GOES AROUND COMES AROUND

Do not say, "I'll pay you back for this wrong!"
Wait for the Lord, and he will avenge you.
Proverbs 20:22 (NIV)

Anger is the corrosive emotion that blackens your heart with hard pits of resentments that will weaken your emotional and mental health. Eventually, if you continue to give anger free reign over you, it will maliciously destroy you!

Give up the plan you have in your mind to seek revenge on someone who has wronged you. *Wait for the LORD, and He will avenge you.* The old saying, "What goes around comes around", can be applied to your situation in a positive way. There are consequences for all behaviors. But those who do wrong to another on purpose, the Lord will punish them. Let Him enact His own judgement on your behalf. He will be your Strong Fortress of physical ease and comfort; alleviating your anger, until it is squashed like an irritating bug underneath the Lord's sandal.

When I see You coming, O Lord, knowing You will shelter me in Your everlasting arms of peace, I will rejoice and shout hallelujahs and praises to My Strong Rock of Refuge and Strength! What goes around comes around in the perfect timing of the Lord! May the heavens and the earth shout for joy, for the unfailing love and compassion given to me by The Lover of My body and soul! He is the Lord God almighty who came, stomped the anger, and squashed it until it died. My body was again in the blessed presence of My Maker. Amen.

November 3

LOOK! HERE COMES THE LORD RIDING ON THE WINGS OF AN HORSE

Let us acknowledge the Lord; let us press on to acknowledge him. As surely as the sun rises he will appear; he will come to us like the winter rains, like the spring rains that water the earth. Hosea 6:3 (NIV)

The morning is here again. May you enjoy this blessed day that the Lord has given you. Don't be lazy; forgetting to praise the Lord in your devotion to Him through prayer this morning. The GREAT I AM is worthy to be honored by your thankful heart. Rise above your own needs. Look! Here comes the Lord riding on the wings of an horse, seeking your presence! *Acknowledge the Lord;* He has honored you with His holy presence. Fall to your face and worship Him. Sing and dance, rejoicing in the honor and privilege the King has bestowed upon you today. Jump into His gentle, compassionate arms and ride on His everlasting wings, soaring in exhilaration; the wings of joy playfully calling to the child within.

As you ride on the wings of a horse Lord, and take me up into Your strong arms of unfailing love, I am singing and dancing with joy and thankfulness Lord for the thoughtfulness of Your heart; rejoicing, anticipating the time we will spend together this morning. When I sit quietly and pray to You, My Devoted Friend, I find peace and joy, as I start my day in Your holy presence; my problems are blown away by the wings of time! Amen.

November 4

NO GREATER LOVE

The faithful love never ends! His mercies never cease.
Lamentations 3:22 (NLT)

When you think about all that you have endured throughout your life, who could you always depend on to be there for you? Did you answer, "God the Father?" There is no greater love than the love that a parent gives to their child! You are God's child! You are more valuable than any of God's other creations. He adores you! Even when you disobey Him, He still loves you, very much. The super amazing part is Your Father knows what you are going to do, before you do it. *The faithful love of the LORD never ends! His mercies never cease.* When you call to God with any need, He is the top supplier that you can go to for all your spiritual goods.

Gracious Father, I can depend on You for all my needs. But, sometimes, I am selfish and take Your unfailing love for granted, Daddy. There is no greater love, than You, My Awesome Creator! You never, ever would leave me nor forsake me Lord, like I do You, when I do my own will. Even then, You come when I call You to rescue me from the filthy garbage I have found myself covered in; the smelly sins of "self-will – run-riot!" I love You so very, very much, Dad! Amen.

November 5

A WOLF IN SHEEP'S CLOTHING

So be subject to God. Resist the devil [stand firm against him], and he will flee from you.
James 4:7 (AMP)

The devil will appear as a sheep, but is really a wolf in sheep's clothing, ready to devour you. The deceiver will even act like he is helping you, by quoting the Holy Word. You will not know you have been duped until you find yourself down a dark and frightening road, with no way of getting home.

You will know it is the devil when he convinces you to sin against the Lord. If you know the Holy Word of God well, and have it stamped on the inside of your heart, you immediately recognize the evil one twists the Word to fit his agenda. For instance, if you have faith in God and know without a doubt you would be disobeying His word if you put anything before Him in life, you will recognize the enemy saying, "It is ok to overeat today. You are upset. Get the chocolate you want to comfort you." Or the deceiver may say, "Looking at pornography is OK. Everyone does it. You are doing nothing wrong." See how innocent the evil one's words are? But they will lead you far from God.

I have been distressed lately, Lord! I have been far away from your presence and can't find my way home to You, Precious Savior. I was led astray by the evil one. He came as a gentle lamb, but was really a wolf in sheep's clothing. Please forgive me, Jesus. I crave Your Comforting Presence and I am desperate to be held by You, O Lord! Amen.

November 6

REPRESENT JESUS TO EVERYONE YOU COME IN CONTACT WITH

The purpose of my instruction is that all believers would be filled with love that comes from a pure heart, clean conscious, and genuine faith.
1 Timothy 1:5 (NASB)

God was disappointed and angry at the detestable things His children were doing. Evil was running through their hearts and souls, leaving a stench on every area of their innermost parts. God could have destroyed the world with a flick of His finger. Instead, He forgave the transgressions of His children with the birth of His Only Son Jesus.

Do you believe you were forgiven of all your sins by God's mercy and grace? If you do, how are you going to show the Lord you are filled with gratitude for Him setting you free from the bondage of your sins? An easy way to show God how grateful you are for the blessings in your life is to represent Jesus to everyone you come in contact with. Loving them the way Jesus loved you, by forgiving them for wrongs done to you. Or maybe the Lord is speaking to you to become a missionary, helping the less fortunate by showing them Jesus through love. God is sending you to people who need the light of the Holy Spirit in their lives.

I pray I can represent Jesus to everyone I come in contact with. I would feel so blessed to be able to help the less fortunate see the love of Jesus, by the light of the Holy Spirit that shines through my heart to theirs. I am thankful and filled with gratitude for Your unfailing love, which saved my life from internal darkness. Amen.

November 7

FEELING CONFIDENT THAT THE LORD IS WITH YOU

Draw near to God, and He will draw near to you. Cleanse your hands, you sinners; and purify your hearts, you double minded. James 4:8 (NKJV)

How do you handle conflicts in your life? Do you get upset and anxious when conflicts present themselves to you, allowing your flesh to take over; anger and sarcastic remarks flying off your tongue? Or do your remain calm and peaceful, feeling confident that the Lord is with you? *Draw near to God, and He will draw near to you.* It is like God is your favorite robe that you lounge in.

I am reassured in Your Presence, Lord. When conflicts present themselves to me, I am confident that Lord that You are with me. Thank You, Lord Jesus, for keeping me calm through the storms of life. You are the steady boat that gets me safely to shore when the oceans waves sweep over me. Amen.

November 8
UNPROTECTED PROGRAM

If you openly declare that Jesus is Lord and believe in your heart that God raised him from the dead, then you will be saved. Romans 10:9 (NLT)

Has your mind been defiled by the world's corruptive forces? Does it feel like you are stumbling through life, and nothing makes sense anymore? Could it be that you strayed away from Jesus, and now you are lost in the day to day repetitiveness of living your life as a carbon copy of the world's accepted demoralization.

If you openly declare that Jesus is Lord and believe in your heart that God raised Him from the dead, you will be saved. The mind is like a computer. You can save anything you safely store there like a document. God can be your strong firewall, keeping out the viruses of sin that attach themselves to an unprotected memory in your mind. But you first need to admit you have a problem with sin corrupting your thoughts. Watch the Computer Ace come clean out the bugs, making your computer run better than before. He placed a special program of His Holy Word, which if used correctly, will be a life time warranty of day to day blessings.

God, you are the best computer programmer in the world! When my thoughts get corrupted by the world I crash, because I am overloaded with dirty viruses of sin which attach themselves to the unprotected program in my mind. I will call You Lord to come and fix it for me. You are Firewall of Strength, Jesus, when my computer needs a reboot of spiritual programming. Amen.

November 9

OFFER UP TO GOD A SACRIFICE OF PRAISE

Through Him, therefore, let us constantly and at all times offer up to God a sacrifice of praise, which is the fruit of the lips that thankfully acknowledge and confess and glorify His name. Hebrews 13:15 (AMP)

To be in the presence of the King of kings, and Lord of lords, is time to celebrate; dancing and singing, making a joyful noise to the glory of His Majesty! Hallelujah, hallelujah, *offer up a sacrifice of praise to God,* from the highest of mountains, exulting Him to all the world, proclaiming the blessings you receive when you sought God the Father, first and foremost above all else in your life.

From the highest of mountains, I will shout your praises, O Lord, proclaiming Your goodness so the whole world can sing with me. I want to offer up a sacrifice of praise to the One True King! The Sovereign Lord over all the nations. I love You, Great and Awesome Provider of infinite blessings, as I put my total trust in You, My God! Amen.

November 10

GOD IS A CONSIDERATE AND LOVING FRIEND

I lift up my eyes to the mountains—where does my help come from? My help comes from the LORD, the Maker of heaven and earth. Psalm 121:1-2 (NIV)

God is a considerate and loving Friend! He never puts demands on you. He has given you free will to live your life the way you choose. However, when you seek God for any purpose, He will come running to help you immediately. God doesn't make you wait, because you forgot to pray to Him this morning. Or He would never say to you, *"My child, I am helping someone else out right now who is more worthy than you. They followed my leading and you decided to go off and travel far away from me."* As long as you seek the presence of your Best Friend humbly with a heart of repentance, God will be more then glad to help you. Your *help comes from the LORD, the Maker of heaven and earth.* He is slow to anger and abounding in love. You don't ever have to fear and be anxious when seeking the presence of God. He is always gentle and loving to His children when they seek Him.

God, You are a considerate and loving friend, who always has my best interest at heart. Your arms are opened wide, welcoming me into Your Holy Presence, Lord, when I come to You humbly with a heart of repentance for straying away from Your guidance for my life. I am so filled with Joy and gladness God, for Your unfailing love for me! Amen.

November 11

LIBERATED IN CHRIST

Stand fast therefore in the liberty by which Christ has made us free, and do not be entangled again with a yoke of bondage. Galatians 5:1 (NKJV)

The evil one is prowling around like a lion to destroy your soul. He doesn't want you to be liberated in Christ! *Do not be entangled again with a yoke of bondage.* The deceiver of the world, will try to convince you, you are unworthy of the unfailing love Jesus freely gave you by His mercy and grace. The enemy has no power over you! Christ graciously set you free, as His blood sealed your sins to the cross upon His death. Live unhindered from your past sins. Walk in the righteousness of Jesus, who paid the highest price, dying a prisoner's death for the liberation of your soul.

I am so very thankful for Your unfailing love Jesus, which set this prisoner free from the chains that bound me. I was a nothing; disgraced and ashamed! I didn't feel worthy enough to look upon Your Holy Presence Lord. You came that fatal, horrible day, and surrendered Yourself to death Jesus, liberating me from my sins. I am so very grateful, Precious Savior of my soul! I love You so very much Christ Jesus! Amen.

November 12
LIVE IN THE PRESENCE OF THE LORD

Surely your goodness and unfailing love will pursue me all days of my life, and I will live in the house of the Lord forever. Psalm 23:6 (NLT)

Holy Father God, I am so thankful for everything that you do for me. Nothing that I have belongs to me! I am so grateful that I have a Wonderful Comforter who considers me more important than Himself. My needs are always met. I lack nothing! The blessings keep coming beyond anything I could have dreamed I deserved to ask You for, Lord God.

I am so in need of Your Presence, Father. I can't wait to live in the presence of the Lord, My Best Friend! *Surely your goodness and unfailing love will pursue me all the days of my life, and I will live in the house of the Lord forever.* I crave Your gentle presence, where Your compassionate arms of grace surround me when I seek You, My Quiet Haven of Peace!

I dedicate this above song of praise to You Father God! I want to live in the presence of the Lord, My God, forever and ever! My delight comes when Your unfailing love and kindness washes over me with gladness and joy, O Lord of my heart! I will praise You, My Best Friend, all the days of my life! Amen.

November 13

ARE YOU WISER THAN THE LORD?

Who is wise? Let him understand these things. Who is prudent? Let him know them. For the ways of the LORD are right; the righteous walk in them, but transgressors stumble in them. Hosea 14:8 (NKJV)

It is very simple for a believer in the Lord to discern: *For the ways of the LORD are right; the righteous walk in them, but transgressors stumble in them.* It is evident by the way you conduct your life whether you follow in the ways of the Lord. If you continue to do what you want, without having any regard for living righteously in the Lord, not following His commandments that He has directed you through His Holy Word, then He will not come to help you out of the mess you have made of your life. Are you wiser than the Lord?

On the other hand, if you live the way the Lord has guided you to live through His Holy Word, trying to follow all His commandments for your life, then the Lord with come when you call Him immediately to help you. He will never leave you nor forsake you.

Holy Father God, I wasn't too wise in how I have lived my life. I have really made a mess of things O Lord! I am not wiser than You Lord! I have been a fool! I've had no regard for doing what Your Holy Word has guided me to do, Precious Comforter. I surrender humbly, Lord, my life over into Your keeping. I am repenting of all my transgressions against You, Lord God. Please forgive me Everlasting Father. Amen.

November 14

THE BODY OF CHRIST

And the church is his body; it is made full and complete by Christ, who fills all things everywhere with himself. Ephesians 1:23 (NLT)

Feel the living waters of Christ wash all your worries and fears away. As the purified waters seep deep into the pores of your skin, Christ will rid your body of all the poisonous toxins of powerlessness, defeat, helplessness, and anger. You are Christ's treasured creation; Christ, *who fills all things everywhere with himself,* will bless you with a fragrant herb from His heavenly gardens. When mixed with His living waters, it will refresh your heart and soul, as you sit quietly, with the steaming mist of the body of Christ surrounding you with encouragement, confidence, strength, hope, and tranquility,

Precious Heavenly Father, I am so blessed to have the body of Christ surround me with confidence and assurance that I am not alone in tackling all the problems of the day. I was so frightened and scared when I awoke; the darkness coating my heart and soul with terror! I couldn't escape from the gloom and doom that had me trapped. Then I remembered that Christ would come and set me free with His living waters of hope and encouragement. Thank You, Father God, for Your Son Jesus Christ living inside of my heart and soul! Hallelujah, hallelujah, praise the Lord of Salvation, who will walk beside me today! Amen.

November 15

THE MERCIFUL GRACE OF GOD

I am the LORD your God, who brought you out of Egypt so that you would no longer be slaves to the Egyptians; I broke the bars of your yoke and enabled you to walk with heads held high.
Leviticus 26:13 (NIV)

The Israelites remained bound to their past, even though the Lord freed them from the Egyptians. They didn't obey God's commands and remained trapped in their minds, fearfully bound in chains of oppression to the Egyptians. An example of their fear and enslavement to the past was when God wanted them to take possession of Canaan. They rebelled and refused to conquer the Amalekites and Canaanites, thinking God would leave them to fend for themselves. So God punished them by making them wander the desert for 40 years.

What is God directing you to do? Are you hesitant to follow the commands of God out of fear? Are you still enslaved, bound in chains in your mind from the past? If so, your past is part of your future. You will never be free to experience the blessings God has for you, until you surrender your past and live free. The merciful grace of God wants to see you rise above your past and achieve the goals He has set for you.

Dear God, I am so fearful at times! Everything You have done for me, shows me I can trust in You, O Lord. But my fear washes away all the faith and trust, like rivers wash into the ocean. Your merciful Grace, God, that has set this prisoner free, I am thankful for. Please, Father God, help me to trust You more. Amen.

November 16

STAND STRONG IN THE LORD, AND NEVER FEAR OPPOSITION

Who is going to harm you if you are eager to do good? But even if you should suffer for what is right, you are blessed. "Do not fear their threats: do not be frightened." But in your hearts revere Christ as Lord.
1 Peter 3:13-15 (NIV)

Do not faint or be weary when you are condemned by others for your faith in Jesus Christ. Stand strong in the Lord, and never fear opposition! *Who is going to harm you if you are eager to do good?* Keep walking with your feet steady and upright along the narrow road that leads to heaven.

Never feel contrite about your strong faith in the Lord. You never know when the same people who opposed your faith in Jesus Christ will be the very ones who are walking behind you to life eternal with the Lord. All because you never gave up, and refused to denounce Jesus Christ, as Your LORD and Savior. You never know who you will lead to Jesus just by walking in the light of faith! The blessings received from leading someone to the Lord are more valuable than all the gold in the world!

Glory, glory, hallelujah! Praise the LORD GOD ALMIGHTY! I have stood strong in You, Lord! I refuse to fear those who oppose You Lord. I will keep praising My Jesus, and hopefully continue to bring more people to You because I love You! Amen.

November 17

GIVE THANKS TO THE LORD FOR HE IS GOOD

You are my God and I will praise you! You are my God, and I will exalt you! Give thanks to the LORD, for he is good! His faithful love endures forever.
Psalm 118:28-29 (NLT)

The lord has taken all your sins upon Himself. He wasn't selfish or self-centered when He submitted to Pilate that horrible day in history two thousand years ago. Your Lord was under the authority of His Father in heaven, who wanted His Precious Son to pay the penalty for your transgressions. *Give thanks to the LORD, for he is good! His faithful love endures forever.* Jesus loved you so much that He was willing to die for you. That is a love that is everlasting to everlasting! His love will never be trampled on the ground like a piece of paper. Jesus' love is in your heart, and will remain there forever!

Praise the King of Glory, who came to my rescue with unfailing love and mercy to fix my blackened soul by taking all my sins away with the light of redemption. Now my soul is healed by the gentle hands of the Lord's mercy and grace! Amen.

November 18
FOREVER IN INTERCESSION

Therefore He is able also to save forever those who draw near to God through Him since He always lives to make intercession for them. Hebrews 7:25 (NASB)

Don't lose heart when you are going through a rough day. Nothing that causes worry and confusion will be able to saturate your mind, like syrup on a pancake, as you absorb the presence of the Lord into your thoughts. He will take all the many problems you have allowed to coat your mind with stress, soaking them all into the sponge of His refreshing, comforting arms of reassurance and relief. Christ Jesus is forever in *intercession for* you, if you seek His presence at all times and on all occasions in your life.

Jesus, You are forever in intercession for me, especially, more so, when I call on Your Precious Name to come help me when problems cause me to worry and feel confused. I can feel Your gentle hand touch my thoughts and relieve all of the pressure. The problems all squeeze into my mind and cause me to become faint, as the stress builds up, then I feel like I am ready to explode. I love You, O Lord, for taking the time to care for all of my needs! Amen.

November 19

OCEANS

Have you no respect for me? Why don't you tremble in my presence? I, the LORD, define the ocean's sandy shoreline as an everlasting boundary that the waters cannot cross. The waves may toss and roar, but they can never pass the boundaries I set.
Jeremiah 5:22 (NLT)

Are you desperate to be in the presence of the Lord? Or are you too busy with life to seek His presence? Maybe He is a fleeting thought in your mind, which you are too preoccupied to catch and hold on to!

"*I, the LORD, define the ocean's sandy shoreline as an everlasting boundary that the waters cannot cross.*" In quoting this Holy Word from the Lord, can you identify the boundaries He has set for you? Do you feel the Lord is asking too much when He expects you to worship Him above everything else in your life? When you decide to carry on as if the Lord is not important, you are bowing down and worshipping everything He has blessed you with. Those things can become your god instead of the Lord.

My Lord, I am so very sorry for making my life into a god! Everything I have belongs to You, O Life Mate! I am so blessed that You want my life to be joyous and fulfilled with many blessings which You divinely created for me. But I continue to violate the boundaries shared between you and me when I worship my possessions instead of humbly worshipping You, O Loving Father. I appreciate the gifts you continually bestow upon me daily. I am asking for forgiveness in Your Glorious Name! Amen.

November 20
A NEW LIFE

Therefore, if anyone is in Christ, he is a new creation; old things have passed away; behold, all things have become new. 2 Corinthians 5:17 (NKJV)

Do you feel overjoyed knowing the Lord has complete control over each day of your life? Does it make you want to throw a party and invite all your friends to help you celebrate the exciting news you have received in your special relationship you have with Christ? The old life has *passed away; behold, all things have become new.* The liberation that you have in Christ has given you a new deed in life. One that can never be stolen from you! You have a legal deed to a spiritual mansion which you inherited from Your Father, the King of Righteousness, the day you allowed the blood of Jesus to enter your soul and cover all your sins, to heal your soul with the spiritual surgery of atonement. Your new life entitles you to all the blessings that a child of royalty is privileged to receive: unfailing love, compassion, kindness, peace, comfort, security, hope, strength, forgiveness, joy, happiness, guidance, and the presence of the Everlasting Father always with you forever.

Gracious and merciful Father, I have never been so happy! Since I have given You complete control over my life, I am given everything I need! Thank you for saving my soul! Out of the ashes of death to the sins which were destroying my soul, has come a new life in You, Everlasting Father. The blessings You give me, are very exciting! I live my life in anticipation, knowing I will spend it in Your Comforting Presence! Thank You, Jesus, for giving me a new life with You forever. Amen.

November 21

BLUNDERS

I can do all things through Christ who strengthens me.
Philippians 4:13 (NKJV)

When you communicate with God about your plans for tomorrow, do you listen to Him when He tells you that your plans are not going to work out? Or do you override God's plans for your life and do what you want anyway, like a defiant child who disobeys their parents.

God is a forgiving God! He will help you fix your blunders, once you realize you have made a mistake. You can ask God to speak through you, giving you the correct words to say as you apologize. By accepting the consequences for your actions, realize you can do all things through God who strengthens you. Don't forget to thank God for being there for you!

I have made many blunders in my life, God, but you always will come with me when I ask you to speak through me, as I make my apology for the mistake. I am so thankful I have a Best Friend who will never leave me in my imperfections, but will walk with me and hold my hand, guiding me through the mistake, giving me the strength to humble myself when I err, and hold my head up high, no matter what happens. I love You God, for being My Constant Companion. Amen.

November 22
PRIDE GOES BEFORE DESTRUCTION

Pride goes before destruction, and a haughty spirit before a fall. Proverbs 16:18 (AMP)

God is Omnipotent! When you are going through a crisis, turn to Him first, before you get anxious and overwhelmed about the situations in your life that you can't control. The outcome of these situations belongs to God. You can't fix anything on your own will power. *Pride goes before destruction.* When you try to control anything, it is like you put your life under construction, and you alone are saying you know just how to fix your life, making it better than it was before. This leads to everything that you constructed to fall apart, because you were cutting corners with your life because of your faulty thinking. Your mind is a bad neighborhood to be caught in! You just got ghetto slapped by God! DID IT WAKE YOU UP TO THE REALITY THAT GOD IS IN CHARGE OF YOUR LIFE?

Pride goes before destruction, you point out in Your Holy Word, God. I need to read a verse in Your Holy Word, Lord, so it stays fresh in my mind. I am so worn out from trying to construct my life the way I want it to be. You are the Expert Carpenter over my life. When I allow You, Wonderful Counselor, to guide me through life it is constructed perfectly. Nothing falls apart. The interior is perfect! I can live comfortable for the rest of my life, Lord, with Your continued construction of my innermost parts. Amen.

November 23

YOU DON'T HAVE TO GO TO EVERY FIGHT YOU ARE INVITED TO

For I know the thoughts that I think toward you, says the LORD, thoughts of peace and not of evil, to give you a future and hope. Jeremiah 29:11 (NKJV)

Conflicts come between you and other people when your expectations are not fulfilled the way you wanted them to be. You don't have to go to every fight you are invited to! You can ask God to help you overcome the desire to get into the boxing ring and fight every opponent that disagrees with your point of view. God will give you *thoughts of peace and not of evil,* if you consult Him before you put on your boxing gloves and fight every one that didn't anticipate your every need. The truth is, only God knows what you need, before you tell Him what you need.

God, I have been in too many boxing rings lately! I am tired of fighting with everyone who doesn't meet my needs, O Lord. I have to learn not to go to every fight that I am invited to. I will consult You God, the Perfect Manager of my life. I will only expect You from now on Father, to meet all of my needs! Other people with never be able to satisfy me like You do, Wonder Comforter! Amen.

November 24

THE GATE OF THE SHEPHERD

I tell you the truth, the man who does not enter the sheep pen by the gate but climbs in by some other way, is a thief and a robber. The man who enters by the gate is the shepherd of his sheep.
John 10:1-2 (NIV)

The enemy is always trying to enter the gate of your soul, but isn't able to because he is not the Shepherd. Be alert and on the lookout for the deceiver to try to enter *by some other way*. He may use the Holy Word of God to gain entry, using it in an underhanded way to corrupt your morals and lead you astray.

The Gate of the Shepherd to your soul can only be opened by the voice of Jesus. You recognize His voice and know when He is entering. He will bring the light of the Holy Spirit with Him and always point you towards His Father. Jesus will never do anything His Father hasn't directed Him to do. The devil, on the other hand, is self-serving and concerned about his own agenda, which is to get you to follow his leading, causing you to stumble and fall. Jesus will guide you along the path that leads to heaven.

Gracious and merciful Father in heaven, the enemy of my soul has tried to come by climbing in some other way, but I have always recognized His voice. That doesn't mean I haven't been tempted and led to feel distress for a time. But I realize what is occurring, and call on your Glorious Name to save me. I love You, Jesus, so much! You have put a lock on the gate to my soul, which is sealed with Your Holy blood. I trust You are faithful to always protect me from the evil one. Amen.

November 25

GOD, WHO IS IN CONTROL OVER EVERYTHING

Casting the whole of your care [all your anxieties, all your worries, all your concerns, once and for all] on Him, for He cares for you affectionately and cares about you watchfully. 1 Peter 5:7 (AMP)

You can choose to be scared and frightened over a situation which has you tied up in knots, continuing to have you to be in a tangled mess. Or, you can seek the presence of God, who is in control over everything, and have Him free you from the tight fastening that is woven around your heart and soul. *Casting the whole of your care [all your anxieties, all your worries, all your concerns, once and for all] on Him.* Then the blood of Christ can flow perfectly through your heart and soul, guiding you day by day to be able to handle situations that used to paralyze you with fear. Now you are relaxed, having confidence in God to take charge over the situation.

God, I am so thankful, You are in control over everything. I am finally at peace, My Confidante and My Best Friend! I know that You affectionately care about me and watchfully make sure I am never left to fend for myself. You are My Constant Companion who is with me wherever I go! I love You Lord, with all of my heart and soul, for your unfailing love which will never, ever, leave me nor forsake me! Amen.

November 26

OVERLAPPING MIRACLES

I am counting on the LORD; yes, I am counting on him. I have put my hope in his word... O Israel, hope in the LORD; for with there is unfailing love. His redemption overflows. Psalm 130:5, 7 (NLT)

Overlapping miracles occur each day in your life. Are you aware of them? Some miracles from God are recorded in His Holy Word: A blind man is given sight, who had been blind from birth; ten lepers were cured of leprosy; a crippled man was able to walk again. How was Jesus able to cure these people? Was it because He was the Son of God? Yes, that is the truth! But also, all of the people had faith in Jesus to heal them.

There are more subtle ways overlapping miracles occur, not always recognized because you take for granted they are going to happen. Some examples are: The sun appearing each morning, seeing the sun set in the evening in preparation for the moon to come out, and the stars to shine in the sky as guide posts for the darkness. Others are mountains that have been standing strong forever; oceans that inhabit and maintain marine life; your needs being taken care of each day. These are profound miracles, which without God overseeing them, wouldn't happen.

O My God, I am desperate for Your Loving Presence! I can't get enough of You! When I wake, I am seeking You, My Friend! All through my day, I am comforted by Your Guiding Presence beside me. As I prepare for bed, I think of You above all else, and humbly get on my knees and thank You for Your Provisions which sheltered me from my enemies! Thank You! Amen.

November 27

WEAR THE THANKFULNESS FOR THE LORD LIKE YOU WEAR YOUR FAVORITE PAJAMAS

Oh give thanks to the LORD, call upon His name; make known His deeds among the peoples. Sing to Him, sing praises to Him; speak of all His wonders.
1 Chronicles 16:8-9 (NASB)

Wear the thankfulness that you feel for the Lord like you wear your favorite pajamas; they are old and comfortable, but perfect when you want to spend a day at home doing nothing.

When you wear the presence of the Lord upon your body, you are the light that shines in His Holy Temple for all of the people who are lost to find hope and shelter for their weary soul. *Oh give thanks to the LORD, call upon His name...sing praises to Him; speak of all His wonders* for what the Lord has done for you in your life.

I delight in praising Your name Lord, above all names. You are my hope and salvation when I am weary and weak in my heart and soul. That is why I wear my thankfulness for You Lord, like my favorite pajamas. You are the comfort I seek when I can't take one more moment without being in Your gentle arms of peace. I feel relaxed lying in Your Presence, God; My Safe Haven, when life becomes too much to deal with! Amen.

November 28

DO ALL TO THE GLORY OF GOD

Therefore, whether you eat or drink, or whatever you do, do all to the glory of God.
1 Corinthians 10:31 (NKJV)

Your life doesn't belong to you. It belongs to God. God bought the life that you enjoy with the blood of His Only Son, Jesus Christ. You can't take credit for the blessings that you receive from God daily. It is through the mercy and grace of God, that your life is so good and fulfilled! *Therefore, whether you eat or drink, or whatever you do, do all to the glory of God.*

You can meekly glorify God by letting your good deeds be so outstanding that everyone who comes in contact with you will praise God in heaven.

I could never thank You enough God, for the blessed life You have graciously given me. I am so very sorry that Your Son, Jesus, had to die so viciously so I could live. I know it was predestined by You God that Jesus had to die so His blood would pay the penalty for my sins. But every time I think about what happened to Jesus, that horrible day God, when He was crucified for my sins, I am grateful, but also sad. I will glorify You God by giving up my life to You, and forever being your servant, helping those in need. I want my light to shine brilliantly, so those in the darkness will see it, and be set free by the Holy Spirit of Jesus inside of my heart. I love You, so much Father! Amen.

November 29
GOD IS COOL!

How precious is your unfailing love, O God! All humanity finds shelter in the shadow of your wings.
Psalm 36:7 (NLT)

The path that you walk upon through life will have obstacles that will hinder your travelling plans. But be reassured, God has already walked ahead of you, and has placed blessings at different spots for you to find. They will help you maneuver safely past the barriers erected to block your passage. God is cool! He has placed delightful surprises mixed in with the obstacles that will stimulate your heart, causing joy and laughter to erupt deeply from within you.

How precious is your unfailing love O God! I am singing and dancing; rejoicing along my path through life. Every day is delightful as I discover love gifts along the way of my journey, O Lord! You are cool, God! Thank You, from the depths of my heart for walking before me, My Life Mate, and helping me through the obstacles of the enemy which are aimed to block my path to eternity with You. I really love You very much, My own Special Clown! Amen.

November 30

A SATISFYING RELATIONSHIP WITH GOD

I keep asking that the God of our Lord Jesus Christ, the glorious Father, may give you the Spirit of wisdom and revelation, so that you know him better.
Ephesians 1:17 (NIV)

When you want something desperately, like the Apple watch, which is compatible with the I-Phone, you have to understand how they work together efficiently. You have to read the instructions on how to pair them together.

If you desire a satisfying relationship with God you will need to read His Holy Word. As you are reading the Bible, it may seem hard to understand at first. But if you study it every day, you will eventually hear God speak to you. You will find the Bible is actually a Life Manual that instructs you to live every day with integrity, no matter what is happening in your life. The amazing part of God's Holy Word is that every time you read it, you will discover something that you missed the first time which will give you a deeper relationship with God. Through the *Holy Spirit of wisdom and revelation* He will help you understand what to search for.

My life-long friend, I can't wait to read Your Holy Word each day. It brings me closer to You, Precious Father of my life! I have such a satisfying relationship with You, God, which can't contain the joy I feel inside of my heart. I am not ashamed to tell everyone that I read the Bible. Even in my work place, everyone knows I read Your Holy Word so I can worship Your Sacred Name. I love You, God of My Heart, so much! Amen.

December 1

JESUS-MESSIAH-IMMANUEL

Look! The virgin will conceive a child! She will give birth to a son, and they will call him Immanuel, which means 'God is with us.' Matthew 1:23 (NLT)

Is Christmas special to you because of the gifts you buy for others? Do you frantically search for that special gift, being willing to pay any amount of money to purchase it? Even if it puts you in debt?

Or, is your heart overjoyed, anticipating the birth of Jesus-Messiah- *Immanuel?* The precious baby boy, who was God in human form, stepped down off of His royal throne because of His unfailing love for you. A love so merciful and filled with an overabundance of grace, that Jesus would die on the cross, suffering horribly, so you could live free from your sins. Now think about what Jesus did for you! Isn't this a special gift that you can give to others this Christmas? Jesus will light up everyone's heart and soul, like a gift wrapped so beautifully, that all who see it, won't be able to wait to open it! It is a gift which keeps on giving!

God, You are the Only present I desire this Christmas! You came down from heaven in the form of a human baby boy, born of a virgin, miraculously conceived, to be the Savior of all humanity! You are My Jesus-Messiah-Immanuel! I am so grateful that You saved a filthy wench like me, who gave up hope of ever being redeemed. Amen.

December 2
THE SERVANT OF GOD

But He was wounded for our transgressions, He was bruised for our guilt and iniquities; the chastisement [needful to obtain] peace and well-being for us was upon Him, and with the stripes [that wounded] Him we are healed and made whole...He was submissive and opened not His mouth; like a lamb that is led to slaughter... Isaiah 53:5, 7 (AMP)

Jesus Christ was born to a virgin on Christmas day. Let all the world shout with praise and rejoicing, celebrating the awaited miracle of God, the Royal Prince of Peace.

Over two thousand years ago, Christ Jesus obeyed His Father and came to earth as a human baby boy. When He was twelve years old, Jesus started preaching His Father's Holy Word in the temple of Jerusalem to all who would listen. As He became a man, He commissioned twelve men to be His disciples, and "walked the talk," teaching them about His Father's will. Even though Jesus had an intimate relationship with His disciples and followers, they still condemned Him to suffer a prisoner's death.

I am guilty of treating You, Jesus, with contempt. All You wanted was to save my life and make my soul whole through Your royal blood. I was so ashamed and filled with such hatred for myself that I hated You for showing kindness to me. But in the end, as a servant of God, Your mercy and grace saved me! I am forever grateful You found me worthy of Your unfailing love. If not, I would be doomed for hell instead of heaven. Amen. and Amen.

December 3

A DOUBTING THOMAS

Jesus told him, "I am the way, the truth, and the life. No one can come to the Father except through me." John 14:6 (NKJV)

Jesus was telling His disciples He was going to be crucified and going to His Father's house (heaven) where there were many rooms. He told them He was going to prepare a room for them. Thomas, "the doubter", as usual, had to question the truth of Jesus' words, *"I am the way, the truth, and the life. No one can come to the Father except through me."* Are you a "doubting Thomas?" Or do you have deep faith in the truth of the Holy Word of God? Jesus is the key that will unlock the door to His Father's house!

This Christmas, if you haven't already, why don't you re-read the greatest story ever told? The biography of a baby boy who left the comfort of His father's home, where everything was at His "beck-and call," and journeyed to a hostile land where He was hated and despised by the very people He came to save. The sensational part of this story that you don't want to miss is that Jesus came anyway to die for your sins!

Jesus, I have been a "doubting Thomas." Even though I have re-read the Holy Word of God many times and even studied it, I still can live life like You are not a huge part of it. When I go without a thought of how You are doing, I am saying You don't matter, which is ridiculous! You died for me, and gave me life. What or who in this world could or would do that for me? No one! This Christmas, I am going to read the greatest story ever told, the Birth of My Lord Jesus! Amen.

December 4

THE SON RADIATES GOD'S OWN GLORY

The Son radiates God's own glory and expresses the very character of God, and he sustains everything by the mighty power of his command. When he had cleansed us from our sins, he sat down in the place of honor at the right hand of the majestic God in heaven. Hebrews 1:3 (NLT)

The story of Jesus should be read often and not limited to when the Christmas holiday comes. *The Son radiates God's own glory and expresses the very character of God, and sustains everything by the mighty power of his command.*

Christmas can be celebrated all year long inside your heart as you reflect on the mercy and grace, which was extended to you by the unfailing love of Jesus. You can begin each day with thankfulness and gratitude for the rich life you live since Jesus Christ paid the atonement price to His Father for your sins. Take gifts of healing to those trapped in the dark pit of despair and hopelessness. They never heard the precious name of Jesus. You are helping them climb out of the dark pit, and into the loving arms of the Lord, where comfort and healing for their souls is waiting for them.

I love thee Jesus! O how I love You! I have such a rich and blessed life today, because of You Jesus. The only way I can show You that I am truly grateful for cleansing my soul with Your blood soaked hands; purifying my soul free of all sins hidden there, is each day, to tell others about the baby boy who brought peace to the world by radiating God's own glory. Amen.

December 5

THE VOICE OF THE SHEPHERDS

And there were shepherds living out in the fields nearby, keeping watch over their flocks at night. An angel of the Lord appeared to them, and the glory of the Lord shone around them, and they were terrified. But the angel said to them, "Do not be afraid. I bring you good news that will cause great joy for all the people. Today in the town of David, a Savior has been born to you; he is the Messiah, the Lord. This will be a sign to you: You will find a baby wrapped in cloths and lying in a manger." Luke 2:8-12 (NIV)

God will use all who are willing to spread the Good News, even lowly shepherds! The shepherds believed the angel who appeared before them and said, *"Today in the town of David a Savior has been born to you; he is the Messiah, the Lord. This is a sign to you: You will find a baby wrapped in cloths and lying in a manager."* The shepherds traveled to Bethlehem and found Jesus lying in a manager, as the angel said they would. After witnessing the Christ Child, the shepherds spread the Good News to people about the *Messiah* living among them. Can you identify with this story? Who told you about Jesus? If it changed your life and Jesus is your Savior, don't take Him for granted. Praise and worship Him by being an example others can follow.

Holy Father God, thank You, for guiding me to the story of the birth of Jesus! Every time I read about the shepherds visiting Your Beloved Son Jesus, as the angels told them to, it is truly amazing to me! I need to read that story more, and not just at Christmastime Lord. It makes me get off my lazy butt, and spread the Good News about Jesus. I love You! Amen.

December 6

A TRAPPED DOE

My God, My God, why have You forsaken Me? Why are You so far from helping Me, and from the words of My groaning? Psalm 22:1 (NKJV)

The human part of Jesus was evident when He cried, *"My God, My God, why have You forsaken me?"* But Jesus had confidence in God to provide freedom from the constant agony and suffering He endured while hanging on the cross near death. He trusted that His Father in heaven would resurrect Him in three days, so Jesus could appear to His apostles providing evidence that He was brought back from death by God, the Father, just as Jesus said would happen.

Do you have complete confidence in God, through strong faith, to take care of your trials and tribulations? Or are you like a trapped doe caught in the headlights of a car? The doe is terrified, but most likely will be hit. Are you like the doe, running away from God, rather than letting Him have control over your life? What is trapping you in the dark, making you afraid to go into the light where Jesus is? There is an old saying: "If nothing changes, then nothing changes!"

As Christmas is approaching, I am reflecting on Your One and Only Son, Jesus. He is precious to You! But God, You gave Him up to suffer terribly for my sins to be redeemed! I am like a doe caught in the headlights of a car. I feel unworthy of His unfailing love for me, so I run and hide. But Jesus is there in the darkness with me. I can't hide from the loving kindness and compassion He has for me, O God! I surrender my will to You. Only You Lord can put my life back together again. Amen.

December 7

YOU ARE MY FRIENDS IF YOU DO WHAT I COMMAND YOU

"Greater love has no one than this, than to lay down one's life for his friends. You are My friends if you do whatever I command you." John 15:13-14 (NASB)

Are you a friend of Jesus? Think about this question before you answer. Jesus gives an explanation of who He considers to be His friends: *"You are My friends if you do what I command you."* Do you do what Jesus commands you to do?

Jesus' commands are easy to follow, but hard to do, especially if you follow the master of this world. Examine your life. Is chaos and mayhem an integral part of your life? Call on the Holy Name of Jesus, the Prince of Peace, who has blessings He wants to give you. He wants to provide peace instead of confusion, faith instead of despair, freedom to live a happy life, instead of bondage to the evil things of this world, and most important, the unfailing love of Jesus, who will never leave you, nor forsake you.

Every Christmas, Lord Jesus, I am reminded You died so I could have eternal life in heaven with You and God forever. Please help me find You. I am lost in this evil world. I need You to come and save me! I am not strong enough to fight the enemy alone! I have heard that I can ask for forgiveness of my sins anytime. Here I am again asking You to be my friend and teach me your commandments for my life. I am prostrate on the floor, humbly giving myself over to Your care, asking for forgiveness of my sins. Please Jesus, come and save me! Amen.

December 8

CHRISTMAS TREASURES

Don't store up treasures here on earth, where moths eat them and rust destroys them, and where thieves break in and steal. Store your treasures in heaven, where moth and rust cannot destroy, and thieves do not break in and steal. Wherever your treasure is, the desires of your heart will also be.
Matthew 6:19-21 (NLT)

It seems people get more heart conscious during the Christmas season. It's as if they were put in a trance for the other eleven months, and not aware of the external stimuli going on around them. Then they suddenly awake all cheery and bubbly, filled with extraordinary amounts of love and caring for those in need of help. Do they think if they do good deeds around Christmas every year, it will guarantee a ticket to heaven? What do you think about this?

God wants people to love one another as He loved us. Do you treat others the way you want to be treated? Helping all in need, no matter the circumstances that brought them to need help? *"Don't store up treasures here on earth, where moths eat them and rust destroys them, and where thieves break in and steal."*

Oh Jesus, teach me to show everyone I meet the presence of You in my life. I don't want to just help those in need during Christmastime. Christmas treasures can be valuable if I give to others from a heart brimming with gratitude for all the blessings I have received from You, Jesus, because I love You, very much! Amen.

December 9

PRAISE GOD

Praise the Lord! Praise God in His sanctuary; praise Him in the heavens of His power. Praise Him for His mighty acts; praise Him according to the abundance of His greatness! Psalm 150:1, 2 (AMP)

Praise God for His mercy and grace. *Praise God* for His gentleness and kindness. *Praise God* for His hope;, the strength that keeps you upright and steady during all that occurs in your day.

Praise God with singing and shouting with joy *according to the abundance of His greatness!* A greatness that is so humble in divinity that you were granted a privilege in Christ Jesus, who showed Himself as a human baby, so weak in His humanness, but without sin or blemish. He was omnipresent as God, but yet was a devoted servant to all humanity. As a servant of God, Jesus was the salvation of healing blood, so potent that it sealed your soul to heaven for eternity. Praise God for His compassion and unfailing love that through mercy and grace you are sanctified through the Holy Spirt to be resurrected in Jesus.

I praise You, God, for loving me unconditionally, that has made me a new creation in Christ Jesus. One that can never be subject to death in a dark grave. I am sealed by the blood of Christ to heaven's glory forever. What peace I am feeling in my heart and soul! I praise and honor your divinity O God! I love You so much for sending Your Son Jesus, to be born on December 25. I can't wait to celebrate the birth of Jesus! I praise You God with my voice. I praise You God, with my life, as I follow your will gladly! Amen.

December 10
CHRISTMAS

It is for freedom that Christ has set us free. Stand firm, then, and do not let yourselves be burdened again by the yoke of slavery. Galatians 5:1 (NIV)

Have you accepted Jesus into your heart? Jesus is the Deliverer from your sins. He is the Salvation for your soul. The LORD is your Redeemer, Healer, and Great Controller! If you haven't accepted Jesus as your Lord and Savior, do so before it is too late. Jesus could return any day! Are you ready for His return?

The first six letters of Christmas is CHRIST! In these letters are found the atonement for your sins. *Stand firm, then, and do not let yourselves be burdened again by the yoke of slavery.* Are you carrying the heavy load of sin upon your shoulders? If you are, why not submit to the authority of Jesus, who can take your sins and rid you of the heavy load? Are your sins weighing you down with guilt, remorse, and shame? In the Holy Presence of Jesus you will discover a compassionate, and loving, devoted friend who will always be available to you. You will no longer have guilt, remorse, and shame holding you prisoner, because Jesus will be your rock of salvation giving you healing peace and contentment for your soul!

Hallelujah My, Redeemer and Healer! You are My Salvation Jesus! In Your royal blood I have found victory over my sins. I am no longer held in chains of shame, remorse, and guilt. I have been set free forever! What a glorious relief my soul feels in your Glorious Presence, Lord! I find such peace and contentment in your arms of tender mercy and grace. Amen. and Amen.

December 11

ARE YOU ELATED THAT JESUS IS COMING BACK FOR YOU?

Behold, He is coming with the clouds, every eye will see Him, even they who pierced Him. And all the tribes of the earth will mourn because of Him. Even so, Amen. Revelations 1:7 (NKJV)

Are you elated Jesus is coming back for you? *Behold, He is coming with the clouds, every eye will see Him, even they who pierced him.* Or do these profound Holy Words from God's mouth put fear into your heart because you are worshipping idols that have control over your life? What will it take for you to surrender to the care of Jesus? Everyone will be judged according to how they lived their lives. Those who don't have an intimate relationship with Jesus s will burn in hell, forever cut off from the light of the Spirit of the LORD!

Jesus, I am coming into Your Perfect Presence, with all my imperfections. I know I have been unclean in my sins! I chose to worship idols of this world, instead of You, the ONE TRUE GOD! I am asking for forgiveness of my sins. I want You, Jesus, to take control over my life. I am so tired of living my life this way. Especially when I know I can seek Your Redeeming Presence. The love and acceptance I have been seeking in the idols I have been worshipping can be found in You Jesus. And the best part is I will never be dissatisfied again because You will fulfill all my needs. As I give total control to You, my fears and anxieties will go away, and I will be elated that You are coming to take me home to heaven with You! I love You Jesus, so much! Amen.

December 12

IT IS WHAT COMES FROM INSIDE THAT DEFILES YOU

And then He added. "It is what comes from inside that defiles you. For from within, out of a person's heart, come evil thoughts, sexual immorality, theft, murder, adultery, greed, wickedness, deceit, lustful desires, envy, slander, pride, and foolishness. All these vile things come from within; they are what defile you."
Mark 7:20-23 (NLT)

When you read these powerful words, do you think of how much you hurt Jesus by the nasty habits you revisit each day? It is like you have an old man living inside your mind that you don't want there, but refuse to evict, no matter how often he destroys your property. Jesus bought this property with His blood. *And then he added, "It is what comes from inside that defiles you."* Jesus' unfailing love for you is the reason your life is so blessed and overflowing with peace, joy, happiness, serenity, and harmony most of the time. When you allow the old man inside your mind control you, you disregard everything Jesus lovingly gave you. He surrendered His life so yours could be free of sin. Why revisit the same sins Jesus took to His death?

Jesus, please help me! I am lost in my old sinful ways. I allow the old man which lives in my mind to control my life. Help me evict him. When I live my life any way I want to, I renege on our agreement. I am saying I don't care how You feel! I am sorry for being self-centered and only thinking about what I want. I ask for forgiveness for stepping all over Your unfailing love for me. I do love You Jesus, very much! Amen.

December 13

A CONTROL FREAK

What then shall we say to these things? If God is for us, who can be against us? He who did not spare His own Son, but delivered Him up for us all, how shall He not with Him, also freely give us all things?
Romans 8:31-32 (NKJV)

Are you a control freak? Is your control so bad, that you slip and slide on it, like ice on a sidewalk after an ice storm, unable to pull yourself up? So you lay there in helpless desperation until you submit your pride to God and humbly admit defeat over your problem asking for help from your Awesome Comforter. *If God is for us, who can be against us?* Absolutely nothing that happens in your day will deter God! He is the Almighty God; more powerful than anything that tries to harm you. You can conquer anything with God fighting beside you!

God, You did not spare Your own Son, Jesus for me. You gave Him up gladly so I could have peace in my life from my sins. But when I am a control freak, trying to control every aspect of my life, there is no peace in my life. I am giving over my prideful ways to You, Father. Do what You want with my life! I humbly thank You O Lord, with praises of joy; hands lifted up to the heavens, singing songs of worship to My Marvelous Creator, the GREAT I AM! I rejoice that in twelve days, I can celebrate the birth of the King of Glory, My Everlasting Father, and Prince of Peace! Amen.

December 14

CHILD OF GOD COME FORTH AND CLAIM YOUR INHERITENCE

God decided in advance to adopt us into his own family by bringing us to himself through Christ Jesus. This is what he wanted to do, and this gave him great pleasure. Ephesians 1:5 (NLT)

Child of God, come forth and claim your inheritance! An inheritance so rich in mercy, grace, and everlasting love, that the finest pearls can't match its value. There is no price tag on God's unfailing love for you! *God decided in advance to adopt us into his own family by bringing us to himself through Christ Jesus.* No amount of money would ever be enough to satisfy the desires of your heart, as the check written and signed in the blood of Christ Jesus, which finalized your adoption into God's family forever.

I can't wrap my mind around the agony you felt Father, when You sent Your Son, Christ Jesus to die in my place on the old rugged cross of Calvary! The confusing thing for me is You had great delight in adopting me into Your royal family through the blood that was shed on the cross through Jesus. You gladly called me to come forth and claim my inheritance as Your precious child, to come back home to live with You forever Father. I love You, so very much, Great Redeemer of My Soul! Praise Jesus! Hallelujah, praise Jesus! Amen.

December 15

SPREAD THE WORD

Paul, a bond servant of God, and an apostle (a special messenger) of Jesus Christ (the Messiah) to stimulate and promote the faith of God's chosen ones and to lead them on to accurate discernment and acquaintance with the Truth which belongs to and harmonizes with and tends to godliness.
Titus 1:1 (AMP)

Saul was a Pharisee who took delight in hunting Christians and watching them die before the Lord called him to serve His kingdom. God had to blind Saul first so he could see that Jesus was the way, the truth, and the life of salvation for Saul's brokenness. God changed Saul's name to Paul and he became the faithful Apostle who wrote much of the New TestAmen.t. As he grew in faith and was filled with the Holy Spirit, he went from city to city preaching, wanteing all men and women to be rescued and set free from their sins.

What are you willing to do for Christ Jesus? Are you willing to spread the word of salvation through the Holy Spirit of Christ; *to stimulate and promote the faith of God's chosen ones and lead them to accurate discernment* that they have a Savior delighted to have them come into His supreme presence of glory to receive a pardon for their transgressions?

My Father God, I love You and I am willing to spread the word of the eternal kingdom that is available for Your chosen ones. Please use me as a devoted servant, like You did Paul, to bring people out of the darkness of evil and into the light of the Holy Spirit. I humbly submit my mind, body, and soul to You God! Amen.

December 16

STRENGTH ARISES AS YOU WAIT UPON THE LORD

You have eyes—can't you see? You have ears—can't you hear? Don't you remember anything at all?
Mark 8:18 (NLT)

Has Jesus been talking to you about what He wants you to do for Him today? *"You have ears—can't you hear?"* The Lord's people can be deaf when it comes to listening and accomplishing His purpose for their lives! Especially when the world's obligations interfere with their spiritual focus on seeking the presence of God. Are you one of those people who allow the day to day monotony of your life to snatch away the spiritual seeds in your heart? Jesus has put them there for you to discover and use to accomplish the goals He has for you today. They will benefit His kingdom on Earth. Strength arises as you wait upon the Lord's voice to direct your paths today!

I know I have become lax in studying Your Holy Word God! I have allowed the hustle and bustle of my Christmas obligations to snatch away the spiritual seeds that Jesus has planted in my heart, hindering them from growing into His plans for my life to benefit His kingdom on earth. Please guide me through Your voice in the Holy Words of the Bible, to allow the strength to arise as I wait upon You Lord, to guide me to follow Your leading for today. I love You, My Constant Companion! Amen.

December 17
PRACTICE WHAT YOU PREACH

He has told to you, O man, what is good; and what does the LORD require of you but to do justice, love kindness, and to walk humbly with your God?
Micah 6:8 (NASB)

Words just flow from your mouth, like water from Niagara Falls. But are they words that preface the Holy Word of God? You can't speak something you never studied yourself. You can't quote Holy Scripture to people, telling them to apply it to their lives, if you haven't applied these principles of truth into your own life. In other words, practice what you preach!

God deserves more from you than falsehoods! He surrendered His beloved Son so His healing blood that poured from His wounds on to the cross could dissolve the shackles around your soul. Decayed, rotten flesh and wrong practices prevents the Holy Spirit from filling your soul with His shining light of goodness! *Do justice, love kindness, and walk humbly with your God,* and you will be able to share with others countless miracles from your life. This happens when you make the Word of God a priority. Then God's truths pour from your mouth, helping those in need of a Savior.

It is a shame that around Christmas I seem to get all Christian-like, as I am reminded how much I have rejected You God! You open my heart to the truth of my laziness in seeking Your Divine, Holy Presence, Lord! Please, Father, help me to be more vigilant in seeking You through honest prayer and meditation of Your Holy Word. I want to practice what I preach, so I can be a worthy servant to others who need a Savior! Amen.

December 18
WHO RULES WITH PEACE

His government and its peace will never end. He will rule with fairness and justice from the throne of the ancestor David for all eternity. The compassionate commitment of the LORD of Heaven's Armies will make this happen! Isaiah 9:7 (NLT)

Who rules with peace? Do you know? Or are you wrapped up and entangled with the ruler of this world with no time for anything else? When you obey and give allegiance to the evil one and his armies from hell, you are trapped on the pathway to destruction and death; a gruesome massacre of your soul!

His government and its peace will never end...the compassionate commitment of the Lord of Heaven's Armies will make this happen! This is a guarantee in writing you can be sure of! If you believe the Holy Bible was divinely inspired by God, you will walk the road less travelled with Jesus by your side. The choice is yours! You can continue to worship the ruler of this world and let the devil have full control over your soul until there is no turning back for you. Or you can bow down and reverently atone for your sins. As you walk with Jesus you will find your life has never run smoother.

Holy Father God, I humbly give control of my soul into your trusting hands. I want to submit to the government of heaven where You and Your Son Jesus rule. I know the Lord of Heaven's armies will protect me from the evil clutches of the devil and his armies. I want to walk with You guiding me with Your righteous right hand to mercy and grace, which is the forgiveness of my sins. Amen.

December 19

SELF WILL RUN RIOT

The Lord is near to all who call upon Him, all who call upon Him sincerely and in truth. Psalm 145:18 (AMP)

Do you have "your" day planned? Are you contemplating in your mind, how this and that is going to turn out? Therefore, because "you" know how to run your day effectively, "your" day will be the most perfect day ever, right? Only one very important part that you forgot to include in the equation. "You" are trying to figure out and solve, concerning how "your" day will turn out: *The Lord is near to all who call upon Him, all who call upon Him sincerely and in truth.* Self-will-run-riot is the motto for this day "you" have planned! No God, no peace! Know God, have peace!

God, You are My Provider and Constant Companion for each day You so graciously grant me on this earth! When I go about my day without consulting You first Lord, self-will-run-riot, is the motto for my day! How can I be so foolish as to think, Lord Jesus, I am the one controlling my day? Please God, forgive me for excluding You from being part of my day. I want to follow alongside You Jesus, and follow where You lead me! Anywhere You lead me will turn out blessings, even in the worst of times! Amen.

December 20

REPENT AND LIVE

For I take no pleasure in the death of anyone, declares the Sovereign LORD. Repent and live!
Ezekiel 18:32 (NIV)

Jesus was innocent of any wrong doing. He was without sin! Yet He died a prisoner's death; crucified amongst convicts who committed atrocious crimes. Why did Jesus allow Pilot and his men to capture Him and inflict excruciating pain upon Him? Jesus was beaten, spit upon, with nails driven into His hands and feet to hold Him on the cross. Jesus suffered gladly with unfailing love, mercy and grace for sinners to be healed of their sins!

God sent Jesus to be born of a virgin more than two thousand years ago to save your life. He took your sins upon Himself to do so. Thank God for His mercy and grace for you. He didn't want you to be lost in the darkness. *For I take no pleasure in the death of anyone, declares the Sovereign LORD. Repent and live!* The Great Physician healed your poisonous wounds which were causing death and decay to obliterate your soul. By the indwelling of the light of the Holy Spirit, God rebuked the darkness of the devil from your innermost parts. You were given a new life in Jesus!

Over two thousand years ago You sent Your Only Son, Jesus, to save me from my sins, God. You wanted me to repent and live through the blood of Jesus! I know I fall short of Your Glory every day by sinning against Your will for me. My selfish pride and arrogance lead me to believe I can control my life. My ego gets me in trouble all the time! I surrender all to You. Amen.

December 21

MARY THE MOTHER OF JESUS

Then the angel said to her, "Do not be afraid, Mary, for you have found favor with God. You will conceive in your womb and bring forth a Son, and shall call His name Jesus." Luke 1:30-31 (NKJV)

"Do not be afraid, Mary, for you have found favor with God." Mary, mother of Jesus, was approximately sixteen years old when the angel Gabriel came to her. He proclaimed the Good News that she would conceive a Son who was the King of kings, and Lord of lords, a Ruler over the nations of the world.

Think about the fact that Mary was a virgin when the angel told her she would get pregnant and give birth to a Son she would call Jesus. Was she thinking, "You must have lost your mind." Or, "How is this possible?" Nevertheless, Mary was honored and rejoiced God had chosen her above all other women to carry His Son. Little did Mary know then that when her baby boy was thirty-three years old, she would stand helpless while Jesus was crucified in front of her! Do you think if she knew this before-hand that she still would have rejoiced and sang praises to God in worship for the miraculous gift He bestowed upon her?

Dear Lord Jesus, only four more days to Christmas morning when I will be celebrating with praises of thanksgiving for the baby Jesus' birth. Every time I read about Jesus' birth in the Holy Bible I get so excited with anticipation knowing You sent Jesus to me as a gift of salvation for my sins. Hallelujah, hallelujah! I praise You God for giving me a Best Friend who delights in taking care of me! Amen.

December 22
"HOLY, HOLY, HOLY"

I saw the Lord sitting on a throne, high and lifted up, and the train of His robe filled the temple. Above it stood seraphim; each one had six wings: with two He covered His face, with two He covered His feet, and with two He flew. And one cried to another: "Holy, holy, holy, is the LORD of hosts; the whole earth is full of His glory." Isaiah 6:1-3 (NKJV)

The Lord is the King of Glory with unlimited power to wipe out the whole Earth and everyone in it because they won't stop worshipping their evil practices! Yet He still provides opportunities for repentance.

The amazing part is God's love is so potent that He takes great pleasure in you. He wants to see you achieve your full unique potential which He created. But something terrible happened! You were stranded for a time in this evil society where temptation clouded your mind, preventing you from seeing God's hand reaching down to pull you free. *"Holy, holy, holy, is the LORD of hosts; the whole earth is full of His glory."* God didn't destroy the earth because He was patiently waiting for you to call out to Him in realization of your need for a Savior. In what ways does God want you to serve Him? If you don't know, keep seeking and asking God to reveal to you His purpose for your life.

Jesus, I am incredibly blessed to have You as my partner in life. I never have to walk alone again! You reign as my Supreme Majesty, but by dying for me You served me as a slave serves their master! Please help me to serve my purpose and use my talents to love others the way you loved me. Amen.

December 23

FIGHTING THROUGH TONS OF LINEBACKERS

"Now this is eternal life: that they know you, the only true God, and Jesus Christ, whom you have sent."
John 17:3 (NIV)

To get to the special gift you want to buy for a special person in your life is hard. It's like trying to break through the line of scrimmage in a football game. You get exhausted fighting through linebackers who are guarding the same gift they want for themselves.

It is not wrong to buy gifts for family and friends who you love! But, it is wrong to merely concentrate on buying presents without a thought of expressing the real meaning of Christmas. Christmas has become more about commercialism instead of the birth of Jesus Christ. *"Now this is eternal life: that they know you, the one true God, and Jesus Christ, whom you have sent."* Light up the hearts of those you love by sharing the Christmas blessing. It may very well be the redeemable gift they will want for Christmas from now on! You started your own Christmas tradition that everyone will look forward to sharing with you.

Precious Father of My Heart, I enjoy sharing the birth of Jesus with those I love! It has become a special part of my Christmas blessing! It used to be that I would exhaust myself trying to fight to protect the gift I wanted so badly to buy. You know I still buy presents for my family and friends, but it has been my greatest pleasure to see the light shining in my family and friends eyes when we talk about your birth every Christmas. Amen.

December 24

A PRAYER TO MY DEVOTED LIFE MATE

Grace to you and peace, from Him who is and who was and who is to come...and from Christ Jesus, the faithful witness, the first born of the dead, and the ruler of the kings of the earth. To Him who loved us and released us from our sins by His blood.
Revelation 1:4, 5 (NASB)

Jesus I love you with all my heart and soul! You are My One True Friend who will never leave nor forsake me. You are My Shelter through the storms of life! I can hide in Your comforting arms of security.

You are My Jesus, *Him who is and who was and who is to come... who loved us and released us from our sins by His blood.* Here I am living an incredible life, with unmeasurable blessings I don't deserve! But, Your heart overflows with love and compassion. You value me more than the stars You created in the sky and the creatures You created to fill the earth! When I am upset You give peace that defies all understanding. When I need guidance, You are never too busy to show me the right route. I know I am safe and secure in Your trusting presence forever!

Jesus, this prayer is a love hymn dedicated to You, for loving me even when I sin and make mistakes in life! You come running when I call You to rescue me. I love to seek Your presence. I need to feel the loving compassion of Your comforting arms of peace and contentment surround me. I enjoy our talks together, Jesus. Praise and honor and glory, tomorrow is Your birthday! I can't wait to celebrate it with You! Amen.

December 25

THE CHRISTMAS STORY

After they had heard the king, they went on their way, and the star they had seen when it rose went ahead of them until it stopped over the place where the child was. When they saw the star, they were overjoyed. On coming to the house, they saw the child with his mother Mary, and they bowed down and worshipped him. Then they opened their treasures and presented him with gifts of gold and frankincense and myrrh.
Matthew 2:9-12 (NIV)

The magi came to inquire of King Herod, who reigned in Jerusalem during the time Jesus was born in Bethlehem in Judea. Where could the King of the Jews be found? Herod was disturbed when he heard the news from the Magi, that Jesus was born. Unbeknownst to the Magi, Herod even plotted Jesus' death. When he asked them to come after their visit to see Jesus and tell him where he was so he could go and worship him but they didn't go. The magi were warned by God in a dream to return back to their country by another route. King Herod was furious when the Magi didn't return and ordered all babies under two years old in Bethlehem to be put to death.

The Magi followed the star of God which led them to the place where Jesus was born. Upon seeing Jesus with His mother *they bowed down and worshipped him. Then they opened their treasures and presented him gifts of gold and frankincense and myrrh.* After the Magi left the place where Jesus was, an angel of the Lord appeared to Joseph and told him to leave and take Mary and Jesus to Egypt because Herod was searching for Him in Bethlehem.

Sue Reidell

It wasn't time for You to die for my sins Jesus, so Your Father protected You until the appointed time. He sanctioned Your death to complete the requirement of my inheritance to be final with the blood that dripped onto my wounded heart and healed my soul. Happy birthday to You Jesus. Happy birthday to You Jesus, My awaited King of the Jews. I have been reading the Christmas story this morning and am overwhelmed that You loved me with an unlimited amount of mercy and grace. That is the whole reason that I have a life worth living today! Thank You, Thank You, Thank You, for giving me the gift of Yourself to enjoy! Amen.

December 26

WHEN YOUR FAITH IS TESTED

Dear brothers and sisters, when troubles of any kind come your way, consider it an opportunity for great joy. For you know that when your faith is tested, your endurance has a chance to grow. James 1:2-3 (NLT)

Snap out of the funky mood you are in! Don't allow your feelings to call the shots! Take off the dark shroud that has enveloped your mind and come out of that casket of depression you have buried yourself in. God is calling you to come back to the land of the living where the light of His tranquility will calm all your fears. *For when your faith is tested, your endurance has a chance to grow* in the solace of God's presence.

Precious Heavenly Father, my thoughts have been so dark and dreary and suffocating the light of Your wisdom until only smelly grave clothes of decay and ashes remain. Help me find my way back to Your harmonious presence of tranquility Father God. My faith has been tested beyond what I can endure without Your bright light of endurance advising me how to conquer the ugly demons of distress. They stole my joy away! I need You My Comforter, to hold me tightly in Your gentle arms of love and make me feel alive again. In Your hope of positive possibilities nothing is too big to dream about. Amen.

December 27

FAITH IN GOD = ANSWERED PRAYER

There has never been a day like this one before or since, when the LORD answered such a prayer. Surely the Lord fought for Israel that day! Joshua 10:14 (NLT)

Joshua took command of the Israelites after Moses died. God promised the Israelites that if they followed His commands they would occupy all the land they put their feet upon. They had to have courage and walk with the Lord to defeat their enemies and conquer the land the Lord had given them. The Israelites came up against the formidable army of the Amorites whose five kings came together to fight them. The Israelites, with God's help, slaughtered them. *There has never been a day like this one before or since, when the LORD answered such a prayer.* The Lord caused the Amorites to be confused and brought huge hail stones down, making it easy for the Israelites to defeat them.

In what ways has the LORD answered your prayers? Has it been supernaturally evident that it was the hand of the Lord interceding against formidable opposition? Did you get what you asked for in prayer? Faith in God = answered prayer! When you use these combinations, you have an unbeatable Champion who will fight for you and give you victory over anything.

Dear Heavenly Father, I am very distraught over this situation I am facing off against. I have a champion who is mighty to save me from the strongest foes who dare come up against me. I need help, Lord! I am stuck in my mind where the enemies of doubt and fear are ruling over me. Faith in God = answered prayer. I love You, My Conqueror of life's problems! Amen.

December 28

THE HEAD FOREMAN

Submit to God, and you will have peace; then things will go well for you. Listen to his instructions, and store them in your heart. Job 22:21-22 (NLT)

God has been in the business of constructing hearts for a long time. You could say He is the Head Foreman over His work crew! *Submit to God and you will have peace and then things will go well for you. Listen to his instructions and store them in your heart.* Unfortunately, His work crew wants to do things their own way and they make mistakes. They break God's commandments and don't follow what the Bible says because they feel they can run their own lives. "What does the boss know anyway?" they say. Because they don't follow God's blueprint, their lives collapse around them. But their boss is slow to anger and abounding in love and shows them mercy and grace. He will make them new in Christ Jesus! But, first, His work crew has to admit their mistakes. Second, they must repent of their sins. Third, they must follow the boss's commandments for their lives. Are you following God's commandments? Or do you feel God's commandments don't pertain to you? Try reading them again with a humble heart and submit to God. Then see if that makes a difference in your life!

Father, for a lont time I have been running my life. I thought I didn't need Your help. What an idiot I was! Please forgive me. I humbly repent of my sins, Holy Father. You are my Head Foreman and I want to be part of Your work crew. Please fix my heart and make it run perfectly for You. As I allow Your Holy Spirit to guide my life, I will complete my job You have asked me to do. I love You, Jesus! Amen.

December 29

SILENT BUT DEADLY

Not faith is the assurance (the confirmation, the title deed) of the things [we] do not see and the conviction of their reality [faith perceiving as a real fact what is not revealed to the senses]. Hebrews 11:1 (AMP)

As you walk each day in faith, convinced God will keep you steadfast and upright, you may stumble and fall over obstructions in the road you are travelling on. You will seek the hand of God to pick you up, dust you off, and prepare you for anything that may get in your way during the day *[Faith perceiving as a real fact what is not revealed to the senses).*

The enemy is silent but deadly! You don't know when he will strike; tearing apart your heart and soul with his evil tongue of poisonous venom. He will make each step you take labored by his insidious accusations aimed to rip out the spiritual lining of your soul. He will continue the assault until you are so weak you can't even call out to the Powerful Rescuer! But don't give up! God is with you, waiting to devour the evil serpent. Just utter Jesus' name over and over again, and the evil one will have no choice but to flee. With God fighting your battles, the evil one can't harm you!

Glorious Heavenly Father, I love You with an everlasting love! You are my hope and salvation for a day filled with Your unfailing love and delightful presence. You are always glad to see me. Please help me keep my armor of Your Mighty Presence upright and indestructible against the destroyer of my peace. If I have You covering me with Your Everlasting Coat of Armor, the evil one can't get at me! Amen.

December 30

THE ELECT OF GOD, HOLY AND BELOVED

Therefore, as the elect of God, holy and beloved, put on tender mercies, kindness, humility, meekness, longsuffering; bearing with one another, and forgiving one another, if anyone has a complaint against one another; even as Christ forgave you, so you must do. But above all things put on love which is the bond of perfection. Colossians 3:12-14 (NKJV)

How you live your life shows the character of God inside your heart and soul. Your character reflects off of you, like a sunbeam filtered through the clouds.

If you have had an argument with another person, *therefore as the elect of God, holy and beloved, put on tender mercies, kindness, humility, meekness, longsuffering; bearing with one another, and forgiving* them, *as Christ forgave you.* To carry strife weighs down your heart and soul! Eventually, if you do not surrender these character defects to God, your heart and soul will carry a stench which will eat away the lining of your innermost sanctuary of God. The odor of darkness will come outward from your heart instead of the light of the Holy Spirit reflecting off of you!

Precious Comforter, I need Your touch upon my heart and soul, for healing from the anger, malice, and slander I have emitted out of Your Holy Sanctuary. I want to reflect the light of Your Holy Spirit from the innermost parts of my body. I want to brighten up any person who came in contact with me today. But I need to release the resentments I carry around with me for another person. They cause me to be a negative and bitter person. Please help me surrender them. I want peace and serenity back in my life! Amen.

December 31

BONA-FIDE JESUS FREAK

In Him we have redemption through His blood, the forgiveness of our trespasses, according to the riches of His grace which He lavishes upon us.
Ephesians 1:7-8 (NASB)

Are you a bona-fide Jesus freak? Do you seek Jesus' counsel like a person lost in the desert seeks water? If you said yes, then everything in your life begins and ends with Jesus having total control of it.

In Him we have redemption through His blood, the forgiveness of our trespasses, according to the riches of His grace which He lavishes upon us. The unfailing love that Jesus graciously gave you in His blood soaked hands caresses your soul. God massages it with the healing light through His fingers, circulating mercy into every crevice where sin was hidden. The death of your sins brought the resurrection of a new life. Walking hand in hand with Jesus, where rewarding blessings are given to you, you fall into submission of His will for your life each day.

Jesus, Precious Jesus, O how I love thee! I love thee Jesus with every fiber of my body. I never want to be apart from You ever again! I am only complete in Your loving and compassionate presence. I am a bona-fide Jesus freak! My days are blessed Jesus since I invited You to be a part of my life. Even the bad days are good and overflowing with Your mercy and grace. Amen.